# MILE BY MILE
## On Britain's Railways

Readers please note that S.N. Pike's original numbering of the maps has been faithfully reproduced, and the absence in these original three guides of any maps numbered from 1 onwards does not mean any maps have been omitted.

# MILE BY MILE
# On Britain's Railways

The LNER, LMS, GWR and Southern Railway
as They Were in 1947

S.N. Pike MBE

Great Western Railway maps by Reginald Piggott;
research by Matt Thompson

First published in Great Britain
2011 by Aurum Press Ltd
7 Greenland Street, London NW1 0ND
www.aurumpress.co.uk

*Mile by Mile on the LNER*, *Mile by Mile on the LMS* and *Travelling on the Southern Railway: The Journey Mile by Mile* all originally published in 1947 and 1948 by Stuart N. Pike.

Maps on p. 110-140 by Reginald Piggott
Great Western Railway mile-by-mile research by Matt Thompson

Every effort has been made to trace the copyright holders of material quoted in this book. If application is made in writing to the publisher, any omissions will be included in future editions.

A catalogue record for this book is available from the British Library.

ISBN-13: 978 1 84513 612 3

3  5  7  9  10  8  6  4  2
2011  2013  2015  2014  2012

Design by Tim Peters, www.timpeters.co.uk
Printed by MPG Books, Bodmin, Cornwall

# CONTENTS

# INTRODUCTION

The first intercity passenger railway in Britain, between the north-west's two centres of industry and population, Liverpool and Manchester, heralded the beginnings of 'leisure travel' for the masses. Railways throughout the world would generate and serve industry, but now also create journeys. Access to this form of transport had been democratised.

Whether the purpose of travel was business or leisure, inevitably the railway companies started to cater for the needs of their customers, providing everything from improved rolling stock to better on-board services, waiting rooms, restaurants and even hotels. By November 1879 luxury dining was on offer, with the Great Northern Railway the first to operate a Pullman Car dining service on their 10 a.m. train from Leeds. Thus the journey was becoming as important as the destination.

Speed and levels of luxury competed in advertisements for the various companies' services and enthusiastic travel literature became available. Bradshaw's Guide became a classic independent source of information for travellers. The railways grew up learning that they had a lot to offer those who enjoyed the new-found freedom they promoted, and in due course their marketing and advertising departments came up with innovative ways to entice travellers to their services. Today, historic station railway posters are accepted as a collectable art form, and the world of printed memorabilia includes early travel guides produced by most of the great independent railway companies prior to nationalisation.

Leap forward to the millennium, and we find ourselves in an era where, having lost so much of our railway network, we are reawakened too late to its value. Those of us with a black and white memory card are left recalling with a misty eye those smoke-hung booking hall days of the 50s and 60s. How we cling to an age when we were memorably less well served! We have bought up all the supplies of lamps and memorabilia at Euston's Collector's Corner to the point of ensuring its closure, filled our houses with signal box equipment and old timetables, saved every last steam engine we can, and have even started building new ones! In other words, more successfully than any other generation in history, we have secured the past for our dotage. So starts the story of *Mile by Mile*.

In a dusty drawer some years ago I discovered copies of S. N. Pike's three wonderful railway map books: mile-by-mile audits of the LMS, the LNER and the Southern Railway. They were immediately treasured – because, I perceived, they were known only to me and few others. Why should they be so valuable? Well, privately created in 1947, with an evident and ardent enthusiasm, they served the purpose of providing fascinating route information about our main lines when the newly nationalised companies operating them had lost interest in doing so. They memorialise an age before Dr Beeching's attempt to improve the railways by closing down so very many of them, and they remind me of Saturdays spent train spotting, those smoky booking halls, the long-gone water troughs and 'passenger luggage in advance'. The maps themselves, containing a wealth of railway information for anyone interested in what went by the window, are to my mind unique. And whilst some of the routes depicted no longer exist today, they live on in these books as a historical record of what was there. Thanks to S. N. Pike, then, for a timeless portrait of somewhere many of us have been.

But I could find no fourth *Mile by Mile* volume by S. N. Pike on the Great Western Railway. I did some research on the life and times of Stuart Nelson Pike, but was able to find out very little about him. He was a fighter ace in the Royal Flying Corps during World War I. He became Squadron Leader in 20 Squadron RAFVR. During a distinguished flying career, we do know, he shot down one German aircraft whilst flying an FE2B. In 1944 he was awarded the MBE for services unconnected to his wartime achievements. I could trace no surviving family or relatives. And, sadly, I had to accept, Pike had never produced the missing GWR volume – even the reason why remains a mystery.

Now, however, the *Mile by Mile* set is reissued in this single handsome volume, with S. N. Pike's three classic books complemented by a new, fourth section on the Great Western mainline to Penzance and also to Bristol, created in like style by cartographer Reginald Piggott and railway researcher Matt Thompson, and I commend it to you. Complete at long last is what I hope will be a treasured reference work, for both avowed admirers of S. N. Pike and newcomers to his work.

*Nick Dodson*
*Sidmouth*
*Devon*

# MILE by MILE

## ON THE L.N.E.R.

by

S. N. PIKE, M.B.E.

KINGS CROSS EDITION
L.N.E.R.

The journey between London and the North described
detail :—

- GRADIENTS OF THE LINE

- SPEED TESTS AND MILEAGES

- VIADUCTS, BRIDGES AND EMBANKMENTS

- TUNNELS, CUTTINGS AND CROSSOVERS

- STREAMS, RIVERS AND ROADS

- TOWNS, VILLAGES AND CHURCHES

- MINES, FACTORIES AND WORKS

with an account of features of interest and beauty to be seen
from the train.

*Published by*

STUART   N.   PIKE,

Shepperton - on - Thames
Middlesex, England

# ERRATA

**Map 14** (Page 16) : *The true position of mileposts 165, 166 and 167 is slightly north of where indicated on this map, milepost 167 being north of the Goole Canal, not south of the bridge as shown.*

**Map 16** (Page 18) : *The correct name of the Junction 2 miles north of York is Skelton Junct., not Poppleton as shown.*

# Author's Note

The pleasures and thrills of the journey between Kings Cross and Edinburgh are limitless. Every mile of the trip embraces some special feature of interest or beauty to compel the attention of the passenger.

The object of this little book is to encourage the passenger to anticipate his progress, and to enable him to know, to a nicety, what he next will see from the window at any and every stage of the journey. It is such a pity to sacrifice this experience to idle slumber, or to concentration on a magazine that would the better be enjoyed at home.

The beautiful countryside rushes by; beneath the tranquil surface, right beside the line, miners are toiling for the black diamonds essential to feed the great industrial plants we pass.

I acknowledge, with grateful thanks, certain information given me by Officials of the L.N.E.R. Railwaymen of every grade have contributed their share to make this publication as complete as possible. Railwaymen are justly proud of the vast organisation they serve; it is their wish that passengers should enjoy to the full the journeys they make with such speed and safety. The information and advice they have so readily placed at my disposal has been gladly offered with that end in view.

Shepperton, 1947.                                    S. N. P.

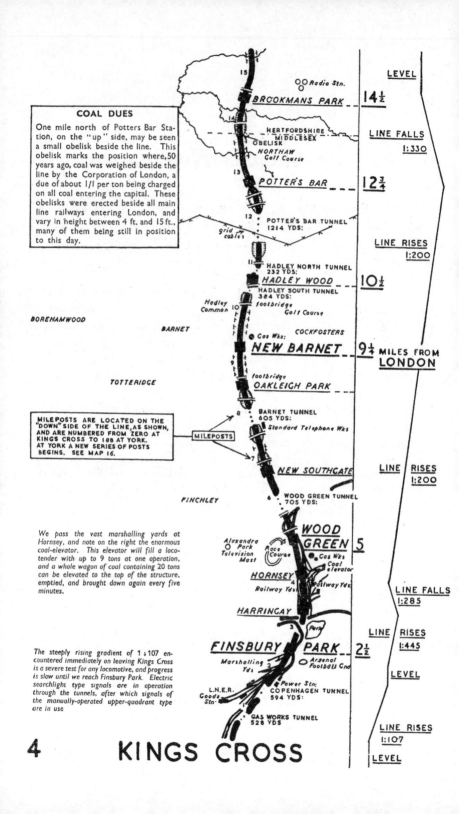

○○ *Radio Stn.*

BROOKMANS PARK — 14½

LINE FALLS
1:330

HERTFORDSHIRE
MIDDLESEX
OBELISK

**COAL DUES**

One mile north of Potters Bar Station, on the "up" side, may be seen a small obelisk beside the line. This obelisk marks the position where, 50 years ago, coal was weighed beside the line by the Corporation of London, a due of about 1/1 per ton being charged on all coal entering the capital. These obelisks were erected beside all main line railways entering London, and vary in height between 4 ft. and 15 ft., many of them being still in position to this day.

NORTHAW
*Golf Course*

POTTER'S BAR — 12¾

POTTER'S BAR TUNNEL
1214 YDS:

*grid cables*

LINE RISES
1:200

HADLEY NORTH TUNNEL
232 YDS:

HADLEY WOOD — 10½

HADLEY SOUTH TUNNEL
384 YDS:

*footbridge*

BOREHAMWOOD

*Hadley Common*

*Golf Course*

BARNET

● *Gas Wks.*          COCKFOSTERS

**NEW BARNET** — 9¼ MILES FROM LONDON

TOTTERIDGE

*footbridge*

OAKLEIGH PARK

BARNET TUNNEL
605 YDS:

MILEPOSTS ARE LOCATED ON THE "DOWN" SIDE OF THE LINE, AS SHOWN, AND ARE NUMBERED FROM ZERO AT KINGS CROSS TO 188 AT YORK. AT YORK A NEW SERIES OF POSTS BEGINS. SEE MAP 16.

MILEPOSTS

*Standard Telephone Wks.*

NEW SOUTHGATE

LINE RISES
1:200

WOOD GREEN TUNNEL
705 YDS:

FINCHLEY

**WOOD GREEN** — 5

*Alexandra Park Television Mast*          *Race Course*

● *Gas Wks.*
*Coal elevator*

We pass the vast marshalling yards at Hornsey, and note on the right the enormous coal-elevator. This elevator will fill a loco-tender with up to 9 tons at one operation, and a whole wagon of coal containing 20 tons can be elevated to the top of the structure, emptied, and brought down again every five minutes.

HORNSEY
*Railway Yds.*          *Railway Yds.*

LINE FALLS
1:285

HARRINGAY

*Park*

LINE RISES
1:445

**FINSBURY PARK** — 2½

*Marshalling Yds.*          ○ *Arsenal Football Gnd.*

LEVEL

The steeply rising gradient of 1:107 encountered immediately on leaving Kings Cross is a severe test for any locomotive, and progress is slow until we reach Finsbury Park. Electric searchlight type signals are in operation through the tunnels, after which signals of the manually-operated upper-quadrant type are in use

L.N.E.R.
Goods Stn.

● *Power Stn.*
COPENHAGEN TUNNEL
594 YDS:

GAS WORKS TUNNEL
528 YDS:

LINE RISES
1:107

**4**          **KINGS CROSS**          LEVEL

# LONDON—EDINBURGH

## EXACT DISTANCES BETWEEN STATIONS—EXPRESS TRAIN RUNNING TIMES

| (1) STATION | (2) Distance Between Stations | | (3) Express Train Running Times | (4) Actual Running Times | | | (5) NOTES and Average Speeds over each Section |
|---|---|---|---|---|---|---|---|
| | Miles | Yards | Minutes | Minutes | Early | Late | |
| KING'S CROSS to HATFIELD | 17 | 1,199 | 27 | | | | From a standing start the heavily laden express encounters a severe 1 : 107 gradient through the Gasworks and Copenhagen tunnels, to be followed by a steep 1 : 200 climb for 8 miles from milepost 4 to Potters Bar, where the summit is reached. From here we rush through Hatfield at really high speed. *Average speed 39.0 m.p.h.*, the low figure being due to the difficult start. (See Maps 4 and 5.) |
| HATFIELD to HITCHIN | 14 | 424 | 14 | | | | The summit on this section is at Woolmer Green Box, near milepost 24. The junction of the lines at Langley are passed at 65 to 70 m.p.h. Water is taken on at the Troughs at milepost 27 at this speed, which we maintain through Hitchin. *Average speed 61 m.p.h.* (See Maps 5 and 6.) |
| HITCHIN to HUNTINGDON | 26 | 1,672 | 26 | | | | This is a really fast section of the line, and, except for a slowing down for curves near Offord, a very high speed is maintained. *Average speed 62.3 m.p.h.* (See Maps 6 and 7.) |
| HUNTINGDON to PETERBOROUGH | 17 | 863 | 19 | | | | An exceptionally fast section of the line. The **necessity** for approaching Peterborough at a minimum pace reduces our average speed to 55.2 m.p.h. (See Maps 7 and 8.) |
| PETERBOROUGH to GRANTHAM | 29 | 165 | 44 | | | | From a standing start at Peterborough we encounter a series of rising gradients from milepost 85 for the next 15 miles. Over the summit we pass through Great Ponton at very high speed, slowing down slightly for Grantham. *Average speed 39.5 m.p.h.* (See Maps 8, 9 and 10.) |
| GRANTHAM to NEWARK | 14 | 1,138 | 14 | | | | Very high speeds are attained on the falling gradients. *Average over the section 63.2 m.p.h.* (See Maps 10 and 11.) |
| NEWARK to RETFORD | 18 | 902 | 24 | | | | Between Newark and milepost 128 the line is dead level, but rising gradients up to Askham tunnel lower the average. Speed is sharply reduced approaching Retford. *Average speed 46.2 m.p.h.* (See Maps 12 and 13.) |

(Continued on page 13)

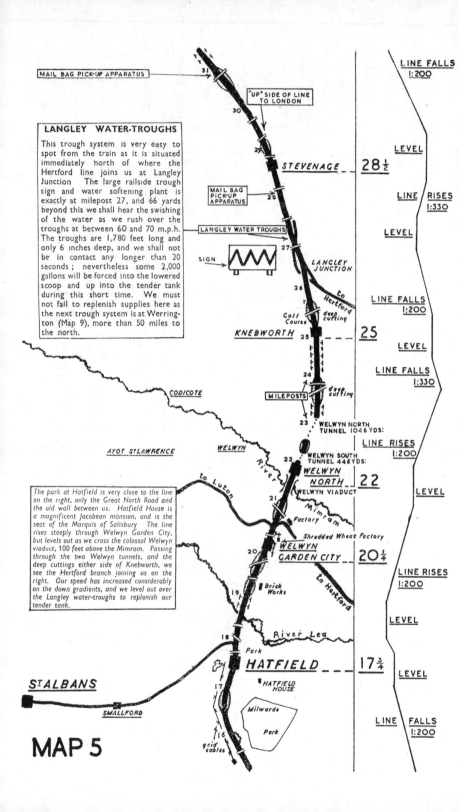

MAIL BAG PICK-UP APPARATUS

31

"UP" SIDE OF LINE
TO LONDON

30

29

*STEVENAGE* — 28½

MAIL BAG
PICK-UP
APPARATUS

28

LANGLEY WATER TROUGHS

27

SIGN

**LANGLEY WATER-TROUGHS**

This trough system is very easy to spot from the train as it is situated immediately north of where the Hertford line joins us at Langley Junction  The large railside trough sign and water softening plant is exactly at milepost 27, and 66 yards beyond this we shall hear the swishing of the water as we rush over the troughs at between 60 and 70 m.p.h. The troughs are 1,780 feet long and only 6 inches deep, and we shall not be in contact any longer than 20 seconds ; nevertheless some 2,000 gallons will be forced into the lowered scoop and up into the tender tank during this short time.  We must not fail to replenish supplies here as the next trough system is at Werrington (Map 9), more than 50 miles to the north.

*LANGLEY
JUNCTION*

to
Hertford

26

*Golf
Course*

deep
cutting

*KNEBWORTH* 25 — 25

24

MILEPOSTS

deep
cutting

23

WELWYN NORTH
TUNNEL 1046 YDS:

WELWYN SOUTH
TUNNEL 446 YDS:

22

*WELWYN
NORTH* — 22

21

WELWYN VIADUCT

*Mimram*

*Factory*

*Shredded Wheat Factory*

The park at Hatfield is very close to the line on the right, only the Great North Road and the old wall between us.  Hatfield House is a magnificent Jacobean mansion, and is the seat of the Marquis of Salisbury  The line rises steeply through Welwyn Garden City, but levels out as we cross the colossal Welwyn viaduct, 100 feet above the Mimram.  Passing through the two Welwyn tunnels, and the deep cuttings either side of Knebworth, we see the Hertford branch joining us on the right.  Our speed has increased considerably on the down gradients, and we level out over the Langley water-troughs to replenish our tender tank.

20

*WELWYN
GARDEN CITY* — 20¼

to Hertford

*Brick
Works*

19

to Luton

*WELWYN*

River

*AYOT St LAWRENCE*

*CODICOTE*

18

River Lea

Park

*HATFIELD* — 17¾

*HATFIELD
HOUSE*

17

*Milwards
Park*

St ALBANS

SMALLFORD

16

grid
cables

**MAP 5**

LINE FALLS
1:200

LEVEL

LINE RISES
1:330

LEVEL

LINE FALLS
1:200

LEVEL

LINE FALLS
1:330

LINE RISES
1:200

LEVEL

LINE RISES
1:200

LEVEL

LEVEL

LINE FALLS
1:200

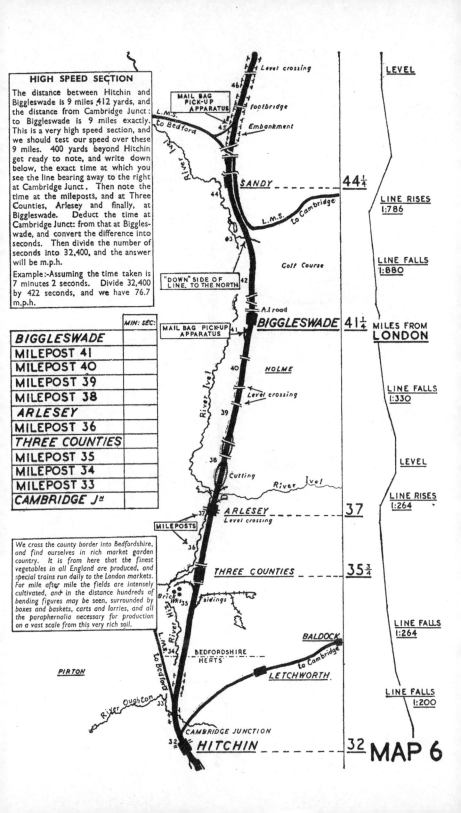

## HIGH SPEED SECTION

The distance between Hitchin and Biggleswade is 9 miles 412 yards, and the distance from Cambridge Junct: to Biggleswade is 9 miles exactly. This is a very high speed section, and we should test our speed over these 9 miles. 400 yards beyond Hitchin get ready to note, and write down below, the exact time at which you see the line bearing away to the right at Cambridge Junct. Then note the time at the mileposts, and at Three Counties, Arlesey and finally, at Biggleswade. Deduct the time at Cambridge Junct: from that at Biggleswade, and convert the difference into seconds. Then divide the number of seconds into 32,400, and the answer will be m.p.h.

Example:—Assuming the time taken is 7 minutes 2 seconds. Divide 32,400 by 422 seconds, and we have 76.7 m.p.h.

|  | MIN: SEC: |
|---|---|
| **BIGGLESWADE** | |
| MILEPOST 41 | |
| MILEPOST 40 | |
| MILEPOST 39 | |
| MILEPOST 38 | |
| **ARLESEY** | |
| MILEPOST 36 | |
| **THREE COUNTIES** | |
| MILEPOST 35 | |
| MILEPOST 34 | |
| MILEPOST 33 | |
| **CAMBRIDGE Jⁿ** | |

We cross the county border into Bedfordshire, and find ourselves in rich market garden country. It is from here that the finest vegetables in all England are produced, and special trains run daily to the London markets. For mile after mile the fields are intensely cultivated, and in the distance hundreds of bending figures may be seen, surrounded by boxes and baskets, carts and lorries, and all the paraphernalia necessary for production on a vast scale from this very rich soil.

Level crossing

MAIL BAG PICK-UP APPARATUS

footbridge

Embankment

L.M.S. to Bedford

SANDY

L.M.S. to Cambridge

Golf Course

"DOWN" SIDE OF LINE, TO THE NORTH

A.1 road

MAIL BAG PICK-UP APPARATUS

BIGGLESWADE

HOLME

River Ivel

Level crossing

Cutting

River Ivel

MILEPOSTS

ARLESEY
Level crossing

THREE COUNTIES

Brick Wks

sidings

BALDOCK

to Cambridge

LETCHWORTH

PIRTON

L.M.S. to Bedford

River Hitchin

BEDFORDSHIRE
HERTS

River Oughton

CAMBRIDGE JUNCTION

HITCHIN

LEVEL

44¼

LINE RISES 1:786

LINE FALLS 1:880

41¼ MILES FROM LONDON

LINE FALLS 1:330

LEVEL

LINE RISES 1:264

37

35¾

LINE FALLS 1:264

LINE FALLS 1:200

32 MAP 6

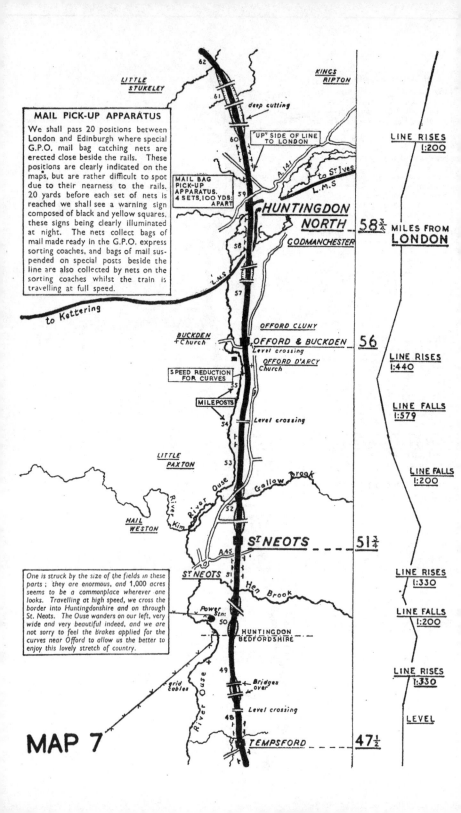

## MAIL PICK-UP APPARATUS

We shall pass 20 positions between London and Edinburgh where special G.P.O. mail bag catching nets are erected close beside the rails. These positions are clearly indicated on the maps, but are rather difficult to spot due to their nearness to the rails. 20 yards before each set of nets is reached we shall see a warning sign composed of black and yellow squares, these signs being clearly illuminated at night. The nets collect bags of mail made ready in the G.P.O. express sorting coaches, and bags of mail suspended on special posts beside the line are also collected by nets on the sorting coaches whilst the train is travelling at full speed.

LITTLE STUKELEY

KINGS RIPTON

deep cutting

"UP" SIDE OF LINE TO LONDON

A.141

to St Ives L.M.S

MAIL BAG PICK-UP APPARATUS. 4 SETS, 100 YDS. APART

## HUNTINGDON NORTH __ 58¾

GODMANCHESTER

to Kettering

L.M.S

OFFORD CLUNY

BUCKDEN + Church

## OFFORD & BUCKDEN __ 56

Level crossing

OFFORD D'ARCY Church

SPEED REDUCTION FOR CURVES

MILEPOSTS

Level crossing

LITTLE PAXTON

MAIL WESTON

River Kim

River Ouse

Gallow Brook

## St NEOTS _ _ _ 51¾

One is struck by the size of the fields in these parts ; they are enormous, and 1,000 acres seems to be a commonplace wherever one looks. Travelling at high speed, we cross the border into Huntingdonshire and on through St. Neots. The Ouse wanders on our left, very wide and very beautiful indeed, and we are not sorry to feel the brakes applied for the curves near Offord to allow us the better to enjoy this lovely stretch of country.

St NEOTS

A.45

Hen Brook

Power Stn:

HUNTINGDON BEDFORDSHIRE

River Ouse

grid cables

Bridges over

Level crossing

## MAP 7

## TEMPSFORD _ _ _ 47½

LINE RISES 1:200

MILES FROM LONDON

LINE RISES 1:440

LINE FALLS 1:579

LINE FALLS 1:200

LINE RISES 1:330

LINE FALLS 1:200

LINE RISES 1:330

LEVEL

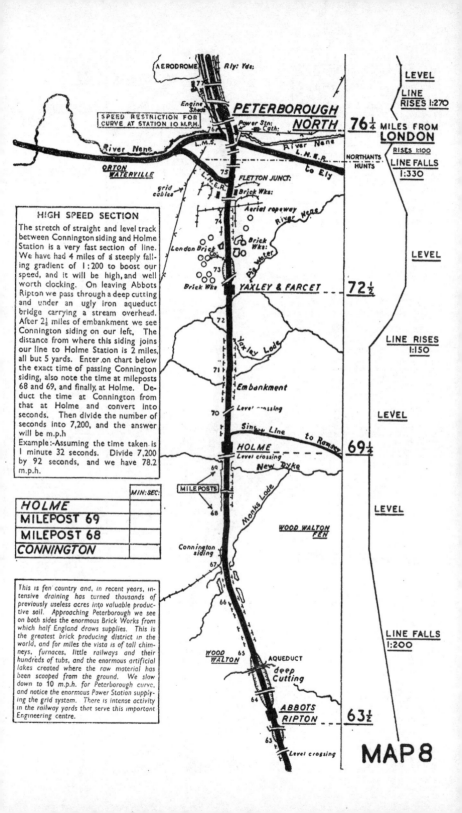

AERODROME  Rly. Yds.

**PETERBOROUGH NORTH** — **76¼** MILES FROM **LONDON**

SPEED RESTRICTION FOR CURVE AT STATION 10 M.P.H.

Engine Sheds

Power Stn.  Cath.

River Nene  L.M.S.  River Nene  L.N.E.R.  to Ely

ORTON WATERVILLE

L.N.E.R.  75

grid cables

FLETTON JUNCT.

Brick Wks.

Aerial ropeway  River Nene

74

Brick Wks.

London Brick Co.  Pig Water

73

Brick Wks.

**YAXLEY & FARCET** — — **72½**

72

Yaxley Lode

71

Embankment

70  Level crossing

Single Line  to Ramsey

**HOLME** — — **69½**
Level crossing

69  New Dyke

MILE POSTS

68  Monks Lode

**WOOD WALTON FEN**

Connington siding

67

66

WOOD WALTON  65  AQUEDUCT  deep Cutting

64  **ABBOTS RIPTON** — — **63½**

63  Level crossing

**MAP 8**

### Right margin gradient profile
LEVEL
LINE RISES 1:270
RISES 1:100
NORTHANTS HUNTS
LINE FALLS 1:330
LEVEL
LINE RISES 1:150
LEVEL
LEVEL
LINE FALLS 1:200

### HIGH SPEED SECTION

The stretch of straight and level track between Connington siding and Holme Station is a very fast section of line. We have had 4 miles of a steeply falling gradient of 1:200 to boost our speed, and it will be high, and well worth clocking. On leaving Abbots Ripton we pass through a deep cutting and under an ugly iron aqueduct bridge carrying a stream overhead. After 2½ miles of embankment we see Connington siding on our left. The distance from where this siding joins our line to Holme Station is 2 miles, all but 5 yards. Enter on chart below the exact time of passing Connington siding, also note the time at mileposts 68 and 69, and finally, at Holme. Deduct the time at Connington from that at Holme and convert into seconds. Then divide the number of seconds into 7,200, and the answer will be m.p.h

Example:-Assuming the time taken is 1 minute 32 seconds. Divide 7,200 by 92 seconds, and we have 78.2 m.p.h.

|  | MIN.SEC.: |
|---|---|
| *HOLME* | |
| MILEPOST 69 | |
| MILEPOST 68 | |
| *CONNINGTON* | |

This is fen country and, in recent years, intensive draining has turned thousands of previously useless acres into valuable productive soil. Approaching Peterborough we see on both sides the enormous Brick Works from which half England draws supplies. This is the greatest brick producing district in the world, and for miles the vista is of tall chimneys, furnaces, little railways and their hundreds of tubs, and the enormous artificial lakes created where the raw material has been scooped from the ground. We slow down to 10 m.p.h. for Peterborough curve, and notice the enormous Power Station supplying the grid system. There is intense activity in the railway yards that serve this important Engineering centre.

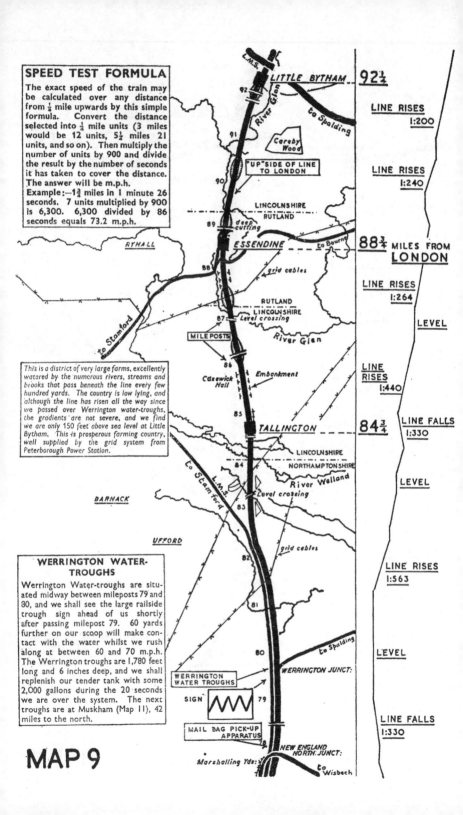

## SPEED TEST FORMULA

The exact speed of the train may be calculated over any distance from $\frac{1}{4}$ mile upwards by this simple formula. Convert the distance selected into $\frac{1}{4}$ mile units (3 miles would be 12 units, $5\frac{1}{4}$ miles 21 units, and so on). Then multiply the number of units by 900 and divide the result by the number of seconds it has taken to cover the distance. The answer will be m.p.h.
Example:—$1\frac{3}{4}$ miles in 1 minute 26 seconds. 7 units multiplied by 900 is 6,300. 6,300 divided by 86 seconds equals 73.2 m.p.h.

*This is a district of very large farms, excellently watered by the numerous rivers, streams and brooks that pass beneath the line every few hundred yards. The country is low lying, and although the line has risen all the way since we passed over Werrington water-troughs, the gradients are not severe, and we find we are only 150 feet above sea level at Little Bytham. This is prosperous farming country, well supplied by the grid system from Peterborough Power Station.*

## WERRINGTON WATER-TROUGHS

Werrington Water-troughs are situated midway between mileposts 79 and 80, and we shall see the large railside trough sign ahead of us shortly after passing milepost 79. 60 yards further on our scoop will make contact with the water whilst we rush along at between 60 and 70 m.p.h. The Werrington troughs are 1,780 feet long and 6 inches deep, and we shall replenish our tender tank with some 2,000 gallons during the 20 seconds we are over the system. The next troughs are at Muskham (Map 11), 42 miles to the north.

**MAP 9**

L.M.S.

*LITTLE BYTHAM*    $92\frac{1}{4}$

92    *River Glen*    *to Spalding*

91    LINE RISES
1:200

*Careby Wood*

"UP" SIDE OF LINE
TO LONDON    LINE RISES
1:240

90

89    *deep cutting*    LINCOLNSHIRE
RUTLAND

RYHALL    *ESSENDINE*    *to Bourne*    $88\frac{3}{4}$    MILES FROM
LONDON

88    *grid cables*    LINE RISES
1:264

RUTLAND
LINCOLNSHIRE    LEVEL
87    *Level crossing*

MILE POSTS    *River Glen*

86    LINE
RISES
1:440

*Casewick Hall*    *Embankment*

85    *TALLINGTON*    $84\frac{3}{4}$    LINE FALLS
1:330

84    LINCOLNSHIRE
NORTHAMPTONSHIRE

*to Stamford*    *River Welland*    LEVEL

L.M.S.    *Level crossing*
83

BARNACK

82    *grid cables*    LINE RISES
1:563

UFFORD    81

80    *to Spalding*    LEVEL
*WERRINGTON JUNCT:*

WERRINGTON
WATER TROUGHS

SIGN ⋀⋀⋀ 79    LINE FALLS
1:330

MAIL BAG PICK-UP
APPARATUS

*NEW ENGLAND
NORTH. JUNCT:*
*Marshalling Yds:*    *to Wisbech*

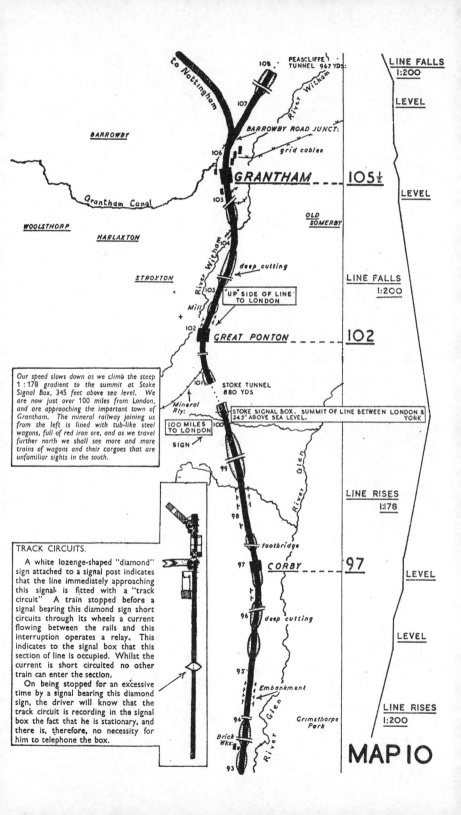

LINE FALLS 1:200

LEVEL

*to Nottingham*

108

PEASCLIFFE TUNNEL 967 YDS:

*River Witham*

107

BARROWBY ROAD JUNCT:

*grid cables*

106

GRANTHAM ___ 105½

LEVEL

105

OLD SOMERBY

*Grantham Canal*

WOOLSTHORP

HARLAXTON

STROXTON

104

*River Witham*

*deep cutting*

103

"UP" SIDE OF LINE TO LONDON

LINE FALLS 1:200

*Mill*

102

GREAT PONTON ___ 102

Our speed slows down as we climb the steep 1 : 178 gradient to the summit at Stoke Signal Box, 345 feet above sea level. We are now just over 100 miles from London, and are approaching the important town of Grantham. The mineral railway joining us from the left is lined with tub-like steel wagons, full of red iron ore, and as we travel further north we shall see more and more trains of wagons and their cargoes that are unfamiliar sights in the south.

101

STOKE TUNNEL 880 YDS

*Mineral Rly:*

STOKE SIGNAL BOX. SUMMIT OF LINE BETWEEN LONDON & YORK 345' ABOVE SEA LEVEL.

100

100 MILES TO LONDON

SIGN →

99

LINE RISES 1:178

98

TRACK CIRCUITS.

A white lozenge-shaped "diamond" sign attached to a signal post indicates that the line immediately approaching this signal is fitted with a "track circuit." A train stopped before a signal bearing this diamond sign short circuits through its wheels a current flowing between the rails and this interruption operates a relay. This indicates to the signal box that this section of line is occupied. Whilst the current is short circuited no other train can enter the section.

On being stopped for an excessive time by a signal bearing this diamond sign, the driver will know that the track circuit is recording in the signal box the fact that he is stationary, and there is, therefore, no necessity for him to telephone the box.

*footbridge*

97

CORBY ___ 97

LEVEL

96

*deep cutting*

LEVEL

95

*Embankment*

94

*River Glen*

*Grimsthorpe Park*

LINE RISES 1:200

*Brick Wks:*

93

MAP 10

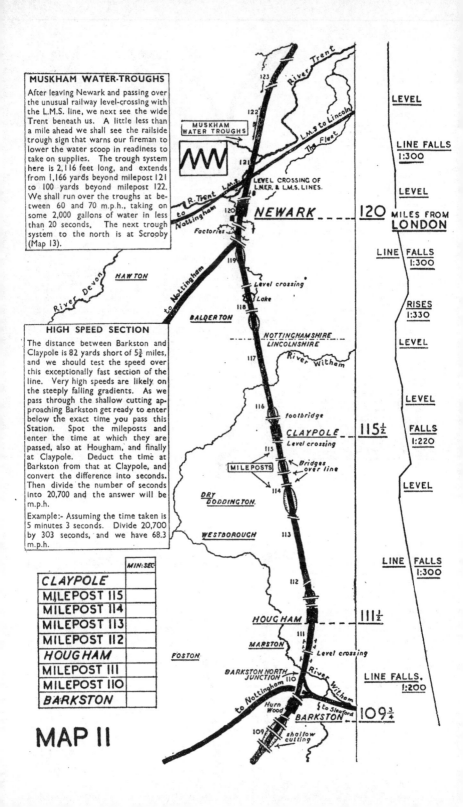

## MUSKHAM WATER-TROUGHS

After leaving Newark and passing over the unusual railway level-crossing with the L.M.S. line, we next see the wide Trent beneath us. A little less than a mile ahead we shall see the railside trough sign that warns our fireman to lower the water scoop in readiness to take on supplies. The trough system here is 2,116 feet long, and extends from 1,166 yards beyond milepost 121 to 100 yards beyond milepost 122. We shall run over the troughs at between 60 and 70 m.p.h., taking on some 2,000 gallons of water in less than 20 seconds. The next trough system to the north is at Scrooby (Map 13).

MUSKHAM WATER TROUGHS

LEVEL CROSSING OF L.N.E.R. & L.M.S. LINES.

**NEWARK**

HAWTON

BALDERTON

NOTTINGHAMSHIRE
LINCOLNSHIRE

River Witham

## HIGH SPEED SECTION

The distance between Barkston and Claypole is 82 yards short of 5¾ miles, and we should test the speed over this exceptionally fast section of the line. Very high speeds are likely on the steeply falling gradients. As we pass through the shallow cutting approaching Barkston get ready to enter below the exact time you pass this Station. Spot the mileposts and enter the time at which they are passed, also at Hougham, and finally at Claypole. Deduct the time at Barkston from that at Claypole, and convert the difference into seconds. Then divide the number of seconds into 20,700 and the answer will be m.p.h.

Example:- Assuming the time taken is 5 minutes 3 seconds. Divide 20,700 by 303 seconds, and we have 68.3 m.p.h.

**CLAYPOLE**

Level crossing

MILEPOSTS

Bridges over line

DRY DODDINGTON.

WESTBOROUGH

footbridge

|  | MIN:SEC |
|---|---|
| *CLAYPOLE* | |
| MILEPOST 115 | |
| MILEPOST 114 | |
| MILEPOST 113 | |
| MILEPOST 112 | |
| *HOUGHAM* | |
| MILEPOST 111 | |
| MILEPOST 110 | |
| *BARKSTON* | |

FOSTON

HOUGHAM

MARSTON

Level crossing

BARKSTON NORTH JUNCTION

River Witham

Hurn Wood

to Nottingham

to Sleaford

**BARKSTON**

shallow cutting

## MAP II

River Trent

L.M.S to Lincoln

The Fleet

LEVEL

LINE FALLS
1:300

LEVEL

**120** MILES FROM **LONDON**

LINE FALLS
1:300

RISES
1:330

LEVEL

LEVEL

**115½**   FALLS
1:220

LEVEL

LINE FALLS
1:300

**111½**

LINE FALLS.
1:200

**109¾**

Level crossing
Lake

to Nottingham

R. Trent L.M.S.

Factories

Level crossing

# LONDON—EDINBURGH

### EXACT DISTANCES BETWEEN STATIONS—EXPRESS TRAIN RUNNING TIMES

| (1) STATION. | (2) Distance Between Stations | | (3) Express Train Running Times | (4) Actual Running Times | | | (5) NOTES and Average Speeds over each Section |
|---|---|---|---|---|---|---|---|
| | Miles | Yards | Minutes | Minutes | Early | Late | |
| RETFORD to DONCASTER | 17 | 611 | 19 | | | | Falling gradients approaching Scrooby water-troughs send us over the water-pick-up at 65 m.p.h. The line rises steeply to milepost 150, but we again make the line speed to the outskirts of Doncaster. Average speed 55.2 m.p.h. (See Maps 12 and 13.) |
| DONCASTER to YORK | 32 | 308 | 42 | | | | The 6 miles of level track between mileposts 158 and 166 is a high speed section, and well worth "clocking." We slow down for the curve and swing bridge at Selby and also for the curve at Chaloner's Whin Junction. The sharp curve at York is approached slowly. Average speed 46.0 m.p.h. (See Maps 14, 15 and 16.) |
| YORK to THIRSK | 22 | 352 | 25 | | | | 12 miles of dead level and dead straight track allows for really fast travelling. By the time we reach Tollerton, speeds are in excess of 75 m.p.h. The standing start at York, however, reduces our average to 53.4 m.p.h. (See Maps 16 and 17.) |
| THIRSK to NORTHALLERTON | 7 | 1,320 | 8 | | | | The line rises very slightly. This section is covered at an average of 58.1 m.p.h. (See Maps 17 and 18.) |
| NORTHALLERTON to DARLINGTON | 14 | 308 | 15 | | | | The Wiske Water-troughs are taken at high speed. Speed is reduced approaching Darlington and we average 57.0 m.p.h. over this 14¼ miles. (See Map 18.) |
| DARLINGTON to FERRY HILL | 12 | 1,496 | 16 | | | | The line rises 1 : 220 and 1 : 203 until we reach the summit by milepost 55, 292 feet above sea level. We average 47.4 m.p.h. over this section. (See Maps 18 and 19.) |
| FERRY HILL to DURHAM | 9 | 330 | 12 | | | | Severe rising and falling gradients and speed restrictions limit our speed on this section, and we average 46.2 m.p.h. (See Maps 19 and 20.) |
| DURHAM to NEWCASTLE | 14 | 66 | 19 | | | | This is not a fast section of the line and our average works out at 44.2 m.p.h. The approach to Newcastle over the King Edward Bridge is taken very slowly. (See Maps 20 and 21.) |

(Continued on page 27)

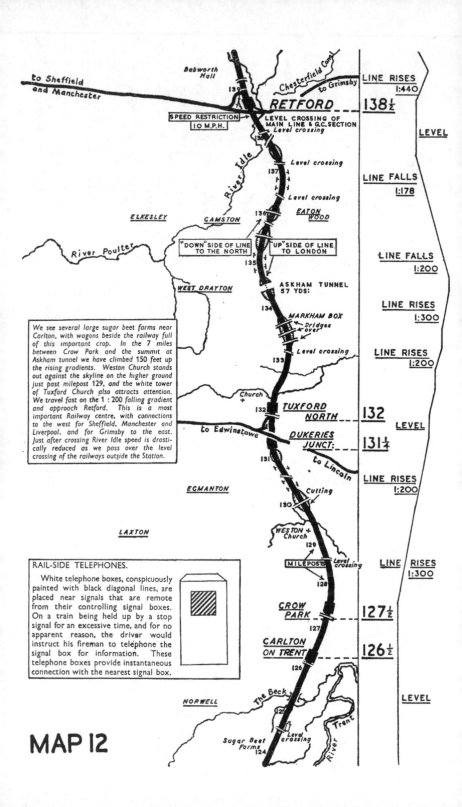

to Sheffield
and Manchester

Babworth Hall

139

Chesterfield Canal

to Grimsby

LINE RISES
1:440

**RETFORD**

138½

LEVEL

SPEED RESTRICTION
10 M.P.H.

LEVEL CROSSING OF
MAIN LINE & G.C. SECTION
*Level crossing*

*Level crossing*

137

*Level crossing*

LINE FALLS
1:178

River Idle

ELKESLEY

GAMSTON

136

**EATON
WOOD**

LINE FALLS
1:200

River Poulter

"DOWN" SIDE OF LINE
TO THE NORTH

"UP" SIDE OF LINE
TO LONDON

135

WEST DRAYTON

ASKHAM TUNNEL
57 YDS:

134

**MARKHAM BOX**
*Bridges
over*

LINE RISES
1:300

133

*Level crossing*

LINE RISES
1:200

> We see several large sugar beet farms near
> Carlton, with wagons beside the railway full
> of this important crop. In the 7 miles
> between Crow Park and the summit at
> Askham tunnel we have climbed 150 feet up
> the rising gradients. Weston Church stands
> out against the skyline on the higher ground
> just past milepost 129, and the white tower
> of Tuxford Church also attracts attention.
> We travel fast on the 1 : 200 falling gradient
> and approach Retford. This is a most
> important Railway centre, with connections
> to the west for Sheffield, Manchester and
> Liverpool, and for Grimsby to the east.
> Just after crossing River Idle speed is drasti-
> cally reduced as we pass over the level
> crossing of the railways outside the Station.

Church
+

132

**TUXFORD
NORTH**

132

LEVEL

to Edwinstowe

**DUKERIES
JUNCT:**

131¼

131

to Lincoln

LINE RISES
1:200

EGMANTON

130

Cutting

**WESTON +
Church**

129

LAXTON

MILEPOSTS

*Level
crossing*

LINE RISES
1:300

128

**CROW
PARK**

127½

127

**CARLTON
ON TRENT**

126½

126

NORWELL

The Beck

River Trent

LEVEL

125

*Level
crossing*

Sugar Beet
Farms

124

# MAP 12

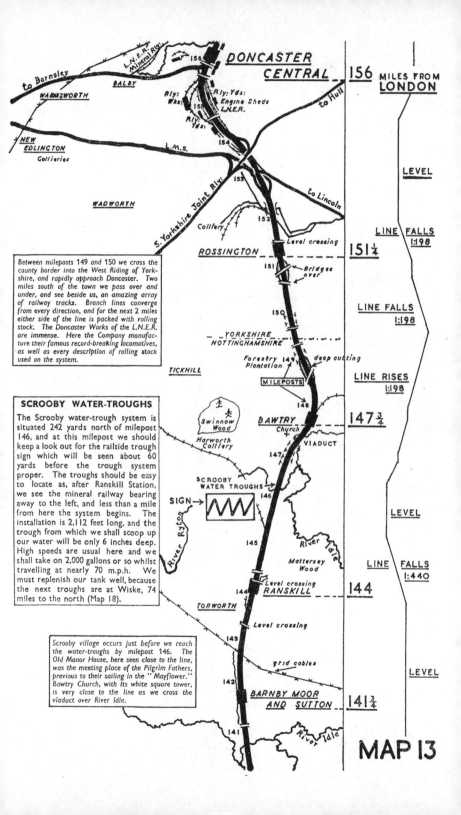

Between mileposts 149 and 150 we cross the county border into the West Riding of Yorkshire, and rapidly approach Doncaster. Two miles south of the town we pass over and under, an amazing array of railway tracks. Branch lines converge from every direction, and for the next 2 miles either side of the line is packed with rolling stock. The Doncaster Works of the L.N.E.R. are immense. Here the Company manufacture their famous record-breaking locomotives, as well as every description of rolling stock used on the system.

### SCROOBY WATER-TROUGHS

The Scrooby water-trough system is situated 242 yards north of milepost 146, and at this milepost we should keep a look out for the railside trough sign which will be seen about 60 yards before the trough system proper. The troughs should be easy to locate as, after Ranskill Station, we see the mineral railway bearing away to the left, and less than a mile from here the system begins. The installation is 2,112 feet long, and the trough from which we shall scoop up our water will be only 6 inches deep. High speeds are usual here and we shall take on 2,000 gallons or so whilst travelling at nearly 70 m.p.h. We must replenish our tank well, because the next troughs are at Wiske, 74 miles to the north (Map 18).

Scrooby village occurs just before we reach the water-troughs by milepost 146. The Old Manor House, here seen close to the line, was the meeting place of the Pilgrim Fathers, previous to their sailing in the "Mayflower." Bawtry Church, with its white square tower, is very close to the line as we cross the viaduct over River Idle.

**MAP 13**

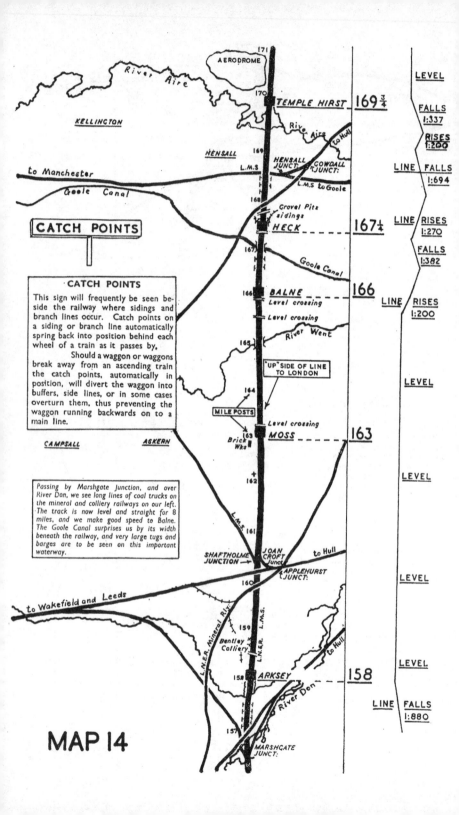

RIVER AIRE

AERODROME                                          171

                                                    170

KELLINGTON                    TEMPLE HIRST         169¾        LEVEL

                                                              FALLS
                                    River Aire                1:337

HENSALL                  169                to Hull           RISES
                                    HENSALL    COWDALL        1:200
to Manchester           L.M.S.      JUNCT.     JUNCT.    LINE FALLS
                                    L.M.S to Goole             1:694
        Goole Canal
                              168
                                    Gravel Pits                LINE RISES
                                    sidings       167½             1:270
        CATCH POINTS                 HECK
                                                              FALLS
                              167                             1:382
                                          Goole Canal
        **CATCH POINTS**
                              166   BALNE           166       LINE RISES
This sign will frequently be seen be-      Level crossing          1:200
side the railway where sidings and
branch lines occur.   Catch points on      Level crossing
a siding or branch line automatically
spring back into position behind each      River Went
wheel of a train as it passes by.
        Should a waggon or waggons   165
break away from an ascending train
the catch points, automatically  in       "UP" SIDE OF LINE     LEVEL
position, will divert the waggon into       TO LONDON
buffers, side lines, or in some cases 164
overturn them, thus preventing the
waggon running backwards on to a    MILE POSTS
main line.
                                           Level crossing
CAMPSALL            ASKERN     163  MOSS            163       LEVEL
                                    Brick
                                    Wks
                              162
                                                              LEVEL
Passing by Marshgate Junction, and over
River Don, we see long lines of coal trucks on
the mineral and colliery railways on our left.
The track is now level and straight for 8  161
miles, and we make good speed to Balne.
The Goole Canal surprises us by its width
beneath the railway, and very large tugs and
barges are to be seen on this important      JOAN
waterway.                           CROFT   to Hull
                        SHAFTHOLME  Junct.
                        JUNCTION →       APPLEHURST
                              160         JUNCT.          LEVEL
to Wakefield and Leeds

                              159
                                    Bentley
                                    Colliery
                                                              LEVEL
                              158  ARKSEY           158
                                                    River Don
                                                              LINE FALLS
                              157                                 1:880
        MAP 14                      MARSHGATE
                                    JUNCT.

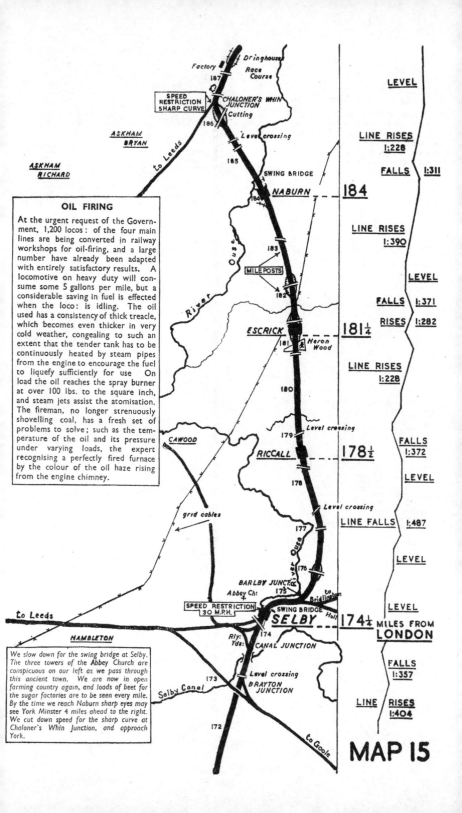

Factory
187

Dringhouses
Race Course

SPEED RESTRICTION SHARP CURVE

CHALONER'S WHIN JUNCTION
Cutting
186

ASKHAM BRYAN

ASKHAM RICHARD

*To Leeds*

Level crossing
185

SWING BRIDGE

NABURN
184
184

LEVEL

LINE RISES 1:228

FALLS 1:311

River Ouse

183

MILE POSTS
182

LINE RISES 1:390

LEVEL

FALLS 1:371

RISES 1:282

ESCRICK
181
Heron Wood
181¼

LINE RISES 1:228

180

CAWOOD

179
Level crossing
RICCALL
178½

178

FALLS 1:372

LEVEL

grid cables

Level crossing
177

LINE FALLS 1:487

LEVEL

176

BARLBY JUNC:
Abbey Ch:
175
to Bridlington

SPEED RESTRICTION 30 M.P.H.
SWING BRIDGE
to Hull
SELBY
174¼

*To Leeds*

174
CANAL JUNCTION

Rly: Yds:

LEVEL

MILES FROM LONDON

FALLS 1:357

HAMBLETON

173
Level crossing
BRAYTON JUNCTION

Selby Canal

LINE RISES 1:404

172

to Goole

## MAP 15

### OIL FIRING

At the urgent request of the Government, 1,200 locos : of the four main lines are being converted in railway workshops for oil-firing, and a large number have already been adapted with entirely satisfactory results. A locomotive on heavy duty will consume some 5 gallons per mile, but a considerable saving in fuel is effected when the loco: is idling. The oil used has a consistency of thick treacle, which becomes even thicker in very cold weather, congealing to such an extent that the tender tank has to be continuously heated by steam pipes from the engine to encourage the fuel to liquefy sufficiently for use  On load the oil reaches the spray burner at over 100 lbs. to the square inch, and steam jets assist the atomisation. The fireman, no longer strenuously shovelling coal, has a fresh set of problems to solve ; such as the temperature of the oil and its pressure under varying loads, the expert recognising a perfectly fired furnace by the colour of the oil haze rising from the engine chimney.

*We slow down for the swing bridge at Selby. The three towers of the Abbey Church are conspicuous on our left as we pass through this ancient town.  We are now in open farming country again, and loads of beet for the sugar factories are to be seen every mile. By the time we reach Naburn sharp eyes may see York Minster 4 miles ahead to the right. We cut down speed for the sharp curve at Chaloner's Whin Junction, and approach York.*

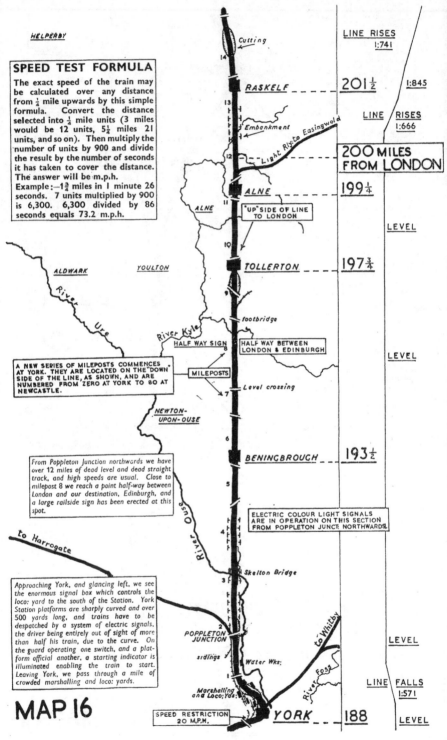

HELPERBY

## SPEED TEST FORMULA

The exact speed of the train may be calculated over any distance from $\frac{1}{4}$ mile upwards by this simple formula. Convert the distance selected into $\frac{1}{4}$ mile units (3 miles would be 12 units, $5\frac{1}{4}$ miles 21 units, and so on). Then multiply the number of units by 900 and divide the result by the number of seconds it has taken to cover the distance. The answer will be m.p.h.
Example:—$1\frac{3}{4}$ miles in 1 minute 26 seconds. 7 units multiplied by 900 is 6,300. 6,300 divided by 86 seconds equals 73.2 m.p.h.

Cutting

14

RASKELF

13

Embankment

12     Light Rly. to Easingwold

ALNE

11     "UP" SIDE OF LINE
TO LONDON

10

TOLLERTON

9

footbridge

River Kyle

HALF WAY SIGN     8     HALF WAY BETWEEN
LONDON & EDINBURGH

A NEW SERIES OF MILEPOSTS COMMENCES AT YORK. THEY ARE LOCATED ON THE "DOWN" SIDE OF THE LINE, AS SHOWN, AND ARE NUMBERED FROM ZERO AT YORK TO 80 AT NEWCASTLE.

MILEPOSTS

7     Level crossing

NEWTON-UPON-OUSE

6

BENINGBROUGH

From Poppleton Junction northwards we have over 12 miles of dead level and dead straight track, and high speeds are usual. Close to milepost 8 we reach a point half-way between London and our destination, Edinburgh, and a large railside sign has been erected at this spot.

5

ELECTRIC COLOUR LIGHT SIGNALS ARE IN OPERATION ON THIS SECTION FROM POPPLETON JUNCT. NORTHWARDS.

to Harrogate

4

3     Skelton Bridge

Approaching York, and glancing left, we see the enormous signal box which controls the loco: yard to the south of the Station. York Station platforms are sharply curved and over 500 yards long, and trains have to be despatched by a system of electric signals, the driver being entirely out of sight of more than half his train, due to the curve. On the guard operating one switch, and a platform official another, a starting indicator is illuminated enabling the train to start. Leaving York, we pass through a mile of crowded marshalling and loco: yards.

2
POPPLETON
JUNCTION

sidings     Water Wks:

to Whitby

River Foss

Marshalling and Loco: Yds:

## MAP 16

SPEED RESTRICTION
20 M.P.H.

YORK     188

LINE RISES
1:741

$201\frac{1}{2}$     1:845

LINE RISES
1:666

**200 MILES
FROM LONDON**

$199\frac{1}{4}$

LEVEL

$197\frac{3}{4}$

LEVEL

$193\frac{1}{2}$

LEVEL

LINE FALLS
1:571

LEVEL

(See Errata note on page ?

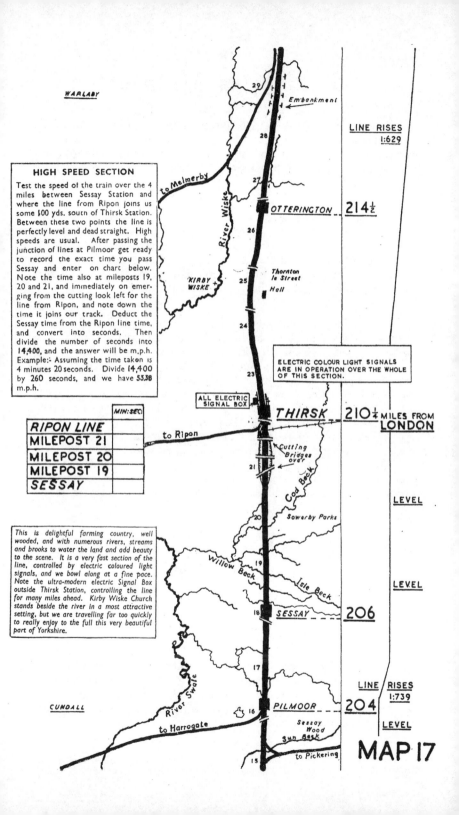

WARLABY

LINE RISES
1:629

to Melmerby

River Wiske

Embankment

29

28

27

OTTERINGTON    214½

26

Thornton
le Street

25

Hall

'KIRBY
WISKE'

24

23

ELECTRIC COLOUR LIGHT SIGNALS
ARE IN OPERATION OVER THE WHOLE
OF THIS SECTION.

## HIGH SPEED SECTION

Test the speed of the train over the 4 miles between Sessay Station and where the line from Ripon joins us some 100 yds. south of Thirsk Station. Between these two points the line is perfectly level and dead straight. High speeds are usual.    After passing the junction of lines at Pilmoor get ready to record the exact time you pass Sessay and enter on chart below. Note the time also at mileposts 19, 20 and 21, and immediately on emerging from the cutting look left for the line from Ripon, and note down the time it joins our track.    Deduct the Sessay time from the Ripon line time, and convert into seconds.    Then divide the number of seconds into 14,400, and the answer will be m.p.h. Example:- Assuming the time taken is 4 minutes 20 seconds.  Divide 14,400 by 260 seconds, and we have 55.38 m.p.h.

ALL ELECTRIC
SIGNAL BOX

THIRSK    210¼ MILES FROM
LONDON

to Ripon

Cutting
Bridges
over

| | MIN:SEC |
|---|---|
| *RIPON LINE* | |
| MILEPOST 21 | |
| MILEPOST 20 | |
| MILEPOST 19 | |
| *SESSAY* | |

21

Cod Beck

LEVEL

20

Sowerby Parks

Willow Beck

19

Isle Beck

This is delightful farming country, well wooded, and with numerous rivers, streams and brooks to water the land and add beauty to the scene.  It is a very fast section of the line, controlled by electric coloured light signals, and we bowl along at a fine pace. Note the ultra-modern electric Signal Box outside Thirsk Station, controlling the line for many miles ahead.  Kirby Wiske Church stands beside the river in a most attractive setting, but we are travelling far too quickly to really enjoy to the full this very beautiful part of Yorkshire.

LEVEL

18    SESSAY    206

17

River Swale

CUNDALL

16    PILMOOR    204

to Harrogate

Sessay
Wood
Sun Beck

LINE RISES
1:739

LEVEL

to Pickering

15

## MAP 17

# Spotting the Mileposts

Where are we now? The pleasures of a railway journey will be immensely increased if, at any given moment, we can tell to a nicety our exact position, and how far it is to the next water-troughs, the next river, junction or Station. Also the exact speed at which we are travelling.

By law, Railway Companies are required to place mile posts alongside the track every ¼ mile throughout the system, and exactly where to look for these posts is shown on every map in this book. ¼, ½ and ¾ posts are omitted but every actual mile post is indicated. They are easily seen, and only at very high speeds will any difficulty be experienced in spotting the clearly numbered posts.

Numbering is effected in four distinct sections and, except between Berwick and Edinburgh, all the posts are on the "down" side of the line—that is, on our left hand side travelling north. Starting at zero at Kings Cross the numbers add up until we reach post 188 at York. Here another series begins numbered from zero at York to 80 at Newcastle. Newcastle starts a third series from zero to 67 at Berwick. Between Berwick and Edinburgh the posts are placed on the opposite side of the line, the "up" side, and are numbered in reverse order from 57 near Berwick down to zero at Edinburgh. The maps in this book show milepost positions as accurately as the scale will allow. By spotting the mileposts we can ascertain and check the speed of the train to very fine limits. The method of so doing is explained on all maps herein where really high speeds are to be expected.

# Average Speeds

Attention is drawn to the Charts on pages 5, 13 and 27, which indicate normal express running times between principal Stations.

By checking actual times against those printed, and making entries in column 4, the passenger is able to tell whether his train running early, late, or to time. Great interest can be added to the journey by comparing the actual average speeds of the train against those given in the Charts.

# On Other Pages

# SEMAPHORE SIGNALS

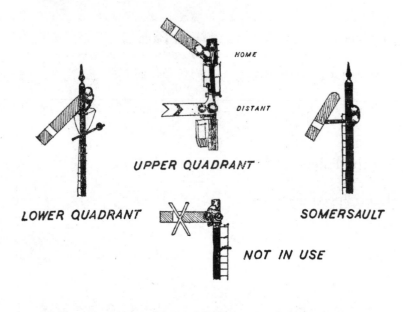

HOME

DISTANT

UPPER QUADRANT

LOWER QUADRANT

SOMERSAULT

NOT IN USE

# COLOUR LIGHT SIGNALS

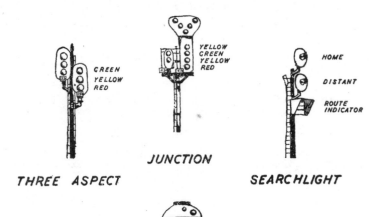

GREEN
YELLOW
RED

YELLOW
GREEN
YELLOW
RED

HOME

DISTANT

ROUTE
INDICATOR

JUNCTION

THREE ASPECT

SEARCHLIGHT

SHUNT SIGNAL

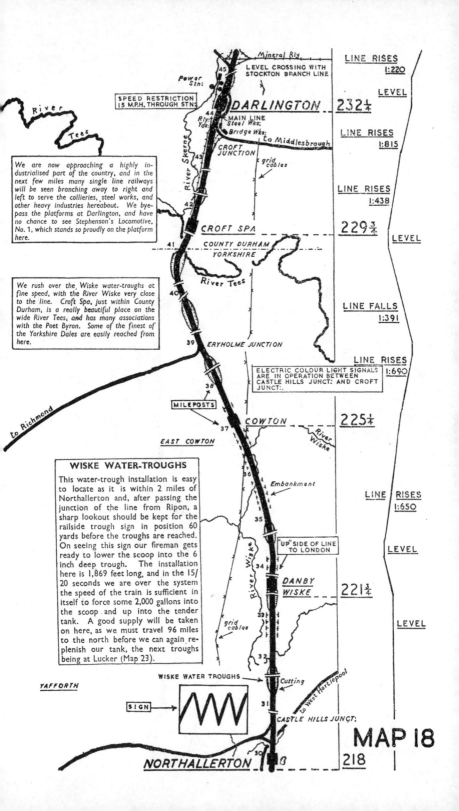

LINE RISES 1:220

LEVEL

LINE CROSSING WITH STOCKTON BRANCH LINE

Mineral Rly.

45

Power Stn:

SPEED RESTRICTION 15 M.P.H. THROUGH STN:

DARLINGTON

232½

44 MAIN LINE
Rly: Yds: Steel Wks:

Bridge Wks:

To Middlesbrough

LINE RISES 1:815

43

CROFT JUNCTION

grid cables

We are now approaching a highly industrialised part of the country, and in the next few miles many single line railways will be seen branching away to right and left to serve the collieries, steel works, and other heavy industries hereabout. We bypass the platforms at Darlington, and have no chance to see Stephenson's Locomotive, No. 1, which stands so proudly on the platform here.

42

LINE RISES 1:438

229¾

CROFT SPA

41

COUNTY DURHAM
YORKSHIRE

LEVEL

We rush over the Wiske water-troughs at fine speed, with the River Wiske very close to the line. Croft Spa, just within County Durham, is a really beautiful place on the wide River Tees, and has many associations with the Poet Byron. Some of the finest of the Yorkshire Dales are easily reached from here.

40

River Tees

LINE FALLS 1:391

39    ERYHOLME JUNCTION

To Richmond

38

MILEPOSTS

LINE RISES 1:690

ELECTRIC COLOUR LIGHT SIGNALS ARE IN OPERATION BETWEEN CASTLE HILLS JUNCT: AND CROFT JUNCT:.

37    COWTON

225¼

EAST COWTON

River Wiske

36

**WISKE WATER-TROUGHS**

This water-trough installation is easy to locate as it is within 2 miles of Northallerton and, after passing the junction of the line from Ripon, a sharp lookout should be kept for the railside trough sign in position 60 yards before the troughs are reached. On seeing this sign our fireman gets ready to lower the scoop into the 6 inch deep trough. The installation here is 1,869 feet long, and in the 15/20 seconds we are over the system the speed of the train is sufficient in itself to force some 2,000 gallons into the scoop and up into the tender tank. A good supply will be taken on here, as we must travel 96 miles to the north before we can again replenish our tank, the next troughs being at Lucker (Map 23).

Embankment

35

LINE RISES 1:650

LEVEL

"UP" SIDE OF LINE TO LONDON

34

DANBY WISKE

221¾

River Wiske

33

LEVEL

grid cables

32

WISKE WATER TROUGHS    Cutting

YAFFORTH

SIGN

31    CASTLE HILLS JUNCT:

To West Hartlepool

**MAP 18**

30    B    218

**NORTHALLERTON**

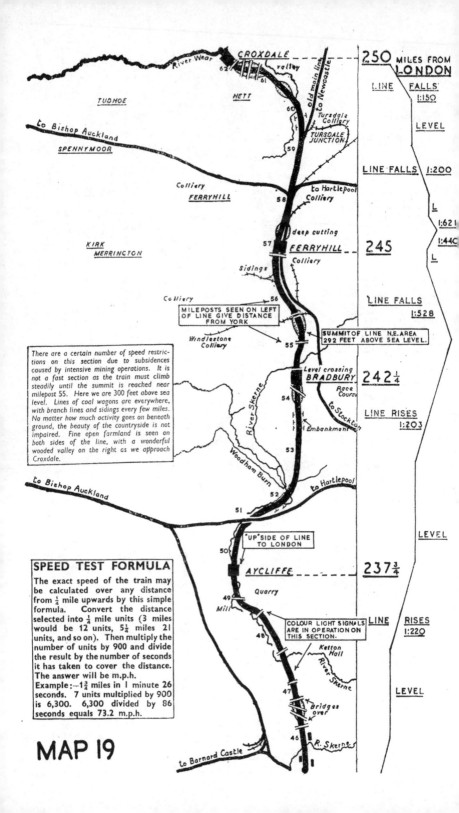

**250** MILES FROM **LONDON**

CROXDALE

River Wear

62

61 valley

old main line to Newcastle

TUDHOE

HETT

60

to Bishop Auckland

SPENNYMOOR

Tursdale Colliery

TURSDALE JUNCTION

59

LINE FALLS 1:150

LEVEL

LINE FALLS 1:200

Colliery FERRYHILL

58

to Hartlepool Colliery

L 1:621

1:440

L

deep cutting

57 FERRYHILL Colliery

**245**

KIRK MERRINGTON

Sidings

Colliery

56

MILEPOSTS SEEN ON LEFT OF LINE GIVE DISTANCE FROM YORK

LINE FALLS 1:528

Windlestone Colliery

55

SUMMIT OF LINE N.E.AREA 292 FEET ABOVE SEA LEVEL.

> There are a certain number of speed restrictions on this section due to subsidences caused by intensive mining operations. It is not a fast section as the train must climb steadily until the summit is reached near milepost 55. Here we are 300 feet above sea level. Lines of coal wagons are everywhere, with branch lines and sidings every few miles. No matter how much activity goes on beneath ground, the beauty of the countryside is not impaired. Fine open farmland is seen on both sides of the line, with a wonderful wooded valley on the right as we approach Croxdale.

Level crossing BRADBURY

54

Race Course

to Stockton

Embankment

53

Woodham Burn

52

to Hartlepool

51

to Bishop Auckland

50

"UP" SIDE OF LINE TO LONDON

**242¼**

LINE RISES 1:203

LEVEL

**237¾**

AYCLIFFE

## SPEED TEST FORMULA

The exact speed of the train may be calculated over any distance from ¼ mile upwards by this simple formula. Convert the distance selected into ¼ mile units (3 miles would be 12 units, 5¼ miles 21 units, and so on). Then multiply the number of units by 900 and divide the result by the number of seconds it has taken to cover the distance. The answer will be m.p.h.
Example:—1¾ miles in 1 minute 26 seconds. 7 units multiplied by 900 is 6,300. 6,300 divided by 86 seconds equals 73.2 m.p.h.

Quarry

49

Mill

48

COLOUR LIGHT SIGNALS ARE IN OPERATION ON THIS SECTION.

Ketton Hall

River Skerne

LINE RISES 1:220

47

Bridges over

46

R. Skerne

LEVEL

to Barnard Castle

# MAP 19

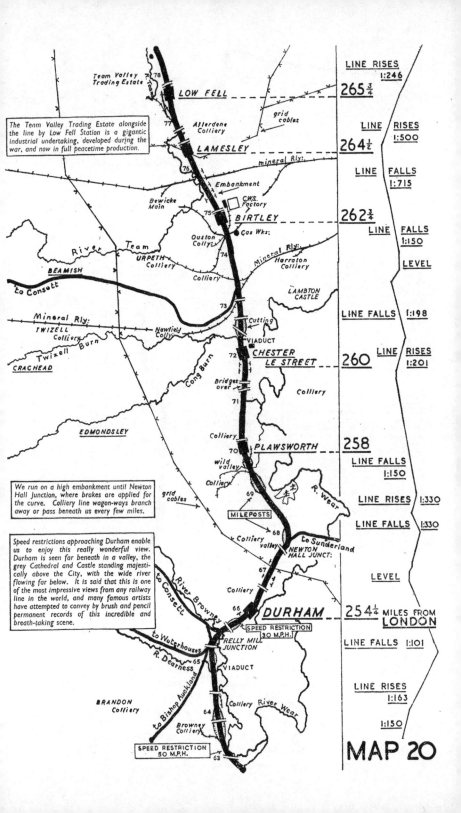

**MAP 20**

Team Valley Trading Estate

78

LOW FELL — — — — 265¾ LINE RISES 1:246

77

Allerdene Colliery

grid cables

LAMESLEY — — — — 264½ LINE RISES 1:500

The Team Valley Trading Estate alongside the line by Low Fell Station is a gigantic industrial undertaking, developed during the war, and now in full peacetime production.

76

mineral Rly:

Embankment

Bewicke Main

LINE FALLS 1:715

75

C.W.S. Factory

BIRTLEY — — — — 262¾

Gas Wks:

Outton Colly:

LINE FALLS 1:150

River Team

URPETH Colliery

BEAMISH

to Consett

74

Colliery

Mineral Rly:

Harraton Colliery

LEVEL

LAMBTON CASTLE

73

Mineral Rly:

TWIZELL Colliery

Twizell Burn

Nawfield Colly:

Cong Burn

Cutting

VIADUCT

72

CHESTER LE STREET — — — 260 LINE RISES 1:201

CRACHEAD

LINE FALLS 1:198

Colliery

Bridges over

71

Colliery

EDMONDSLEY

70

Colliery

PLAWSWORTH 258

wild valley

Colliery

LINE FALLS 1:150

We run on a high embankment until Newton Hall Junction, where brakes are applied for the curve. Colliery line wagon-ways branch away or pass beneath us every few miles.

grid cables

69

R. Wear

LINE RISES 1:330

MILEPOSTS

Colliery valley

68

LINE FALLS 1:330

to Sunderland

NEWTON HALL JUNCT:

Speed restrictions approaching Durham enable us to enjoy this really wonderful view. Durham is seen far beneath in a valley, the grey Cathedral and Castle standing majestically above the City, with the wide river flowing far below. It is said that this is one of the most impressive views from any railway line in the world, and many famous artists have attempted to convey by brush and pencil permanent records of this incredible and breath-taking scene.

67

Colliery

LEVEL

River Browney

to Consett

66

DURHAM 254¼ MILES FROM LONDON

SPEED RESTRICTION 30 M.P.H.

RELLY MILL JUNCTION

to Waterhouses

LINE FALLS 1:101

R. Dearness

65

VIADUCT

BRANDON Colliery

to Bishop Auckland

64

Colliery

River Wear

LINE RISES 1:163

Browney Colliery

1:150

SPEED RESTRICTION 50 M.P.H.

63

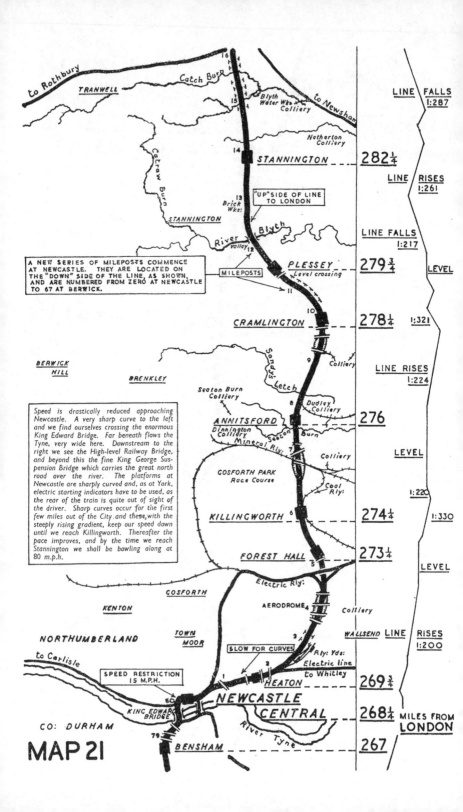

to Rothbury

TRANWELL

Catch Burn

to Newsham

Blyth
Water Wks
Colliery

Netherton
Colliery

LINE FALLS
1:287

16

15

14    STANNINGTON    282¼

LINE RISES
1:261

13
Brick
Wks.

"UP" SIDE OF LINE
TO LONDON

STANNINGTON

River    Blyth

valley    12

LINE FALLS
1:217

A NEW SERIES OF MILEPOSTS COMMENCE
AT NEWCASTLE. THEY ARE LOCATED ON
THE "DOWN" SIDE OF THE LINE, AS SHOWN,
AND ARE NUMBERED FROM ZERO AT NEWCASTLE
TO 67 AT BERWICK.

MILEPOSTS

PLESSEY    279¾

Level crossing

LEVEL

11

10    CRAMLINGTON    278¼    1:321

9    Colliery

BERWICK
HILL

BRENKLEY

Sandys Letch

Seaton Burn
Colliery

8    Dudley
Colliery

LINE RISES
1:224

ANNITSFORD    276

Speed is drastically reduced approaching
Newcastle. A very sharp curve to the left
and we find ourselves crossing the enormous
King Edward Bridge. Far beneath flows the
Tyne, very wide here. Downstream to the
right we see the High-level Railway Bridge,
and beyond this the fine King George Sus-
pension Bridge which carries the great north
road over the river. The platforms at
Newcastle are sharply curved and, as at York,
electric starting indicators have to be used, as
the rear of the train is quite out of sight of
the driver. Sharp curves occur for the first
few miles out of the City and these, with the
steeply rising gradient, keep our speed down
until we reach Killingworth. Thereafter the
pace improves, and by the time we reach
Stannington we shall be bowling along at
80 m.p.h.

Dinnington
Colliery

Seaton Burn

Mineral Rly.    7    Colliery

LEVEL

GOSFORTH PARK
Race Course

Cool
Rly.    1:220

KILLINGWORTH    6    274¼    1:330

FOREST HALL    273¼

5

LEVEL

Electric Rly.

GOSFORTH

KENTON

AERODROME    4    Colliery

TOWN
MOOR

WALLSEND    LINE RISES
1:200

NORTHUMBERLAND

to Carlisle

Rly. Yds.
Electric line
to Whitley

SPEED RESTRICTION
15 M.P.H.

SLOW FOR CURVES

1

3

80    2

HEATON    269¾

KING EDWARD
BRIDGE

NEWCASTLE    268¼

CO: DURHAM    CENTRAL    MILES FROM
LONDON

MAP 21    79    River Tyne    267

BENSHAM

# LONDON—EDINBURGH

## EXACT DISTANCES BETWEEN STATIONS—EXPRESS TRAIN RUNNING TIMES

| (1) STATION | (2) Distance Between Stations | | (3) Express Train Running Times | (4) Actual Running Times | | | (5) NOTES and Average Speeds over each Section |
|---|---|---|---|---|---|---|---|
| | Miles | Yards | Minutes | Minutes | Early | Late | |
| NEWCASTLE to MORPETH | 16 | 1,100 | 28 | | | | From a standing start we commence slowly, and for several miles our speed is restricted by curves. Rising gradients for 10 miles keep down our progress. High speeds are attained after Cramlington, but we must slow down for the curve at Morpeth. Average 35.5 m.p.h. (See Maps 21 and 22.) |
| MORPETH to ALNMOUTH | 18 | 418 | 20 | | | | This is quite a fast section, particularly between Widdrington and Acklington, and on testing we shall find we are travelling at nearer 80 than 70 m.p.h. We average 54.7 m.p.h. over this 18¼ miles. (See Maps 22 and 23.) |
| ALNMOUTH to BELFORD | 16 | 1,385 | 18 | | | | After climbing for 4 miles we make fine speed down the 1 : 150 gradient and pass over the Lucker Water-troughs at nearly 70 m.p.h., maintaining this speed to Belford. Average speed 55.8 m.p.h. (See Maps 23 and 24.) |
| BELFORD to BERWICK | 15 | 616 | 18 | | | | The line falls all the way to Goswick and we make fine speed. The approach to Berwick through Tweedmouth and over the Royal Border Bridge is taken very slowly. (Average speed 51.6 m.p.h. (See Maps 24 and 25.) |
| BERWICK to RESTON | 11 | 484 | 17 | | | | From a standing start we travel slowly up the 1 : 190 gradient past the border of England and Scotland. Once over the summit, near Ayton, we make fine progress. Average speed only 39.7 m.p.h. (See Map 25.) |
| RESTON to DUNBAR | 17 | — | 21 | | | | Speed is not high for the first 5 miles of this section due to the rising gradients, but it is very high from Penmanshiel tunnel onwards. We approach Dunbar slowly. Average speed 48.5 m.p.h. (See Maps 25 and 26.) |
| DUNBAR to DREM | 11 | 880 | 13 | | | | Although the gradients are not favourable, this is, nevertheless, a fast 11¼ miles, and we average 53 m.p.h. (See Maps 26 and 27.) |
| DREM to WAVERLEY | 17 | 1,320 | 30 | | | | Speed is high as far as Inveresk, but from here we slow down considerably as we approach Edinburgh. We climb a severe 1 : 98 gradient over the last 1¼ miles. Average speed works out at 35.5 m.p.h. (See Maps 27 and 28.) |

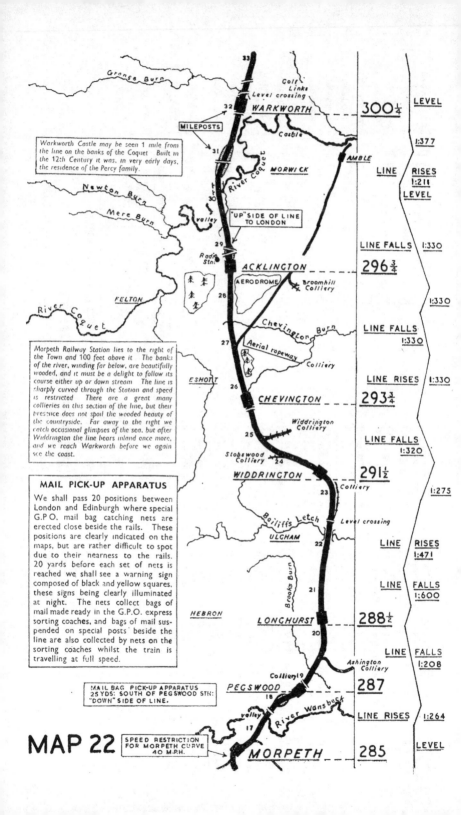

MAP 22

Warkworth Castle may be seen 1 mile from the line on the banks of the Coquet. Built in the 12th Century it was, in very early days, the residence of the Percy family.

MILEPOSTS

"UP" SIDE OF LINE TO LONDON

Morpeth Railway Station lies to the right of the Town and 100 feet above it. The banks of the river, winding far below, are beautifully wooded, and it must be a delight to follow its course either up or down stream. The line is sharply curved through the Station and speed is restricted. There are a great many collieries on this section of the line, but their presence does not spoil the wooded beauty of the countryside. Far away to the right we catch occasional glimpses of the sea, but after Widdrington the line bears inland once more, and we reach Warkworth before we again see the coast.

## MAIL PICK-UP APPARATUS

We shall pass 20 positions between London and Edinburgh where special G.P.O. mail bag catching nets are erected close beside the rails. These positions are clearly indicated on the maps, but are rather difficult to spot due to their nearness to the rails. 20 yards before each set of nets is reached we shall see a warning sign composed of black and yellow squares, these signs being clearly illuminated at night. The nets collect bags of mail made ready in the G.P.O. express sorting coaches, and bags of mail suspended on special posts beside the line are also collected by nets on the sorting coaches whilst the train is travelling at full speed.

MAIL BAG PICK-UP APPARATUS 25 YDS. SOUTH OF PEGSWOOD STN: "DOWN" SIDE OF LINE.

SPEED RESTRICTION FOR MORPETH CURVE 40 M.P.H.

Grange Burn
Golf Links
Level crossing
WARKWORTH — 300¼ — LEVEL — 1:377
Castle
AMBLE — LINE RISES 1:211 — LEVEL
MORWICK
River Coquet
Newton Burn
Mere Burn
valley
Radio Stn.
ACKLINGTON — 296¾ — LINE FALLS 1:330
AERODROME
Broomhill Colliery — 1:330
FELTON
River Coquet
Chevington Burn
Aerial ropeway — LINE FALLS 1:330
Colliery
ESHOTT
CHEVINGTON — 293¾ — LINE RISES 1:330
Widdrington Colliery — LINE FALLS 1:320
Stobswood Colliery
WIDDRINGTON — 291½
Colliery — 1:275
Bailiff's Letch — Level crossing
ULCHAM
LINE RISES 1:471
Brooks Burn
LINE FALLS 1:600
HEBRON
LONGHURST — 288½
Ashington Colliery — LINE FALLS 1:208
Colliery
PEGSWOOD — 287
River Wansbeck — LINE RISES 1:264
valley
MORPETH — 285 — LEVEL

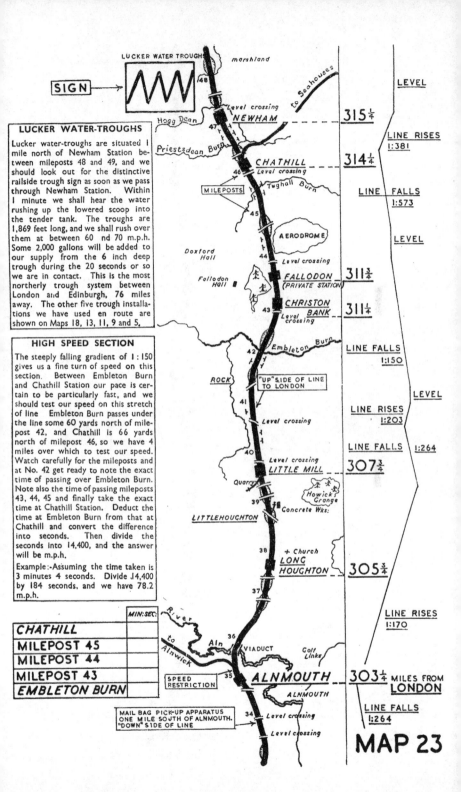

SIGN → LUCKER WATER TROUGH

## LUCKER WATER-TROUGHS

Lucker water-troughs are situated 1 mile north of Newham Station between mileposts 48 and 49, and we should look out for the distinctive railside trough sign as soon as we pass through Newham Station. Within 1 minute we shall hear the water rushing up the lowered scoop into the tender tank. The troughs are 1,869 feet long, and we shall rush over them at between 60 nd 70 m.p.h. Some 2,000 gallons will be added to our supply from the 6 inch deep trough during the 20 seconds or so we are in contact. This is the most northerly trough system between London and Edinburgh, 76 miles away. The other five trough installations we have used en route are shown on Maps 18, 13, 11, 9 and 5.

## HIGH SPEED SECTION

The steeply falling gradient of 1 : 150 gives us a fine turn of speed on this section. Between Embleton Burn and Chathill Station our pace is certain to be particularly fast, and we should test our speed on this stretch of line Embleton Burn passes under the line some 60 yards north of milepost 42, and Chathill is 66 yards north of milepost 46, so we have 4 miles over which to test our speed. Watch carefully for the mileposts and at No. 42 get ready to note the exact time of passing over Embleton Burn. Note also the time of passing mileposts 43, 44, 45 and finally take the exact time at Chathill Station. Deduct the time at Embleton Burn from that at Chathill and convert the difference into seconds. Then divide the seconds into 14,400, and the answer will be m.p.h.

Example:- Assuming the time taken is 3 minutes 4 seconds. Divide .14,400 by 184 seconds, and we have 78.2 m.p.h.

| | MIN: SEC: |
|---|---|
| CHATHILL | |
| MILEPOST 45 | |
| MILEPOST 44 | |
| MILEPOST 43 | |
| EMBLETON BURN | |

MILEPOSTS

marshland

to Seahouses

Hogg Dean

Level crossing
NEWHAM

Priestsdean Burn

CHATHILL
Level crossing

Tughall Burn

AERODROME

Doxford Hall

Level crossing

Fallodon Hall

FALLODON
(PRIVATE STATION)

CHRISTON BANK
Level crossing

Embleton Burn

ROCK

"UP" SIDE OF LINE TO LONDON

Level crossing

Level crossing
LITTLE MILL

Quarry

Howick Grange

Concrete Wks:

LITTLEHOUGHTON

+ Church
LONG HOUGHTON

River

to
Alnwick

Aln

VIADUCT

Golf Links

SPEED RESTRICTION

ALNMOUTH

ALNMOUTH

MAIL BAG PICK-UP APPARATUS
ONE MILE SOUTH OF ALNMOUTH.
"DOWN" SIDE OF LINE

Level crossing

Level crossing

LEVEL

315¼

LINE RISES 1:381

314¼

LINE FALLS 1:573

LEVEL

311¾

311¼

LINE FALLS 1:150

LEVEL

LINE RISES 1:203

LINE FALLS 1:264

307¾

305¾

LINE RISES 1:170

303¼ MILES FROM LONDON

LINE FALLS 1:264

MAP 23

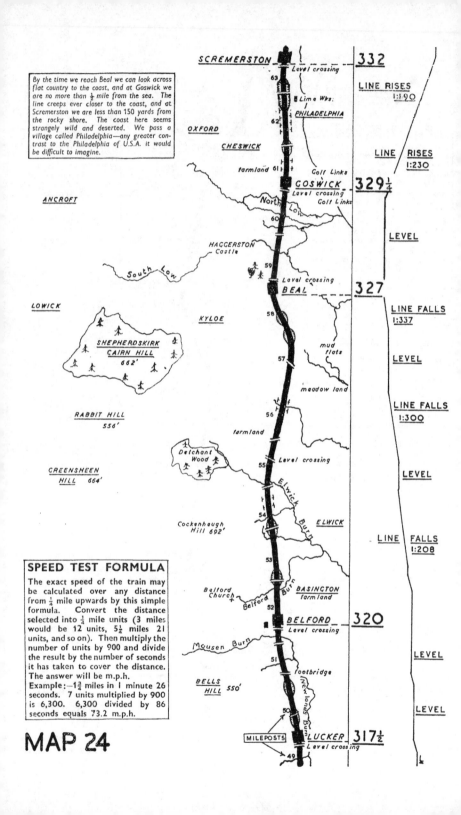

SCREMERSTON
*Level crossing*
332

LINE RISES
1:190

63

Lime Wks.
PHILADELPHIA

62

OXFORD

CHESWICK

LINE / RISES
1:230

*farmland* 61

Golf Links

GOSWICK
*Level crossing*
329¼

ANCROFT

North Low

Golf Links

60

LEVEL

HAGGERSTON
Castle

59

South Low

*Level crossing*
BEAL
327

LOWICK

KYLOE

58

LINE FALLS
1:337

SHEPHERDSKIRK
CAIRN HILL
662'

*mud flats*

57

LEVEL

*meadow land*

LINE FALLS
1:300

RABBIT HILL
556'

56

*farmland*

Delchant
Wood

55

*Level crossing*

LEVEL

GREENSHEEN
HILL 664'

Elwick Burn

54

ELWICK

Cockenhaugh
Hill 692'

LINE FALLS
1:208

53

Belford
Church

Belford Burn

BASINGTON
*farmland*

52

BELFORD
*Level crossing*
320

Mousen Burn

51

*footbridge*

LEVEL

BELLS
HILL 550'

Newlands Burn

50

LEVEL

MILEPOSTS

LUCKER
*Level crossing*
317½

49

## SPEED TEST FORMULA

The exact speed of the train may be calculated over any distance from ¼ mile upwards by this simple formula. Convert the distance selected into ¼ mile units (3 miles would be 12 units, 5¼ miles 21 units, and so on). Then multiply the number of units by 900 and divide the result by the number of seconds it has taken to cover the distance. The answer will be m.p.h.
Example:—1¾ miles in 1 minute 26 seconds. 7 units multiplied by 900 is 6,300. 6,300 divided by 86 seconds equals 73.2 m.p.h.

# MAP 24

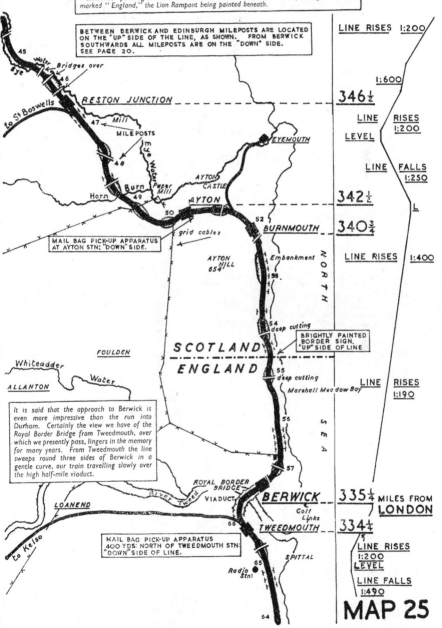

**THE BORDER**

Three miles north of Berwick, between mileposts 54 and 55, a brightly painted sign indicates the exact position of the boundary between England and Scotland. The sign is placed against a low stone wall on the "up" side of the line, and is easily visible from the train. Deep cuttings occur both to the north and south of the boundary, momentarily spoiling our view of the sea. On emerging into the clear from either cutting we should keep a sharp look out. On one side of the sign is painted the Scottish Unicorn, with above an arm marked "Scotland," pointing northwards. The other side shows a similar arm pointing southwards marked "England," the Lion Rampant being painted beneath.

BETWEEN BERWICK AND EDINBURGH MILEPOSTS ARE LOCATED ON THE "UP" SIDE OF THE LINE, AS SHOWN. FROM BERWICK SOUTHWARDS ALL MILEPOSTS ARE ON THE "DOWN" SIDE. SEE PAGE 20.

LINE RISES 1:200

1:600

RESTON JUNCTION

346½

LINE RISES 1:200

LINE LEVEL

EYEMOUTH

LINE FALLS 1:250

MILEPOSTS

342½

AYTON

BURNMOUTH

340¾

MAIL BAG PICK-UP APPARATUS AT AYTON STN: "DOWN" SIDE.

grid cables

AYTON HILL 654

Embankment

53

LINE RISES 1:400

NORTH

54 deep cutting

BRIGHTLY PAINTED BORDER SIGN. "UP" SIDE OF LINE

FOULDEN

SCOTLAND

ENGLAND

Whiteadder

55 deep cutting

Marshall Meadow Bay

LINE RISES 1:190

ALLANTON

Water

It is said that the approach to Berwick is even more impressive than the run into Durham. Certainly the view we have of the Royal Border Bridge from Tweedmouth, over which we presently pass, lingers in the memory for many years. From Tweedmouth the line sweeps round three sides of Berwick in a gentle curve, our train travelling slowly over the high half-mile viaduct.

56

S E A

57

ROYAL BORDER BRIDGE

LOANEND

VIADUCT

River Tweed

BERWICK

335¼ MILES FROM LONDON

Golf Links

66

TWEEDMOUTH

334¼

MAIL BAG PICK-UP APPARATUS 400 YDS. NORTH OF TWEEDMOUTH STN: "DOWN" SIDE OF LINE.

to Kelso

SPITTAL

LINE RISES 1:200

LEVEL

Radio Stn.

65

LINE FALLS 1:490

64

**MAP 25**

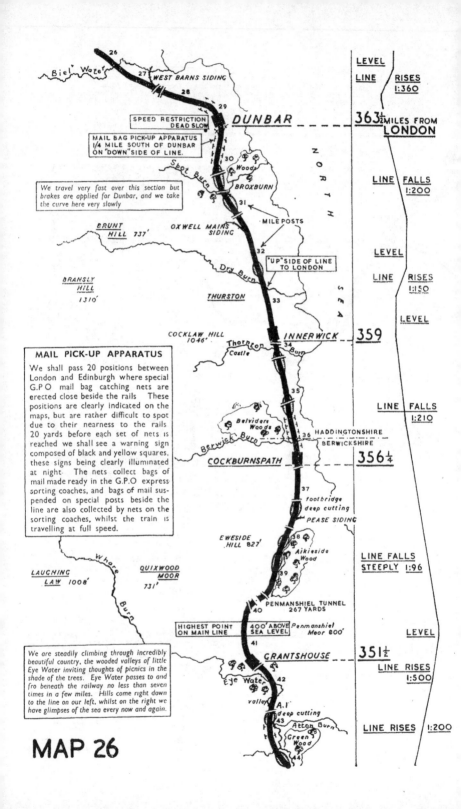

26

Biel Water

27 WEST BARNS SIDING

28

29

SPEED RESTRICTION
DEAD SLOW

MAIL BAG PICK-UP APPARATUS
1/4 MILE SOUTH OF DUNBAR
ON "DOWN" SIDE OF LINE.

DUNBAR

*We travel very fast over this section but
brakes are applied for Dunbar, and we take
the curve here very slowly*

Spot Burn

30 Woods

BROXBURN

BRUNT
HILL 737'

OXWELL MAINS
SIDING

31

MILE POSTS

BRANSLY
HILL
1310'

32

Dry Burn

THURSTON

33

"UP" SIDE OF LINE
TO LONDON

COCKLAW HILL
1046'

Thornton
Castle

34

INNERWICK

Burn

35

## MAIL PICK-UP APPARATUS

We shall pass 20 positions between
London and Edinburgh where special
G.P.O mail bag catching nets are
erected close beside the rails   These
positions are clearly indicated on the
maps, but are rather difficult to spot
due to their nearness to the rails
20 yards before each set of nets is
reached we shall see a warning sign
composed of black and yellow squares,
these signs being clearly illuminated
at night.   The nets collect bags of
mail made ready in the G.P.O express
sorting coaches, and bags of mail suspended on special posts beside the
line are also collected by nets on the
sorting coaches, whilst the train is
travelling at full speed.

Belvidere
Woods

36   HADDINGTONSHIRE
BERWICKSHIRE

Berwick Burn

COCKBURNSPATH

37

footbridge
deep cutting

PEASE SIDING

EWESIDE
HILL 827'

38

Aikieside
Wood

LAUGHING
LAW 1008'

QUIXWOOD
MOOR
731'

Whare Burn

39

PENMANSHIEL TUNNEL
267 YARDS

40

HIGHEST POINT
ON MAIN LINE

400' ABOVE
SEA LEVEL

Penmanshiel
Moor 800'

41

*We are steadily climbing through incredibly
beautiful country, the wooded valleys of little
Eye Water inviting thoughts of picnics in the
shade of the trees.  Eye Water passes to and
fro beneath the railway no less than seven
times in a few miles. Hills come right down
to the line on our left, whilst on the right we
have glimpses of the sea every now and again.*

GRANTSHOUSE

Eye Water

42

valley

A.I

43

deep cutting

Atton Burn

Green
Wood

44

# MAP 26

## Right-hand gradient column

LEVEL

LINE   RISES
1:360

363½ MILES FROM
LONDON

LINE FALLS
1:200

LEVEL

LINE   RISES
1:150

LEVEL

359

LINE FALLS
1:210

356¼

LINE FALLS
STEEPLY 1:96

LEVEL

351½

LINE RISES
1:500

LINE RISES   1:200

NORTH   SEA

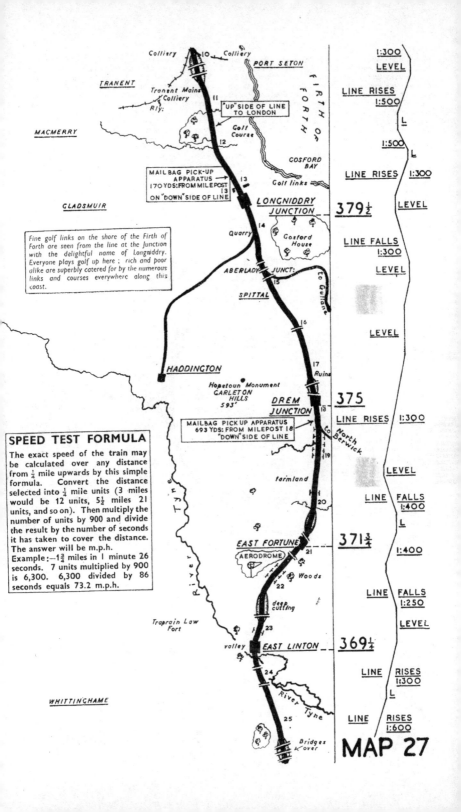

Colliery · 10 · Colliery
PORT SETON
TRANENT
Transent Mains
Colliery
Rly: · 11
"UP" SIDE OF LINE
TO LONDON
MACMERRY
12
Golf Course
GLADSMUIR
MAILBAG PICK-UP
APPARATUS → · 13
170 YDS: FROM MILEPOST
13
ON "DOWN" SIDE OF LINE
GOSFORD BAY
Golf links
LONGNIDDRY
JUNCTION

FIRTH OF FORTH

Fine golf links on the shore of the Firth of Forth are seen from the line at the Junction with the delightful name of Longniddry. Everyone plays golf up here ; rich and poor alike are superbly catered for by the numerous links and courses everywhere along this coast.

14
Quarry
Gosford
House

ABERLADY JUNCT:
15
SPITTAL

16

HADDINGTON
Hopetoun Monument
GARLETON
HILLS
593'
17
Ruins

to Gullane

DREM
JUNCTION
MAILBAG PICK UP APPARATUS
693 YDS: FROM MILEPOST 18
"DOWN" SIDE OF LINE
18
19

to North Berwick

farmland
20

## SPEED TEST FORMULA

The exact speed of the train may be calculated over any distance from $\frac{1}{4}$ mile upwards by this simple formula. Convert the distance selected into $\frac{1}{4}$ mile units (3 miles would be 12 units, $5\frac{1}{4}$ miles 21 units, and so on). Then multiply the number of units by 900 and divide the result by the number of seconds it has taken to cover the distance. The answer will be m.p.h.
Example :— $1\frac{3}{4}$ miles in 1 minute 26 seconds. 7 units multiplied by 900 is 6,300. 6,300 divided by 86 seconds equals 73.2 m.p.h.

EAST FORTUNE
(AERODROME)
21
Woods
22
deep
cutting

Traprain Law
Fort

valley · 23
EAST LINTON

24
WHITTINGHAME
River Tyne

25
Bridges
over

Ty r i v e r

---

1:300
LEVEL

LINE RISES
1:500

L

1:500
L
LINE RISES · 1:300

379½ · LEVEL

LINE FALLS
1:300

LEVEL

LEVEL

375

LINE RISES · 1:300

LEVEL

LINE FALLS
1:400

L

371¾ · 1:400

LINE FALLS
1:250

LEVEL

369½

LINE RISES
1:300

L

LINE RISES
1:600

## MAP 27

*EDINBURGH—When one arrives at Waverley Station one has arrived in Edinburgh—right in Edinburgh. No taxi rides are necessary through dingy streets from the Station to the centre; Waverley Station is the centre. It is as though Kings Cross were at Piccadilly Circus, or Bombay Terminus were on the waterfront. The only Terminus I know to be similarly placed is Central Station in New York; that also is right there. Waverley Station lies deep down in the earth, with Edinburgh rising above on all sides. Climb the granite steps from the platform and one stands in Princes Street in all its glory. Edinburgh is entirely different from any other British City; it is planned differently and built differently. It is incredibly beautiful and dignified, and its natural dignity and atmosphere is reflected right throughout the City and its inhabitants. It is reflected in what the people say and do; in how they dress their shop windows; in how one is received at one's hotel, and how one is served with a bus ticket. If anyone is ever rude or snappy to anyone else in Edinburgh I have yet to experience it. Stroll down the two miles of Princes Street, and note the quiet dignity and solid luxury*

*of the famous shops. Take coffee at Crawford's or Mackie's, and let yourself go on the long low cakes studded with almonds. Note the Banks and Clubs on Princes Street where one ascends steps to gain admittance, and the bookshops off Princes Street with similar steps, except that here one goes down to arrive at the shop door. American visitors will find Edinburgh strangely reminiscent of Philadelphia, with the streets at right angles and the crescents behind with their tall, solid, stone houses. Edinburgh Hotels must be classed as the best in the world. The North British, the Royal British and the Caledonia, to mention only three, receive their visitors with a courtesy and efficiency that, for the moment, seems to be dying out in many cities. One's first visit to Edinburgh is unforgettable, and one always yearns to return. Perhaps it is the soft voices and kind faces of its people, or the feeling of well being one experiences there. Perhaps one gains something from the history steeped atmosphere of the place that so obviously controls the behaviour of its people. Perhaps it is just because it is Scotland.*

# EDINBURGH

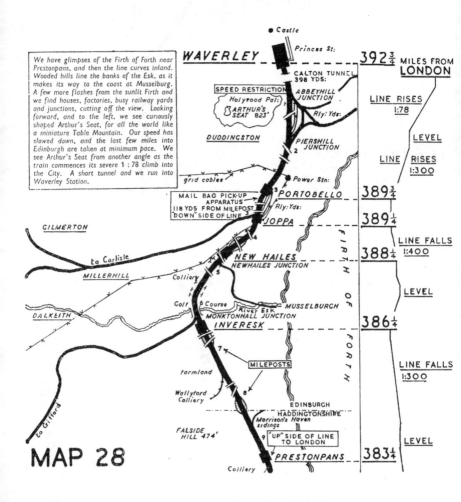

We have glimpses of the Firth of Forth near Prestonpans, and then the line curves inland. Wooded hills line the banks of the Esk, as it makes its way to the coast at Musselburgh. A few more flashes from the sunlit Firth and we find houses, factories, busy railway yards and junctions, cutting off the view. Looking forward, and to the left, we see curiously shaped Arthur's Seat, for all the world like a miniature Table Mountain. Our speed has slowed down, and the last few miles into Edinburgh are taken at minimum pace. We see Arthur's Seat from another angle as the train commences its severe 1 : 78 climb into the City. A short tunnel and we run into Waverley Station.

MAP 28

# The Journey

## "MILE by MILE"

by

### S. N. PIKE, M.B.E.

**WATERLOO EDITION**
**SOUTHERN RAILWAY**

A book of some 10,000 words and 27 maps, describing in detail the main line Railway between London and Towns of the South and South-West; showing :—

- GRADIENTS
- MILEAGES
- SPEEDS
- JUNCTIONS
- VIADUCTS
- TUNNELS
- RIVERS and
- ROADS

with an account of features of interest and beauty to be seen from the train.

*The Author gratefully acknowledges the assistance received from Officials of the Southern Railway in the preparation of this book.*

*Published by*
STUART N. PIKE,
Worthing, Sussex

*SOLE DISTRIBUTORS*
*To whom all enquiries should be addressed :—*
ATLAS PUBLISHING & DISTRIBUTING CO., LTD.,
18, BRIDE LANE, LONDON, E.C.4.

# THE ROUTE OF "MILE BY MILE"

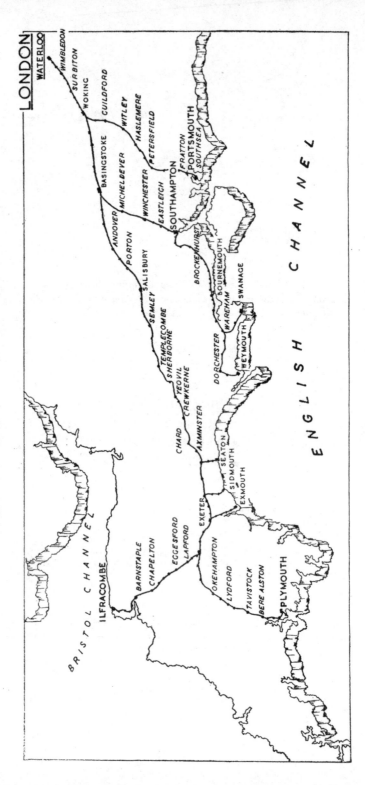

INDEX TO STATIONS & RIVERS PAGE 5.

# The
# *Best Railway Book*
# *ever published*

*This book has been described as the " Best Railway Book ever published." Whether or no it deserves this description is left to the purchaser. Certainly the wealth of detail here collected must give it a high place amongst books about travelling by rail.*

The route is through 149 Stations on the Southern Railway, covering the main line between London and the South and South-west. Each page contains a description of the countryside and what is to be seen of interest on that Section. On the right side of each page is data dear to the heart of the railway enthusiast. Gradients, bridges, viaducts and their height, tunnels and their length, junctions, cuttings, speeds, and approximate running times between Stations.

No less than 60 rivers and streams are encountered and named.

*It is intended that the book be read whilst actually in the train. It may be commenced at any point of the journey. A glance at the name of the Station just passed, a reference to the Index, and what will be seen between there and the next Station is described. Not only what will be seen, but approximately how long it will take to reach that next Station and at what speed, and on what degree of gradient the train will be either climbing up, or coasting down at that moment.*

Small figures indicate the height of the line and that of the surrounding country above sea level, enabling the traveller to anticipate his arrival at a valley, or otherwise. The position of all bridges—even foot bridges—over the line is indicated to enable features mentioned in the commentary to be the more easily pinpointed. For the same reason the position of grid cables near or crossing the line is given.

A gradient of 1 : 80 means that for every 80 yards or feet travelled the line has risen or fallen by one yard or one foot, as indicated on the right of each page.

*To view the countryside as described by the Author, travellers towards the coast should sit facing the engine; those travelling towards London, with their backs to the engine.*

# Rivers we meet

Anton
Avon (Wilts.)
Avon (Hants.)
Axe

Basingstoke Canal
Batts Brook
Beaulieu
Blackwater
Bourne
Bray
Burn

Clyst
Corfe
Creedy
Culm
Culvery

Dalch

East Okement
Ems
Exe

Frome

Hogsmill

Itchen

Lew
Little Dart
Lodden
Loddon
Lumburn
Lyd
Lyde
Lymington
Lynher

Mole
Mude

Nadder

Okement
Otter

Parrett

Rother

Sem
Sid
Sherford
Stour (Dorset)
Stour (Hants.)

Tale
Tamar
Tavy
Taw
Test
Thames
Tilmore
Trent (Dorset)

Umborne

Walkham
Wandle
West Okement
Wey (Dorset)
Wey (Surrey)
Wylye

Yeo

# Counties

London
Surrey
Sussex
Hampshire

Wiltshire
Dorsetshire
Somersetshire
Devonshire

# Index to Stations

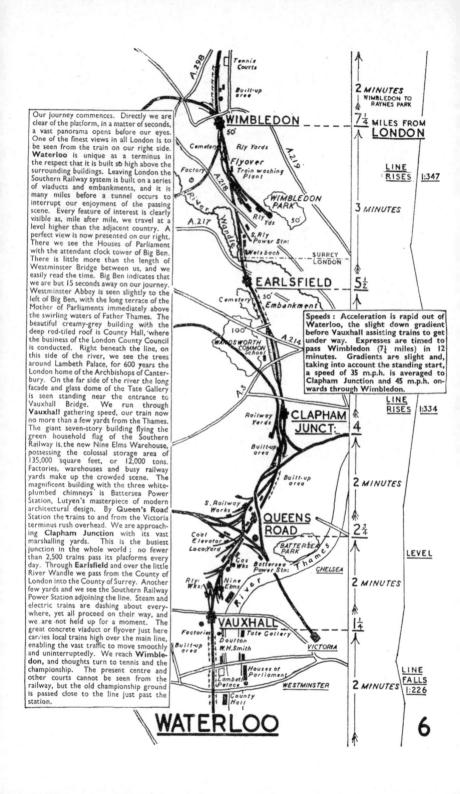

Our journey commences. Directly we are clear of the platform, in a matter of seconds, a vast panorama opens before our eyes. One of the finest views in all London is to be seen from the train on our right side. **Waterloo** is unique as a terminus in the respect that it is built so high above the surrounding buildings. Leaving London the Southern Railway system is built on a series of viaducts and embankments, and it is many miles before a tunnel occurs to interrupt our enjoyment of the passing scene. Every feature of interest is clearly visible as, mile after mile, we travel at a level higher than the adjacent country. A perfect view is now presented on our right. There we see the Houses of Parliament with the attendant clock tower of Big Ben. There is little more than the length of Westminster Bridge between us, and we easily read the time. Big Ben indicates that we are but 15 seconds away on our journey. Westminster Abbey is seen slightly to the left of Big Ben, with the long terrace of the Mother of Parliaments immediately above the swirling waters of Father Thames. The beautiful creamy-grey building with the deep red-tiled roof is County Hall, where the business of the London County Council is conducted. Right beneath the line, on this side of the river, we see the trees around Lambeth Palace, for 600 years the London home of the Archbishops of Canterbury. On the far side of the river the long facade and glass dome of the Tate Gallery is seen standing near the entrance to Vauxhall Bridge. We run through **Vauxhall** gathering speed, our train now no more than a few yards from the Thames. The giant seven-story building flying the green household flag of the Southern Railway is the new Nine Elms Warehouse, possessing the colossal storage area of 135,000 square feet, or 12,000 tons. Factories, warehouses and busy railway yards make up the crowded scene. The magnificent building with the three white-plumbed chimneys is Battersea Power Station, Lutyen's masterpiece of modern architectural design. By **Queen's Road** Station the trains to and from the Victoria terminus rush overhead. We are approaching **Clapham Junction** with its vast marshalling yards. This is the busiest junction in the whole world ; no fewer than 2,500 trains pass its platforms every day. Through **Earlsfield** and over the little River Wandle we pass from the County of London into the County of Surrey. Another few yards and we see the Southern Railway Power Station adjoining the line. Steam and electric trains are dashing about everywhere, yet all proceed on their way, and we are not held up for a moment. The great concrete viaduct or flyover just here carries local trains high over the main line, enabling the vast traffic to move smoothly and uninterruptedly. We reach **Wimbledon**, and thoughts turn to tennis and the championship. The present centre and other courts cannot be seen from the railway, but the old championship ground is passed close to the line just past the station.

Speeds : Acceleration is rapid out of Waterloo, the slight down gradient before Vauxhall assisting trains to get under way. Expresses are timed to pass Wimbledon (7½ miles) in 12 minutes. Gradients are slight and, taking into account the standing start, a speed of 35 m.p.h. is averaged to Clapham Junction and 45 m.p.h. onwards through Wimbledon.

2 MINUTES WIMBLEDON TO RAYNES PARK

7¼ MILES FROM LONDON

LINE RISES 1:347

3 MINUTES

5½

LINE RISES 1:334

4

2 MINUTES

2¾

LEVEL

2 MINUTES

1¼

LINE FALLS 1:226

2 MINUTES

WATERLOO

6

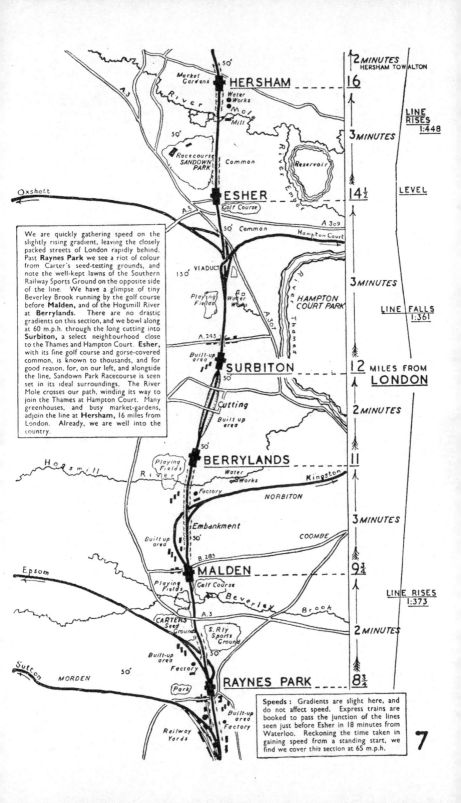

We are quickly gathering speed on the slightly rising gradient, leaving the closely packed streets of London rapidly behind. Past **Raynes Park** we see a riot of colour from Carter's seed-testing grounds, and note the well-kept lawns of the Southern Railway Sports Ground on the opposite side of the line. We have a glimpse of tiny Beverley Brook running by the golf course before **Malden**, and of the Hogsmill River at **Berrylands**. There are no drastic gradients on this section, and we bowl along at 60 m.p.h. through the long cutting into **Surbiton**, a select neighbourhood close to the Thames and Hampton Court. **Esher**, with its fine golf course and gorse-covered common, is known to thousands, and for good reason, for, on our left, alongside the line, Sandown Park Racecourse is seen set in its ideal surroundings. The River Mole crosses our path, winding its way to join the Thames at Hampton Court. Many greenhouses, and busy market-gardens, adjoin the line at **Hersham**, 16 miles from London. Already, we are well into the country.

**2** MINUTES
HERSHAM TO WALTON

**16**

LINE RISES 1:448

**3** MINUTES

**14½**  LEVEL

**3** MINUTES

LINE FALLS 1:361

**12**  MILES FROM **LONDON**

**2** MINUTES

**11**

**3** MINUTES

LINE RISES 1:373

**9¾**

**2** MINUTES

**8¾**

**Speeds:** Gradients are slight here, and do not affect speed. Express trains are booked to pass the junction of the lines seen just before Esher in 18 minutes from Waterloo. Reckoning the time taken in gaining speed from a standing start, we find we cover this section at 65 m.p.h.

**7**

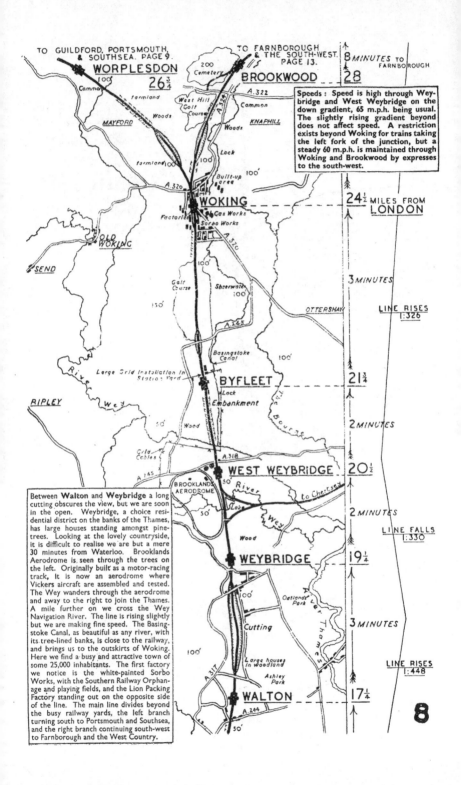

WORPLESDON — 26¾

BROOKWOOD — 28

8 MINUTES TO FARNBOROUGH

**Speeds:** Speed is high through Weybridge and West Weybridge on the down gradient, 65 m.p.h. being usual. The slightly rising gradient beyond does not affect speed. A restriction exists beyond Woking for trains taking the left fork of the junction, but a steady 60 m.p.h. is maintained through Woking and Brookwood by expresses to the south-west.

WOKING — 24½ MILES FROM LONDON

3 MINUTES

LINE RISES 1:326

BYFLEET — 21¾

2 MINUTES

WEST WEYBRIDGE — 20½

2 MINUTES

LINE FALLS 1:330

WEYBRIDGE — 19¼

3 MINUTES

LINE RISES 1:448

WALTON — 17¼

Between **Walton** and **Weybridge** a long cutting obscures the view, but we are soon in the open. Weybridge, a choice residential district on the banks of the Thames, has large houses standing amongst pine-trees. Looking at the lovely countryside, it is difficult to realise we are but a mere 30 minutes from Waterloo. Brooklands Aerodrome is seen through the trees on the left. Originally built as a motor-racing track, it is now an aerodrome where Vickers aircraft are assembled and tested. The Wey wanders through the aerodrome and away to the right to join the Thames. A mile further on we cross the Wey Navigation River. The line is rising slightly but we are making fine speed. The Basingstoke Canal, as beautiful as any river, with its tree-lined banks, is close to the railway, and brings us to the outskirts of Woking. Here we find a busy and attractive town of some 25,000 inhabitants. The first factory we notice is the white-painted Sorbo Works, with the Southern Railway Orphanage and playing fields, and the Lion Packing Factory standing out on the opposite side of the line. The main line divides beyond the busy railway yards, the left branch turning south to Portsmouth and Southsea, and the right branch continuing south-west to Farnborough and the West Country.

**8**

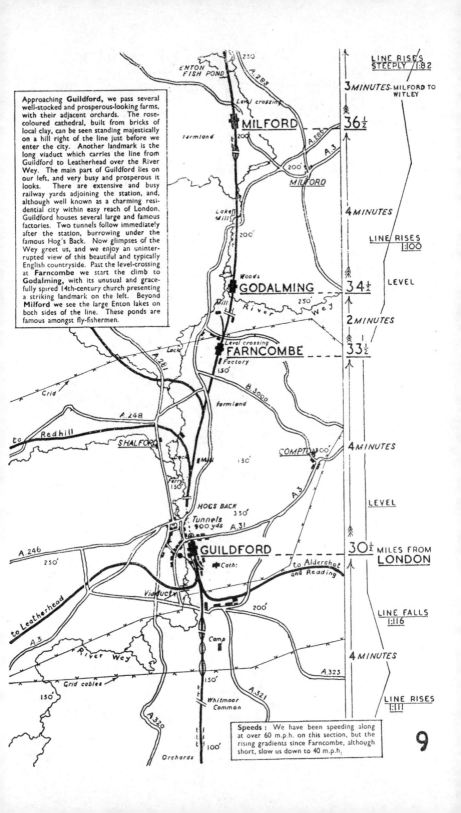

Approaching **Guildford,** we pass several well-stocked and prosperous-looking farms, with their adjacent orchards. The rose-coloured cathedral, built from bricks of local clay, can be seen standing majestically on a hill right of the line just before we enter the city. Another landmark is the long viaduct which carries the line from Guildford to Leatherhead over the River Wey. The main part of Guildford lies on our left, and very busy and prosperous it looks. There are extensive and busy railway yards adjoining the station, and, although well known as a charming residential city within easy reach of London, Guildford houses several large and famous factories. Two tunnels follow immediately after the station, burrowing under the famous Hog's Back. Now glimpses of the Wey greet us, and we enjoy an uninterrupted view of this beautiful and typically English countryside. Past the level-crossing at **Farncombe** we start the climb to **Godalming,** with its unusual and gracefully spired 14th-century church presenting a striking landmark on the left. Beyond **Milford** we see the large Enton lakes on both sides of the line. These ponds are famous amongst fly-fishermen.

ENTON FISH POND

Level crossing

**MILFORD** — $36\frac{1}{2}$

*Farmland*

*MILFORD*

Lake Mill

LINE RISES STEEPLY 1:82

3 MINUTES · MILFORD TO WITLEY

4 MINUTES

LINE RISES 1:100

*Woods*

**GODALMING** — $34\frac{1}{4}$

*River Wey*

LEVEL

2 MINUTES

Level crossing

**FARNCOMBE** — $33\frac{1}{2}$

Factory 150'

farmland

Grid

SHALFORD

COMPTON

4 MINUTES

LEVEL

to Redhill

HOGS BACK 350'

Tunnels 900 yds

**GUILDFORD** — $30\frac{1}{4}$ MILES FROM **LONDON**

Cath:

to Aldershot and Reading

LINE FALLS 1:116

to Leatherhead

Viaduct

200'

Camp

River Wey

4 MINUTES

Grid cables

150'

A.323

Whitmoor Common

LINE RISES 1:111

Orchards

**Speeds :** We have been speeding along at over 60 m.p.h. on this section, but the rising gradients since Farncombe, although short, slow us down to 40 m.p.h.

9

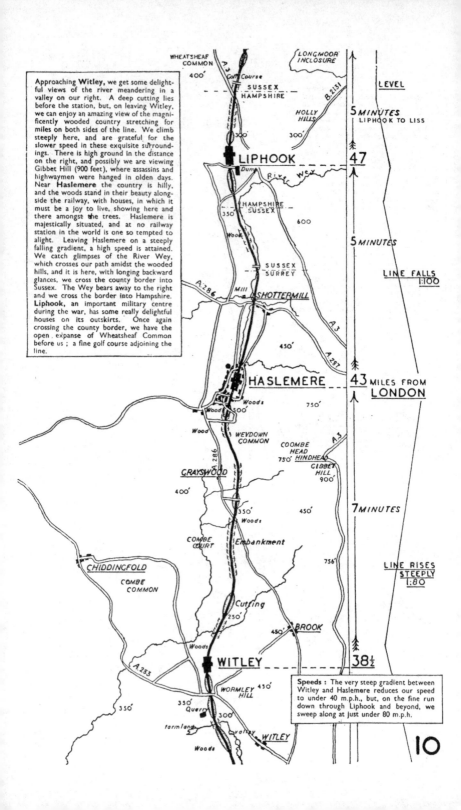

Approaching **Witley**, we get some delightful views of the river meandering in a valley on our right. A deep cutting lies before the station, but, on leaving Witley, we can enjoy an amazing view of the magnificently wooded country stretching for miles on both sides of the line. We climb steeply here, and are grateful for the slower speed in these exquisite surroundings. There is high ground in the distance on the right, and possibly we are viewing Gibbet Hill (900 feet), where assassins and highwaymen were hanged in olden days. Near **Haslemere** the country is hilly, and the woods stand in their beauty alongside the railway, with houses, in which it must be a joy to live, showing here and there amongst the trees. Haslemere is majestically situated, and at no railway station in the world is one so tempted to alight. Leaving Haslemere on a steeply falling gradient, a high speed is attained. We catch glimpses of the River Wey, which crosses our path amidst the wooded hills, and it is here, with longing backward glances, we cross the county border into Sussex. The Wey bears away to the right and we cross the border into Hampshire. **Liphook**, an important military centre during the war, has some really delightful houses on its outskirts. Once again crossing the county border, we have the open expanse of Wheatsheaf Common before us ; a fine golf course adjoining the line.

**Speeds :** The very steep gradient between Witley and Haslemere reduces our speed to under 40 m.p.h., but, on the fine run down through Liphook and beyond, we sweep along at just under 80 m.p.h.

LONGMOOR INCLOSURE

WHEATSHEAF COMMON

400'

Golf Course

SUSSEX
HAMPSHIRE

B.2131

LEVEL

HOLLY HILLS

300'

300'

5 MINUTES
LIPHOOK TO LISS

LIPHOOK

Dump

River Wey

47

HAMPSHIRE
SUSSEX

350'

600'

5 MINUTES

Wood

SUSSEX
SURREY

LINE FALLS
1:100

A.286

Mill

SHOTTERMILL

A.3

450'

A.287

HASLEMERE

43 MILES FROM LONDON

Woods

Wood 500'

750'

Wood

WEYDOWN COMMON

COOMBE HEAD
HINDHEAD 750'

A.3

GIBBET HILL 900

GRAYSWOOD

400'

350'

Woods

450'

7 MINUTES

COMBE COURT

Embankment

756'

CHIDDINGFOLD

COMBE COMMON

LINE RISES STEEPLY
1:80

Cutting

250'

BROOK

450'

Woods

WITLEY

38½

A.283

WORMLEY HILL 450'

350'

350'
Quarry

300'

farmland

valley WITLEY

Woods

10

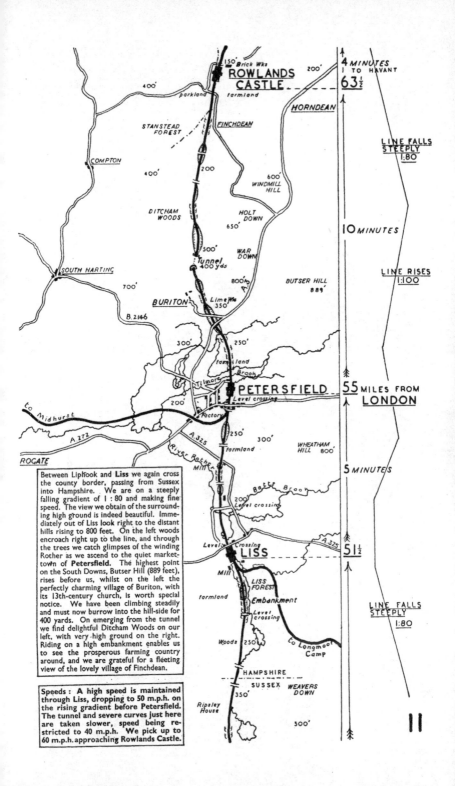

150' Brick Wks

**ROWLANDS CASTLE**

200'

4 MINUTES TO HAVANT

63½

parkland    farmland    400'

_HORNDEAN_

STANSTEAD FOREST

_FINCHDEAN_

200'

COMPTON

400'

600' WINDMILL HILL

DITCHAM WOODS

HOLT DOWN

650'

10 MINUTES

500'

WAR DOWN

Tunnel 400 yds

SOUTH HARTING

700'

800'

_BUTSER HILL 889_

BURITON

Lime Wks 350'

B.2146

A.3

300'

250'

farmland    Brook

to Midhurst

Tilmore

**PETERSFIELD**

55 MILES FROM **LONDON**

200'

Level crossing

A.272

Factory

A.325

250'

300'

_WHEATHAM HILL 800'_

ROGATE

River Rother

farmland

5 MINUTES

Mill

Batts Brook

200' Level crossing

Level Crossing

**LISS**

A.325

51½

Mill

LISS FOREST

farmland

Embankment

Level crossing

Woods

250'

to Longmoor Camp

HAMPSHIRE
SUSSEX    WEAVERS DOWN

350'

Ripsley House

300'

Between Liphook and **Liss** we again cross the county border, passing from Sussex into Hampshire. We are on a steeply falling gradient of 1 : 80 and making fine speed. The view we obtain of the surrounding high ground is indeed beautiful. Immediately out of Liss look right to the distant hills rising to 800 feet. On the left woods encroach right up to the line, and through the trees we catch glimpses of the winding Rother as we ascend to the quiet market-town of **Petersfield**. The highest point on the South Downs, Butser Hill (889 feet), rises before us, whilst on the left the perfectly charming village of Buriton, with its 13th-century church, is worth special notice. We have been climbing steadily and must now burrow into the hill-side for 400 yards. On emerging from the tunnel we find delightful Ditcham Woods on our left, with very high ground on the right. Riding on a high embankment enables us to see the prosperous farming country around, and we are grateful for a fleeting view of the lovely village of Finchdean.

Speeds : A high speed is maintained through Liss, dropping to 50 m.p.h. on the rising gradient before Petersfield. The tunnel and severe curves just here are taken slower, speed being restricted to 40 m.p.h. We pick up to 60 m.p.h. approaching Rowlands Castle.

**11**

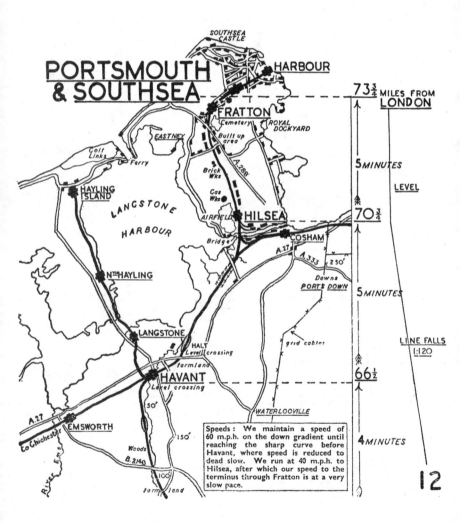

Within 15 minutes we shall have reached the sea. The hills are being left behind, and we are now running through flat farmland where numerous cattle peacefully graze. As we approach the old market town of **Havant**, we see the railway from Chichester approaching the junction. Our speed is now very slow as we take the curve into the station. The line turns sharply to the west here and we proceed slowly over the level crossings to Bedhampton Halt, where, looking left, we have our first view of the sea in Langstone Harbour, with Hayling Island in the distance. Looking right we see the line of disused forts on Ports Down, originally built to defend the harbour, with numerous well-sited houses on the lower slopes of the Downs. Through marshland we cross the junction of the line to Southampton, pass over the creek and on to **Hilsea Halt**. A large aerodrome is on the left and busy railway yards on the right. We notice the very large railway yards at **Fratton**, after which the train runs between rows of houses into **Portsmouth and Southsea** Station. The magnificent building with the tall clock tower is Portsmouth Guildhall. As we travel slowly on to the **Harbour** Station, looking right, we may just see the masts and rigging of Lord Nelson's flagship " Victory," Portsmouth's most famous monument.

ENGLISH CHANNEL

SOUTHSEA CASTLE

# PORTSMOUTH & SOUTHSEA

HARBOUR

**73¾** MILES FROM LONDON

FRATTON

Cemetery

ROYAL DOCKYARD

EASTNEY

Built up area

Golf Links

Ferry

A.288

Brick Wks

HAYLING ISLAND

Gas Wks

LANGSTONE

AIRFIELD

HILSEA

HARBOUR

Bridge

COSHAM

**70¾**

**5** MINUTES

LEVEL

Nᵀᴴ HAYLING

A.27

A.333

250'

Downs

**PORTS DOWN**

**5** MINUTES

LANGSTONE

grid cables

**66½**

HALT
Level crossing

farmland

HAVANT

LINE FALLS
1:120

Level crossing

50'

WATERLOOVILLE

A.27

EMSWORTH

**4** MINUTES

To Chichester

150'

River Ems

Woods

B.2140

100'

farmland

Speeds : We maintain a speed of 60 m.p.h. on the down gradient until reaching the sharp curve before Havant, where speed is reduced to dead slow. We run at 40 m.p.h. to Hilsea, after which our speed to the terminus through Fratton is at a very slow pace.

12

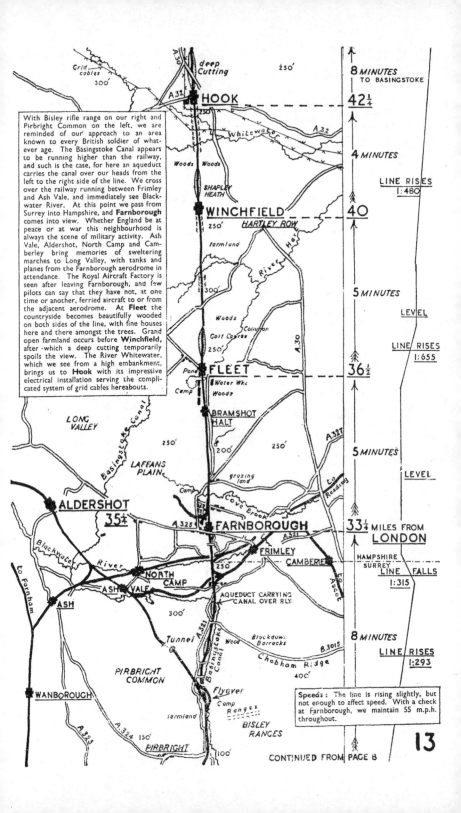

With Bisley rifle range on our right and Pirbright Common on the left, we are reminded of our approach to an area known to every British soldier of whatever age. The Basingstoke Canal appears to be running higher than the railway, and such is the case, for here an aqueduct carries the canal over our heads from the left to the right side of the line. We cross over the railway running between Frimley and Ash Vale, and immediately see Blackwater River. At this point we pass from Surrey into Hampshire, and **Farnborough** comes into view. Whether England be at peace or at war this neighbourhood is always the scene of military activity. Ash Vale, Aldershot, North Camp and Camberley bring memories of sweltering marches to Long Valley, with tanks and planes from the Farnborough aerodrome in attendance. The Royal Aircraft Factory is seen after leaving Farnborough, and few pilots can say that they have not, at one time or another, ferried aircraft to or from the adjacent aerodrome. At **Fleet** the countryside becomes beautifully wooded on both sides of the line, with fine houses here and there amongst the trees. Grand open farmland occurs before **Winchfield**, after which a deep cutting temporarily spoils the view. The River Whitewater, which we see from a high embankment, brings us to **Hook** with its impressive electrical installation serving the complicated system of grid cables hereabouts.

8 MINUTES
TO BASINGSTOKE

42¼ **HOOK**

4 MINUTES

LINE RISES
1:480

40 **WINCHFIELD**

5 MINUTES

LEVEL

LINE RISES
1:655

36½ **FLEET**

5 MINUTES

LEVEL

33¼ **FARNBOROUGH** MILES FROM
**LONDON**

HAMPSHIRE
SURREY
LINE FALLS
1:315

8 MINUTES

LINE RISES
1:293

35¼ **ALDERSHOT**

Speed: The line is rising slightly, but not enough to affect speed. With a check at Farnborough, we maintain 55 m.p.h. throughout.

**13**

CONTINUED FROM PAGE 8

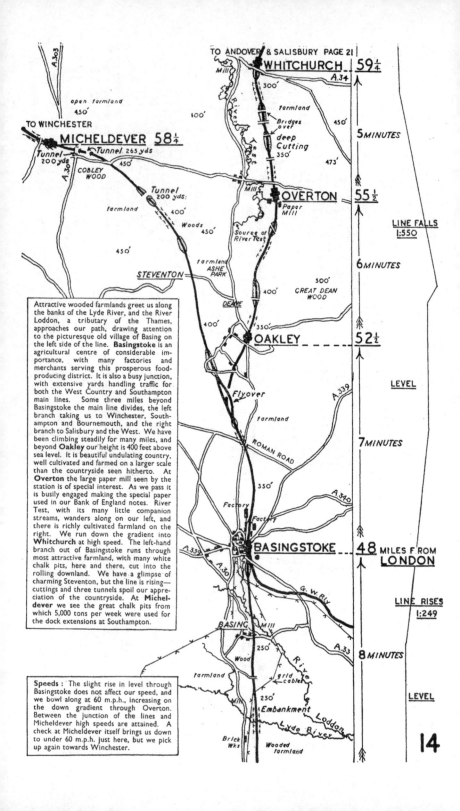

TO ANDOVER & SALISBURY PAGE 21

**WHITCHURCH** 59¼

TO WINCHESTER
**MICHELDEVER** 58¼

**OVERTON** 55½

STEVENTON

**OAKLEY** 52½

**BASINGSTOKE** 48 MILES FROM LONDON

BASING

5 MINUTES

LINE FALLS 1:550

6 MINUTES

LEVEL

7 MINUTES

LINE RISES 1:249

8 MINUTES

LEVEL

Attractive wooded farmlands greet us along the banks of the Lyde River, and the River Loddon, a tributary of the Thames, approaches our path, drawing attention to the picturesque old village of Basing on the left side of the line. **Basingstoke** is an agricultural centre of considerable importance, with many factories and merchants serving this prosperous food-producing district. It is also a busy junction, with extensive yards handling traffic for both the West Country and Southampton main lines. Some three miles beyond Basingstoke the main line divides, the left branch taking us to Winchester, Southampton and Bournemouth, and the right branch to Salisbury and the West. We have been climbing steadily for many miles, and beyond **Oakley** our height is 400 feet above sea level. It is beautiful undulating country, well cultivated and farmed on a larger scale than the countryside seen hitherto. At **Overton** the large paper mill seen by the station is of special interest. As we pass it is busily engaged making the special paper used in our Bank of England notes. River Test, with its many little companion streams, wanders along on our left, and there is richly cultivated farmland on the right. We run down the gradient into **Whitchurch** at high speed. The left-hand branch out of Basingstoke runs through most attractive farmland, with many white chalk pits, here and there, cut into the rolling downland. We have a glimpse of charming Steventon, but the line is rising—cuttings and three tunnels spoil our appreciation of the countryside. At **Micheldever** we see the great chalk pits from which 5,000 tons per week were used for the dock extensions at Southampton.

**Speeds :** The slight rise in level through Basingstoke does not affect our speed, and we bowl along at 60 m.p.h., increasing on the down gradient through Overton. Between the junction of the lines and Micheldever high speeds are attained. A check at Micheldever itself brings us down to under 60 m.p.h. just here, but we pick up again towards Winchester.

14

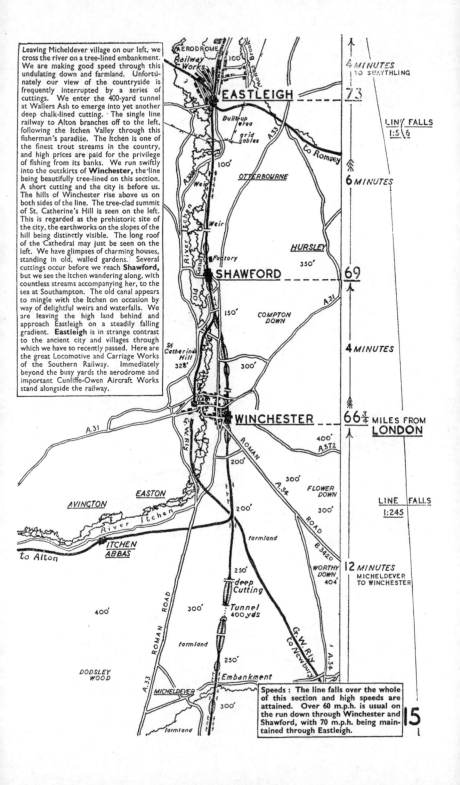

Leaving Micheldever village on our left, we cross the river on a tree-lined embankment. We are making good speed through this undulating down and farmland. Unfortunately our view of the countryside is frequently interrupted by a series of cuttings. We enter the 400-yard tunnel at Wallers Ash to emerge into yet another deep chalk-lined cutting. The single line railway to Alton branches off to the left, following the Itchen Valley through this fisherman's paradise. The Itchen is one of the finest trout streams in the country, and high prices are paid for the privilege of fishing from its banks. We run swiftly into the outskirts of **Winchester**, the line being beautifully tree-lined on this section. A short cutting and the city is before us. The hills of Winchester rise above us on both sides of the line. The tree-clad summit of St. Catherine's Hill is seen on the left. This is regarded as the prehistoric site of the city, the earthworks on the slopes of the hill being distinctly visible. The long roof of the Cathedral may just be seen on the left. We have glimpses of charming houses, standing in old, walled gardens. Several cuttings occur before we reach **Shawford,** but we see the Itchen wandering along, with countless streams accompanying her, to the sea at Southampton. The old canal appears to mingle with the Itchen on occasion by way of delightful weirs and waterfalls. We are leaving the high land behind and approach Eastleigh on a steadily falling gradient. **Eastleigh** is in strange contrast to the ancient city and villages through which we have so recently passed. Here are the great Locomotive and Carriage Works of the Southern Railway. Immediately beyond the busy yards the aerodrome and important Cunliffe-Owen Aircraft Works stand alongside the railway.

**4 MINUTES**
TO SWAYTHLING

**EASTLEIGH**  —  **73**

LINE FALLS
1:5 6

**6 MINUTES**

OTTERBOURNE

HURSLEY
350'

**SHAWFORD**  —  **69**

COMPTON DOWN

**4 MINUTES**

66¾ MILES FROM **LONDON**

**WINCHESTER**

400'
A372
300'
FLOWER DOWN
300'

LINE FALLS
1:245

ROMAN ROAD
B3420

farmland

**12 MINUTES**
MICHELDEVER
TO WINCHESTER

WORTHY DOWN
404'

deep Cutting
250'

Tunnel
400 yds

farmland

250'

Embankment

Speeds : The line falls over the whole of this section and high speeds are attained. Over 60 m.p.h. is usual on the run down through Winchester and Shawford, with 70 m.p.h. being maintained through Eastleigh.

**15**

AERODROME
Railway Works
100'
Built-up area
grid cables
A33
to Romsey
100'
River Itchen
Weir
Weir
Old Canal
Factory
150'
St Catherine's Hill
328'
300'
A31
G.W.R.
ROMAN
200'
A34
300'
200'
AVINGTON
EASTON
River Itchen
ITCHEN ABBAS
to Alton
400'
ROMAN ROAD
A33
DODSLEY WOOD
300'
MICHELDEVER
G.W.R.
to Newbury
A34
farmland

We approach the built-up area of **Sway-thling**. Shortly after passing the water works on the left, we have our last view of the Itchen, now about to become tidal and flow into the sea at Southampton Water. There is a connection between the next station, **St. Denys**, and Paris. It derives its name from the priory founded there, the convent being subject to the Royal Abbey of St. Denys, near Paris. The great timber yards we see on the left mark the site of Clausentum, the Roman South-ampton. Enormous gas holders at **Northam** dwarf all buildings around, and we are now in a highly industrialised and built-up area. We proceed slowly through the tunnel to **Southampton Central**. The enormous Solent Flour Mill on the left was build on land reclaimed from the estuary of the River Test. Up to a few years ago the river ran quite close to the railway—now it is half a mile away. We see the line of giant cranes lining the docks and almost immediately we travel alongside the wonderful " King George V " Graving Dock. This dock, 1,200 feet long, is the largest in the world, 750,000 tons of concrete being used in its construction. Leaving **Totton**, with its numerous oil tanks and busy factories, we very soon reach open country. By the time we reach **Lyndhurst Road** we are well into the New Forest, where William Rufus met his death. For hundreds of years most of the forest has remained untouched and un-spoiled. From our train it seems there are parts where no foot has ever stepped, the only sign of life amongst the ancient trees and clearings being the wild New Forest ponies, grazing timidly close to the line. We reach **Beaulieu Road**, the same wild forest land stretching for miles around us.

TO BROCKENHURST
PAGE 17

LINE FALLS
1:200

6 MINUTES

NEW FOREST
FRAME
HEATH

Bridges over

50'

50'

**BEAULIEU RD** 87½
B. 3056

100'

MATLEY
HEATH

Beaulieu River

50'    forest

forest

5 MINUTES

LINE FALLS
1:300

**LYNDHURST
ROAD** 84¾

to Fawley

**HYTHE**    **MARCHWOOD**
Ferry

SOUTHAMPTON

100'

A.35

farmland

A.336

5 MINUTES

LINE RISES
1:200

Ferry

WATER

WOOLSTON

Cunard Dock    Graving Dock

**DOCKS**    DOCKS'

to Fareham
A.3025

Built-up area

Mill

**SOUTHAMPTON
CENTRAL**

**NORTHAM**

50'    **TOTTON** 82

River Test

6 MINUTES

78¾ MILES FROM
LONDON

4 MINUTES

A.3024

Built-up area

150'

Grid cables

to Romsey
A.3057

76½

A.3067

**St DENYS**

BITTERN

LEVEL

A.27

Itchen

Lock    50'    250'

**SWAYTHLING**

Speeds : We run into Swaythling at high speed, but slow down approaching St. Denys. Through Northam Junction and Southampton speed is reduced to a minimum, and it is only after leaving Totton that we reach 45 m.p.h. A speed of 60 to 65 m.p.h. is reached on the down gradients through Beaulieu Road.

16

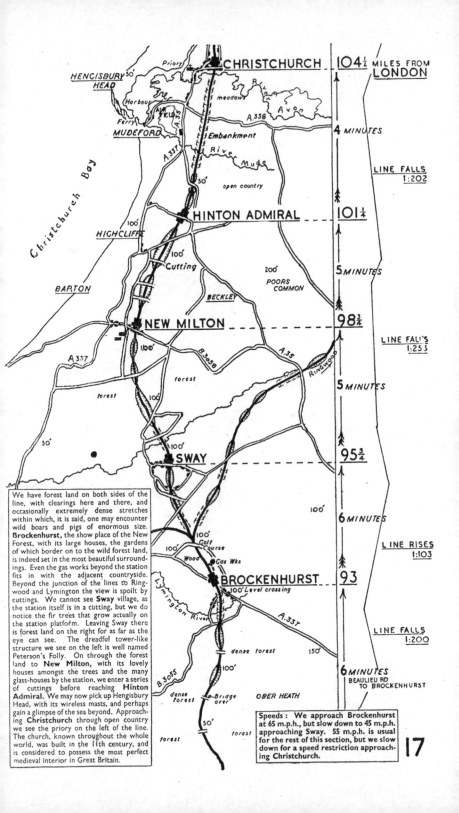

Priory · CHRISTCHURCH — 104½ MILES FROM LONDON

HENGISBURY HEAD · 50'
Harbour · the · R. · meadows · A.338
AIR FIELDS · A.35
Ferry · Embankment
MUDEFORD · River · Mudd · 4 MINUTES
Christchurch Bay · 50' · open country · LINE FALLS 1:202

HINTON ADMIRAL — 101¼
HIGHCLIFFE · 100'
100' · Cutting · 200' · POORS COMMON · 5 MINUTES
BARTON · BECKLEY
NEW MILTON — 98¾
A.337 · B.3058 · A.35 · RINGWOOD · LINE FALLS 1:253
forest · 100'
forest · 100' · 5 MINUTES
50'
100' · SWAY — 95¾
100' · 100' · 6 MINUTES
LINE RISES 1:103
100' · Golf Course
100' · Wood · Gas Wks
BROCKENHURST — 93
Lymington River · 100' Level crossing
A.337 · 6 MINUTES
BEAULIEU RD TO BROCKENHURST
dense forest · 150'
B.3055 · 100' · LINE FALLS 1:200
dense forest · Bridge over · OBER HEATH
50' · forest · forest

We have forest land on both sides of the line, with clearings here and there, and occasionally extremely dense stretches within which, it is said, one may encounter wild boars and pigs of enormous size. **Brockenhurst,** the show place of the New Forest, with its large houses, the gardens of which border on to the wild forest land, is indeed set in the most beautiful surroundings. Even the gas works beyond the station fits in with the adjacent countryside. Beyond the junction of the lines to Ringwood and Lymington the view is spoilt by cuttings. We cannot see **Sway** village, as the station itself is in a cutting, but we do notice the fir trees that grow actually on the station platform. Leaving Sway there is forest land on the right for as far as the eye can see. The dreadful tower-like structure we see on the left is well named Peterson's Folly. On through the forest land to **New Milton,** with its lovely houses amongst the trees and the many glass-houses by the station, we enter a series of cuttings before reaching **Hinton Admiral.** We may now pick up Hengisbury Head, with its wireless masts, and perhaps gain a glimpse of the sea beyond. Approaching **Christchurch** through open country we see the priory on the left of the line. The church, known throughout the whole world, was built in the 11th century, and is considered to possess the most perfect medieval interior in Great Britain.

Speeds : We approach Brockenhurst at 65 m.p.h., but slow down to 45 m.p.h. approaching Sway. 55 m.p.h. is usual for the rest of this section, but we slow down for a speed restriction approaching Christchurch.

17

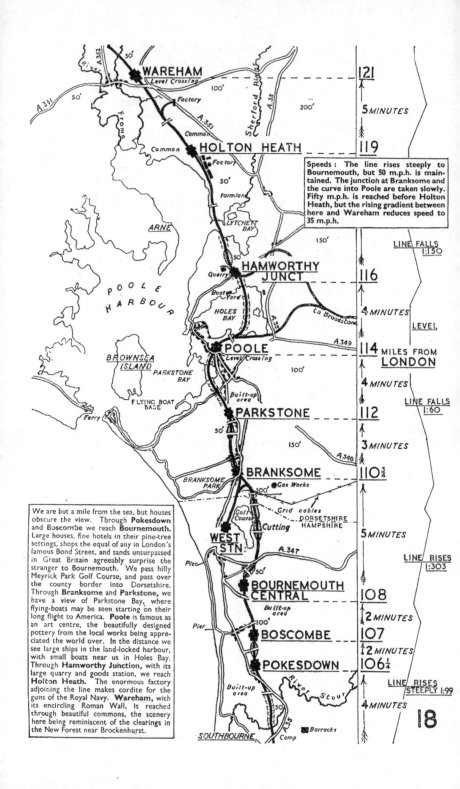

WAREHAM
Level Crossing

A.351
Frome
50'
50'
50'

Sherford River

A.35

A.351

Factory

100'

200'

**121**

5 MINUTES

**119**

Common

HOLTON HEATH

Common

Factory

50'

farmland

LYTCHETT
BAY

ARNE

150'

LINE FALLS
1:150

Quarry

HAMWORTHY
JUNCT

**116**

Boat
Yard

HOLES
BAY

To Broadstone

4 MINUTES

LEVEL

A.35

P O O L E
H A R B O U R

A.349

POOLE
Level Crossing

**114**

MILES FROM
LONDON

100'

4 MINUTES

BROWNSEA
ISLAND

PARKSTONE
BAY

Built-up
area

LINE FALLS
1:60

FLYING BOAT
BASE

Ferry

PARKSTONE

**112**

50'

150'

3 MINUTES

A.348

BRANKSOME
PARK

BRANKSOME

**110¾**

Gas Works

100'

Grid cables
DORSETSHIRE
HAMPSHIRE

5 MINUTES

Golf
Course

Cutting

WEST
STN

A.347

LINE RISES
1:303

Pier

50'

BOURNEMOUTH
CENTRAL

**108**

Built-up
area

2 MINUTES

Pier

100'

BOSCOMBE

**107**

2 MINUTES

POKESDOWN

**106¼**

LINE RISES
STEEPLY 1:99

Built-up
area

River Stour

50'

4 MINUTES

**18**

SOUTHBOURNE

Camp

A.35

Barracks

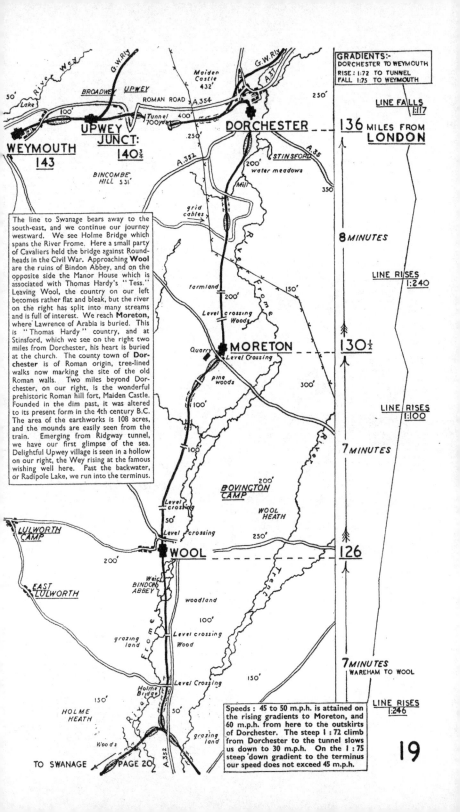

GRADIENTS:-
DORCHESTER TO WEYMOUTH
RISE : 1:72 TO TUNNEL
FALL 1:75 TO WEYMOUTH

LINE FALLS 1:117

**136** MILES FROM **LONDON**

8 MINUTES

LINE RISES 1:240

**130½**

LINE RISES 1:100

7 MINUTES

**126**

7 MINUTES
WAREHAM TO WOOL

LINE RISES 1:246

G.W. RLY
G.W. RLY
RIVER WEY
BROADWEY UPWEY
Maiden Castle 432'
ROMAN ROAD A.354
A.35
UPWEY
Lake 50'
100'
Tunnel 700yds
400'
DORCHESTER
250'
UPWEY JUNCT: **140¾**
A.354
250'
**WEYMOUTH 143**
A.352
STINSFORD
A.35
BINCOMBE HILL 531'
200' water meadows
Mill
350'
grid cables
RIVER FROME
farmland
200'
150'
Level crossing
Woods
**MORETON**
Quarry
Level Crossing
300'
pine woods
100'
Ridgway
Tunnel
100'
200'
BOVINGTON CAMP
WOOL HEATH
Level crossing
50'
Level crossing
250'
LULWORTH CAMP
200'
**WOOL**
Weir
BINDON ABBEY
EAST LULWORTH
woodland
100'
RIVER FROME
Level crossing
Wood
grazing land
Holme Bridge
150'
50'
HOLME HEATH
150'
Woods
grazing land
TO SWANAGE   PAGE 20   A.352

The line to Swanage bears away to the south-east, and we continue our journey westward. We see Holme Bridge which spans the River Frome. Here a small party of Cavaliers held the bridge against Roundheads in the Civil War. Approaching **Wool** are the ruins of Bindon Abbey, and on the opposite side the Manor House which is associated with Thomas Hardy's "Tess." Leaving Wool, the country on our left becomes rather flat and bleak, but the river on the right has split into many streams and is full of interest. We reach **Moreton**, where Lawrence of Arabia is buried. This is "Thomas Hardy" country, and at Stinsford, which we see on the right two miles from Dorchester, his heart is buried at the church. The county town of **Dorchester** is of Roman origin, tree-lined walks now marking the site of the old Roman walls. Two miles beyond Dorchester, on our right, is the wonderful prehistoric Roman hill fort, Maiden Castle. Founded in the dim past, it was altered to its present form in the 4th century B.C. The area of the earthworks is 108 acres, and the mounds are easily seen from the train. Emerging from Ridgway tunnel, we have our first glimpse of the sea. Delightful Upwey village is seen in a hollow on our right, the Wey rising at the famous wishing well here. Past the backwater, or Radipole Lake, we run into the terminus.

Speeds : 45 to 50 m.p.h. is attained on the rising gradients to Moreton, and 60 m.p.h. from here to the outskirts of Dorchester. The steep 1 : 72 climb from Dorchester to the tunnel slows us down to 30 m.p.h. On the 1 : 75 steep down gradient to the terminus our speed does not exceed 45 m.p.h.

**19**

E N G L I S H   C H A N N E L

This is lovely moorland country with woods bordering the line. High ground towers above us on the right, whilst on the left we look across the moorland to Arne and Poole Bay. **Corfe Castle** lies in a gap in the Purbeck Hills. The ruins of the castle stand on a hillock just before the station, completely dominating the quaint and picturesque grey stone village grouped beneath. The origin of the castle is obscure, but, according to tradition, it was the scene of the murder of King Edward in A.D. 978. A busy creamery stands in the station yard, with a hill rising 200 feet sheer behind it. Woods alongside the line intermingle with stretches of gorse-covered common. We are nearly at the seaside. Hills shelter **Swanage** from all but the soft winds from the south, and bathing between Peveril Point and Ballard Point is a delight for those who demand that their swimming and beach idling shall not be spoilt by unkind winds. The population of Swanage is given as 6,000. By the presence of the several fine hotels, and the number of modern shops ready to greet the visitor, it is apparent that a large number of holiday-makers must swell the population both in and out of the season. The reason is not far to seek. A few hours spent in Swanage determines one to come again ; to come again soon, and next time to stay just as long as one's circumstances permit.

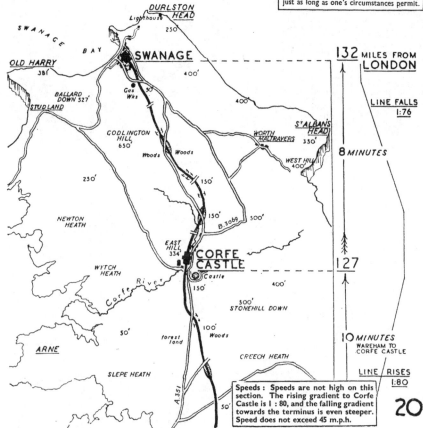

SWANAGE BAY

OLD HARRY
381

BALLARD
DOWN 527
STUDLAND

DURLSTON
HEAD
Lighthouse
250'

SWANAGE

400'

400'

Gas
Wks

GODLINGTON
HILL
650'

Woods    Woods

ST ALBAN'S
HEAD
WORTH
MALTRAVERS
330'

WEST HILL
400'

150'

230'

150'

NEWTON
HEATH

B.3069    500'

EAST
HILL
334

CORFE
CASTLE

Castle

WYTCH
HEATH

Corfe River

150'

400'

500'
STONEHILL DOWN

ARNE

50'

forest
land

100'
Woods

CREECH HEATH

SLEPE HEATH

A.351

50'

**132** MILES FROM **LONDON**

**LINE FALLS**
**1:76**

**8** MINUTES

**127**

**10** MINUTES
WAREHAM TO
CORFE CASTLE

**LINE RISES**
**1:80**

**20**

Speeds : Speeds are not high on this section. The rising gradient to Corfe Castle is 1 : 80, and the falling gradient towards the terminus is even steeper. Speed does not exceed 45 m.p.h.

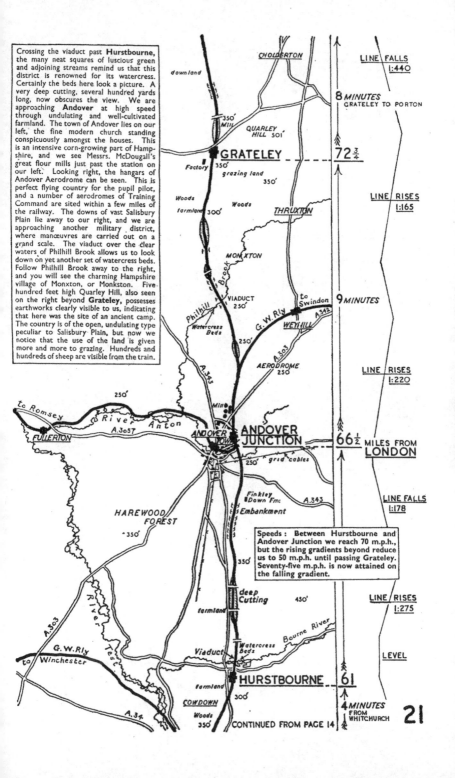

Crossing the viaduct past **Hurstbourne**, the many neat squares of luscious green and adjoining streams remind us that this district is renowned for its watercress. Certainly the beds here look a picture. A very deep cutting, several hundred yards long, now obscures the view. We are approaching **Andover** at high speed through undulating and well-cultivated farmland. The town of Andover lies on our left, the fine modern church standing conspicuously amongst the houses. This is an intensive corn-growing part of Hampshire, and we see Messrs. McDougall's great flour mills just past the station on our left. Looking right, the hangars of Andover Aerodrome can be seen. This is perfect flying country for the pupil pilot, and a number of aerodromes of Training Command are sited within a few miles of the railway. The downs of vast Salisbury Plain lie away to our right, and we are approaching another military district, where manœuvres are carried out on a grand scale. The viaduct over the clear waters of Philhill Brook allows us to look down on yet another set of watercress beds. Follow Philhill Brook away to the right, and you will see the charming Hampshire village of Monxton, or Monkston. Five-hundred feet high Quarley Hill, also seen on the right beyond **Grateley**, possesses earthworks clearly visible to us, indicating that here was the site of an ancient camp. The country is of the open, undulating type peculiar to Salisbury Plain, but now we notice that the use of the land is given more and more to grazing. Hundreds and hundreds of sheep are visible from the train.

**Speeds :** Between Hurstbourne and Andover Junction we reach 70 m.p.h., but the rising gradients beyond reduce us to 50 m.p.h. until passing Grateley. Seventy-five m.p.h. is now attained on the falling gradient.

CHOLDERTON

downland

350' MILL

QUARLEY HILL 501'

**GRATELEY** — 72¾

Factory 350'

grazing land

350'

Woods

farmland 300'

Woods

THRUXTON

MONXTON

to Swindon

VIADUCT 250'

G.W. Rly

WEYHILL A.342

Philhill Brook

Watercress Beds

250'

A.303

AERODROME 250

A.343

LINE FALLS 1:440

**8** MINUTES GRATELEY TO PORTON

LINE RISES 1:165

**9** MINUTES

LINE RISES 1:220

250'

to Romsey

River Anton

A.3057

FULLERTON

ANDOVER TOWN

**ANDOVER JUNCTION** — 66½ MILES FROM **LONDON**

250'

grid cables

Finkley Down Fm.

A.343

Embankment

LINE FALLS 1:178

HAREWOOD FOREST

350'

350'

River Test

deep Cutting

450'

farmland

LINE RISES 1:275

A.303

G.W. Rly

to Winchester

Viaduct

Watercress Beds

Bourne River

LEVEL

farmland

**HURSTBOURNE** — 61

COWDOWN

A.34

Woods 350'

300'

**4** MINUTES FROM WHITCHURCH

CONTINUED FROM PAGE 14

**21**

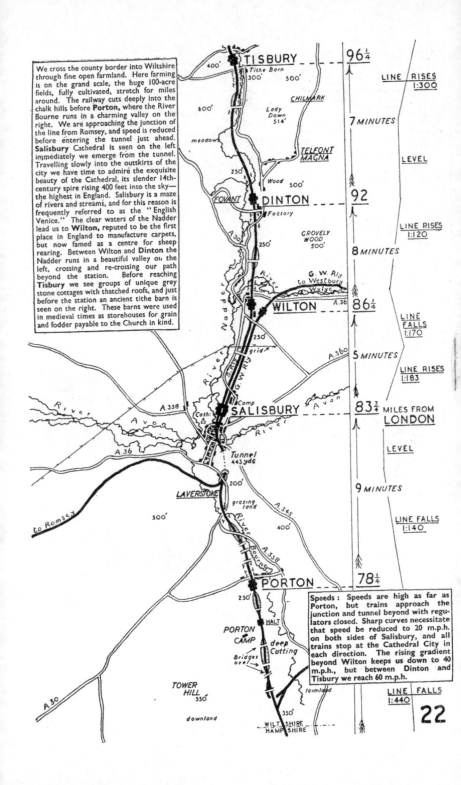

We cross the county border into Wiltshire through fine open farmland. Here farming is on the grand scale, the huge 100-acre fields, fully cultivated, stretch for miles around. The railway cuts deeply into the chalk hills before **Porton**, where the River Bourne runs in a charming valley on the right. We are approaching the junction of the line from Romsey, and speed is reduced before entering the tunnel just ahead. **Salisbury** Cathedral is seen on the left immediately we emerge from the tunnel. Travelling slowly into the outskirts of the city we have time to admire the exquisite beauty of the Cathedral, its slender 14th-century spire rising 400 feet into the sky—the highest in England. Salisbury is a maze of rivers and streams, and for this reason is frequently referred to as the "English Venice." The clear waters of the Nadder lead us to **Wilton**, reputed to be the first place in England to manufacture carpets, but now famed as a centre for sheep rearing. Between Wilton and **Dinton** the Nadder runs in a beautiful valley on the left, crossing and re-crossing our path beyond the station. Before reaching **Tisbury** we see groups of unique grey stone cottages with thatched roofs, and just before the station an ancient tithe barn is seen on the right. These barns were used in medieval times as storehouses for grain and fodder payable to the Church in kind.

**Speeds :** Speeds are high as far as Porton, but trains approach the junction and tunnel beyond with regulators closed. Sharp curves necessitate that speed be reduced to 20 m.p.h. on both sides of Salisbury, and all trains stop at the Cathedral City in each direction. The rising gradient beyond Wilton keeps us down to 40 m.p.h., but between Dinton and Tisbury we reach 60 m.p.h.

TISBURY — 96¼

LINE RISES 1:300

7 MINUTES

LEVEL

DINTON — 92

LINE RISES 1:120

8 MINUTES

WILTON — 86¼

LINE FALLS 1:170

5 MINUTES

LINE RISES 1:183

SALISBURY — 83¾ MILES FROM LONDON

LEVEL

9 MINUTES

LINE FALLS 1:140

PORTON — 78¼

LINE FALLS 1:440

22

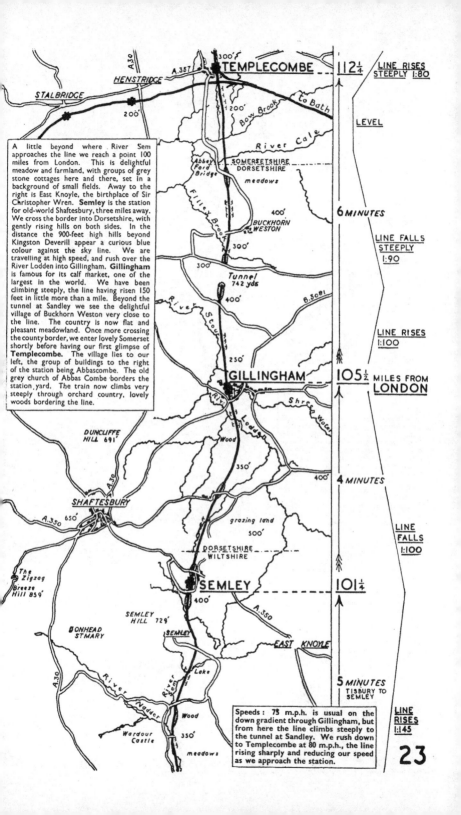

A little beyond where River Sem approaches the line we reach a point 100 miles from London. This is delightful meadow and farmland, with groups of grey stone cottages here and there, set in a background of small fields. Away to the right is East Knoyle, the birthplace of Sir Christopher Wren. **Semley** is the station for old-world Shaftesbury, three miles away. We cross the border into Dorsetshire, with gently rising hills on both sides. In the distance the 900-feet high hills beyond Kingston Deverill appear a curious blue colour against the sky line. We are travelling at high speed, and rush over the River Lodden into Gillingham. **Gillingham** is famous for its calf market, one of the largest in the world. We have been climbing steeply, the line having risen 150 feet in little more than a mile. Beyond the tunnel at Sandley we see the delightful village of Buckhorn Weston very close to the line. The country is now flat and pleasant meadowland. Once more crossing the county border, we enter lovely Somerset shortly before having our first glimpse of **Templecombe**. The village lies to our left, the group of buildings to the right of the station being Abbascombe. The old grey church of Abbas Combe borders the station yard. The train now climbs very steeply through orchard country, lovely woods bordering the line.

Speeds : 75 m.p.h. is usual on the down gradient through Gillingham, but from here the line climbs steeply to the tunnel at Sandley. We rush down to Templecombe at 80 m.p.h., the line rising sharply and reducing our speed as we approach the station.

23

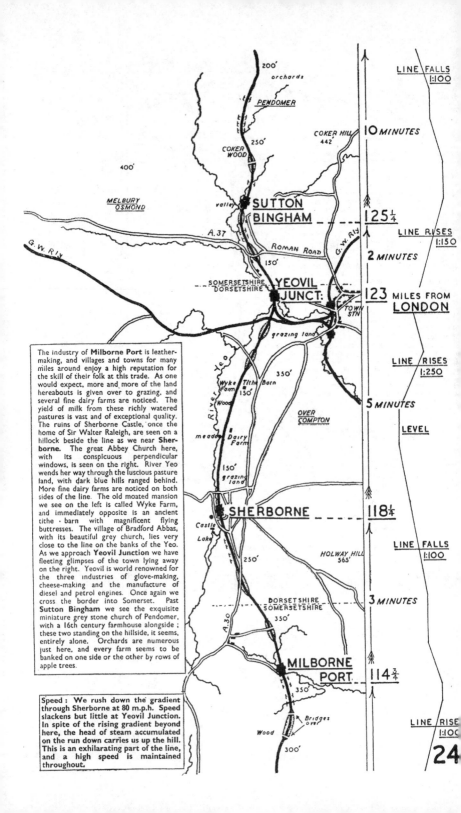

200'
orchards

PENDOMER

COKER HILL
442'

250'

COKER
WOOD

400'

MELBURY
OSMOND

valley

**SUTTON
BINGHAM**

A.37

ROMAN ROAD

150'

SOMERSETSHIRE
DORSETSHIRE

G.W.R'LY

**YEOVIL
JUNCT:**

TOWN
STN

grazing land

River Yeo

Wyke
Farm

Tithe Barn

150'

Wood

350'

OVER
COMPTON

meadow

Dairy
Farm

150'

grazing
land

**SHERBORNE**

Castle
Lake

250'

HOLWAY HILL
563'

DORSETSHIRE
SOMERSETSHIRE

A.30

350'

**MILBORNE
PORT**

350'

Bridges
over

Wood

300'

The industry of **Milborne Port** is leather-making, and villages and towns for many miles around enjoy a high reputation for the skill of their folk at this trade. As one would expect, more and more of the land hereabouts is given over to grazing, and several fine dairy farms are noticed. The yield of milk from these richly watered pastures is vast and of exceptional quality. The ruins of Sherborne Castle, once the home of Sir Walter Raleigh, are seen on a hillock beside the line as we near **Sherborne.** The great Abbey Church here, with its conspicuous perpendicular windows, is seen on the right. River Yeo wends her way through the luscious pasture land, with dark blue hills ranged behind. More fine dairy farms are noticed on both sides of the line. The old moated mansion we see on the left is called Wyke Farm, and immediately opposite is an ancient tithe · barn with magnificent flying buttresses. The village of Bradford Abbas, with its beautiful grey church, lies very close to the line on the banks of the Yeo. As we approach **Yeovil Junction** we have fleeting glimpses of the town lying away on the right. Yeovil is world renowned for the three industries of glove-making, cheese-making and the manufacture of diesel and petrol engines. Once again we cross the border into Somerset. Past **Sutton Bingham** we see the exquisite miniature grey stone church of Pendomer, with a 16th century farmhouse alongside ; these two standing on the hillside, it seems, entirely alone. Orchards are numerous just here, and every farm seems to be banked on one side or the other by rows of apple trees.

Speed : We rush down the gradient through Sherborne at 80 m.p.h. Speed slackens but little at Yeovil Junction. In spite of the rising gradient beyond here, the head of steam accumulated on the run down carries us up the hill. This is an exhilarating part of the line, and a high speed is maintained throughout.

LINE FALLS
1:100

**10** MINUTES

**125¼**

LINE RISES
1:150

**2** MINUTES

**123** MILES FROM
**LONDON**

LINE RISES
1:250

**5** MINUTES

LEVEL

**118¼**

LINE FALLS
1:100

**3** MINUTES

**114¾**

LINE RISE
1:100

**24**

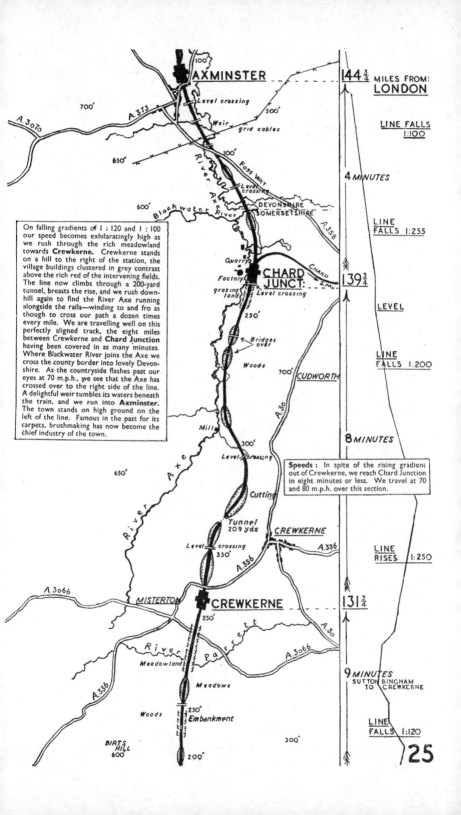

On falling gradients of 1 : 120 and 1 : 100 our speed becomes exhilaratingly high as we rush through the rich meadowland towards **Crewkerne.** Crewkerne stands on a hill to the right of the station, the village buildings clustered in grey contrast above the rich red of the intervening fields. The line now climbs through a 200-yard tunnel, breasts the rise, and we rush downhill again to find the River Axe running alongside the rails—winding to and fro as though to cross our path a dozen times every mile. We are travelling well on this perfectly aligned track, the eight miles between Crewkerne and **Chard Junction** having been covered in as many minutes. Where Blackwater River joins the Axe we cross the county border into lovely Devonshire. As the countryside flashes past our eyes at 70 m.p.h., we see that the Axe has crossed over to the right side of the line. A delightful weir tumbles its waters beneath the train, and we run into **Axminster.** The town stands on high ground on the left of the line. Famous in the past for its carpets, brushmaking has now become the chief industry of the town.

**Speeds :** In spite of the rising gradient out of Crewkerne, we reach Chard Junction in eight minutes or less. We travel at 70 and 80 m.p.h. over this section.

AXMINSTER

144¾ MILES FROM LONDON

LINE FALLS 1:100

4 MINUTES

LINE FALLS 1:255

CHARD JUNCT:

139¾

LEVEL

LINE FALLS 1:200

8 MINUTES

LINE RISES 1:250

CREWKERNE

131¾

9 MINUTES
SUTTON BINGHAM TO CREWKERNE

LINE FALLS 1:120

25

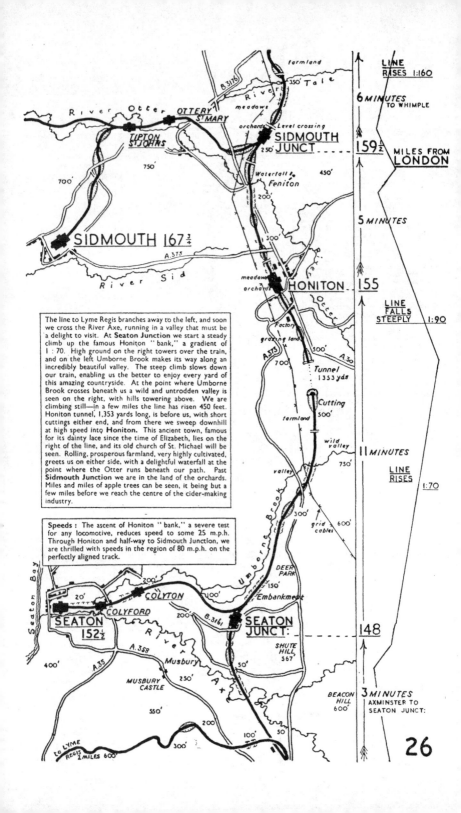

The line to Lyme Regis branches away to the left, and soon we cross the River Axe, running in a valley that must be a delight to visit. At **Seaton Junction** we start a steady climb up the famous Honiton "bank," a gradient of 1 : 70. High ground on the right towers over the train, and on the left Umborne Brook makes its way along an incredibly beautiful valley. The steep climb slows down our train, enabling us the better to enjoy every yard of this amazing countryside. At the point where Umborne Brook crosses beneath us a wild and untrodden valley is seen on the right, with hills towering above. We are climbing still—in a few miles the line has risen 450 feet. Honiton tunnel, 1,353 yards long, is before us, with short cuttings either end, and from there we sweep downhill at high speed into **Honiton**. This ancient town, famous for its dainty lace since the time of Elizabeth, lies on the right of the line, and its old church of St. Michael will be seen. Rolling, prosperous farmland, very highly cultivated, greets us on either side, with a delightful waterfall at the point where the Otter runs beneath our path. Past **Sidmouth Junction** we are in the land of the orchards. Miles and miles of apple trees can be seen, it being but a few miles before we reach the centre of the cider-making industry.

**Speeds :** The ascent of Honiton "bank," a severe test for any locomotive, reduces speed to some 25 m.p.h. Through Honiton and half-way to Sidmouth Junction, we are thrilled with speeds in the region of 80 m.p.h. on the perfectly aligned track.

26

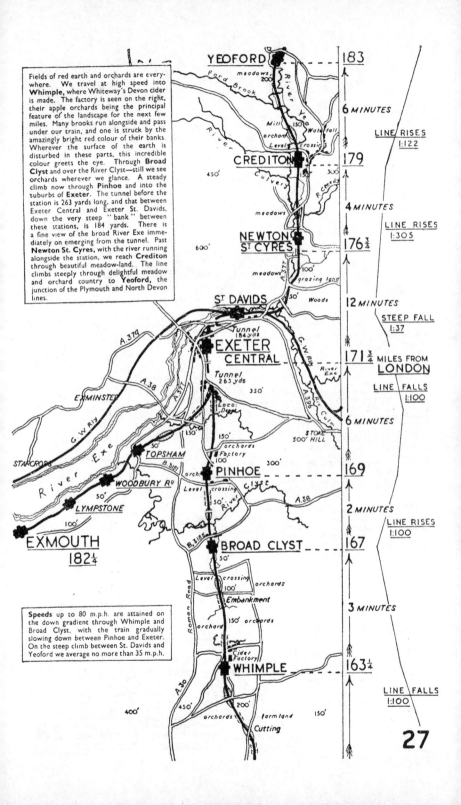

Fields of red earth and orchards are everywhere. We travel at high speed into **Whimple**, where Whiteway's Devon cider is made. The factory is seen on the right, their apple orchards being the principal feature of the landscape for the next few miles. Many brooks run alongside and pass under our train, and one is struck by the amazingly bright red colour of their banks. Wherever the surface of the earth is disturbed in these parts, this incredible colour greets the eye. Through **Broad Clyst** and over the River Clyst—still we see orchards wherever we glance. A steady climb now through **Pinhoe** and into the suburbs of **Exeter**. The tunnel before the station is 263 yards long, and that between Exeter Central and Exeter St. Davids, down the very steep " bank " between these stations, is 184 yards. There is a fine view of the broad River Exe immediately on emerging from the tunnel. Past **Newton St. Cyres**, with the river running alongside the station, we reach **Crediton** through beautiful meadow-land. The line climbs steeply through delightful meadow and orchard country to **Yeoford**, the junction of the Plymouth and North Devon lines.

**Speeds** up to 80 m.p.h. are attained on the down gradient through Whimple and Broad Clyst, with the train gradually slowing down between Pinhoe and Exeter. On the steep climb between St. Davids and Yeoford we average no more than 35 m.p.h.

YEOFORD — 183
6 MINUTES
LINE RISES 1:122
CREDITON — 179
4 MINUTES
LINE RISES 1:305
NEWTON ST. CYRES — 176¾
12 MINUTES
STEEP FALL 1:37
ST DAVIDS
EXETER CENTRAL — 171¾ MILES FROM LONDON
LINE FALLS 1:100
6 MINUTES
Tunnel 184 yds
Tunnel 263 yds
STOKE 500' HILL
PINHOE — 169
2 MINUTES
LINE RISES 1:100
BROAD CLYST — 167
3 MINUTES
WHIMPLE — 163¼
LINE FALLS 1:100

EXMINSTER
TOPSHAM
WOODBURY RD
LYMPSTONE
EXMOUTH 182¼
STARCROSS
River Exe

27

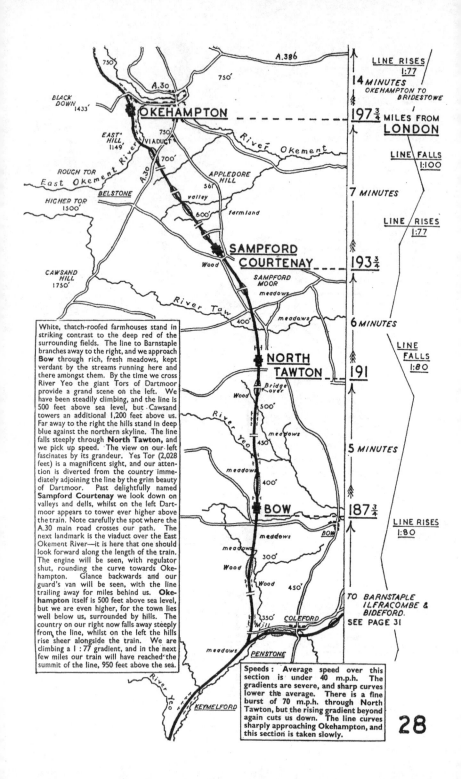

A.386

LINE RISES 1:77

14 MINUTES
OKEHAMPTON TO BRIDESTOWE

750'

750'

BLACK DOWN 1433'

A.30

OKEHAMPTON

197¾ MILES FROM LONDON

River Okement

LINE FALLS 1:100

EAST HILL 1149'

750'

VIADUCT

700'

East Okement River

ROUGH TOR

APPLEDORE HILL 561

BELSTONE

valley

600'

farmland

7 MINUTES

HIGHER TOR 1500'

SAMPFORD COURTENAY

193¾

LINE RISES 1:77

Wood

CAWSAND HILL 1750'

SAMPFORD MOOR

River Taw

meadows

400'

meadows

6 MINUTES

Hill

NORTH TAWTON

191

LINE FALLS 1:80

Bridge over

Wood

River Yeo

500'

meadows

450'

5 MINUTES

meadows

400'

BOW

187¾

LINE RISES 1:80

meadows

BOW

meadows

300'

Wood

Wood

450'

TO BARNSTAPLE ILFRACOMBE & BIDEFORD. SEE PAGE 31

350'

Mill

COLEFORD

meadows

PENSTONE

River Yeo

KEYMELFORD

White, thatch-roofed farmhouses stand in striking contrast to the deep red of the surrounding fields. The line to Barnstaple branches away to the right, and we approach **Bow** through rich, fresh meadows, kept verdant by the streams running here and there amongst them. By the time we cross River Yeo the giant Tors of Dartmoor provide a grand scene on the left. We have been steadily climbing, and the line is 500 feet above sea level, but Cawsand towers an additional 1,200 feet above us. Far away to the right the hills stand in deep blue against the northern skyline. The line falls steeply through **North Tawton,** and we pick up speed. The view on our left fascinates by its grandeur. Yes Tor (2,028 feet) is a magnificent sight, and our attention is diverted from the country immediately adjoining the line by the grim beauty of Dartmoor. Past delightfully named **Sampford Courtenay** we look down on valleys and dells, whilst on the left Dartmoor appears to tower ever higher above the train. Note carefully the spot where the A.30 main road crosses our path. The next landmark is the viaduct over the East Okement River—it is here that one should look forward along the length of the train. The engine will be seen, with regulator shut, rounding the curve towards Okehampton. Glance backwards and our guard's van will be seen, with the line trailing away for miles behind us. **Okehampton** itself is 500 feet above sea level, but we are even higher, for the town lies well below us, surrounded by hills. The country on our right now falls away steeply from the line, whilst on the left the hills rise sheer alongside the train. We are climbing a 1 : 77 gradient, and in the next few miles our train will have reached the summit of the line, 950 feet above the sea.

Speeds : Average speed over this section is under 40 m.p.h. The gradients are severe, and sharp curves lower the average. There is a fine burst of 70 m.p.h. through North Tawton, but the rising gradient beyond again cuts us down. The line curves sharply approaching Okehampton, and this section is taken slowly.

28

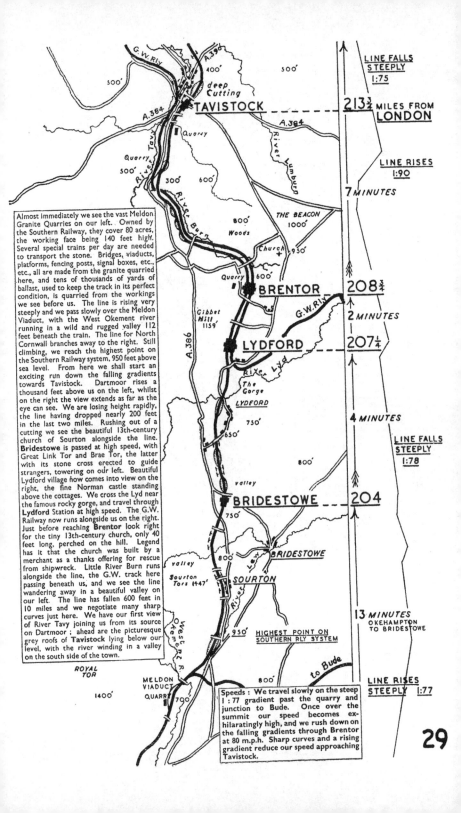

Almost immediately we see the vast Meldon Granite Quarries on our left. Owned by the Southern Railway, they cover 80 acres, the working face being 140 feet high. Several special trains per day are needed to transport the stone. Bridges, viaducts, platforms, fencing posts, signal boxes, etc., etc., all are made from the granite quarried here, and tens of thousands of yards of ballast, used to keep the track in its perfect condition, is quarried from the workings we see before us. The line is rising very steeply and we pass slowly over the Meldon Viaduct, with the West Okement river running in a wild and rugged valley 112 feet beneath the train. The line for North Cornwall branches away to the right. Still climbing, we reach the highest point on the Southern Railway system, 950 feet above sea level. From here we shall start an exciting run down the falling gradients towards Tavistock. Dartmoor rises a thousand feet above us on the left, whilst on the right the view extends as far as the eye can see. We are losing height rapidly, the line having dropped nearly 200 feet in the last two miles. Rushing out of a cutting we see the beautiful 13th-century church of Sourton alongside the line. **Bridestowe** is passed at high speed, with Great Link Tor and Brae Tor, the latter with its stone cross erected to guide strangers, towering on our left. Beautiful Lydford village now comes into view on the right, the fine Norman castle standing above the cottages. We cross the Lyd near the famous rocky gorge, and travel through **Lydford** Station at high speed. The G.W. Railway now runs alongside us on the right. Just before reaching **Brentor** look right for the tiny 13th-century church, only 40 feet long, perched on the hill. Legend has it that the church was built by a merchant as a thanks offering for rescue from shipwreck. Little River Burn runs alongside the line, the G.W. track here passing beneath us, and we see the line wandering away in a beautiful valley on our left. The line has fallen 600 feet in 10 miles and we negotiate many sharp curves just here. We have our first view of River Tavy joining us from its source on Dartmoor; ahead are the picturesque grey roofs of **Tavistock** lying below our level, with the river winding in a valley on the south side of the town.

Speeds : We travel slowly on the steep 1 : 77 gradient past the quarry and junction to Bude. Once over the summit our speed becomes exhilaratingly high, and we rush down on the falling gradients through Brentor at 80 m.p.h. Sharp curves and a rising gradient reduce our speed approaching Tavistock.

LINE FALLS STEEPLY 1:75

213¾ MILES FROM LONDON

LINE RISES 1:90

7 MINUTES

208¾

2 MINUTES

207¼

4 MINUTES

LINE FALLS STEEPLY 1:78

204

13 MINUTES OKEHAMPTON TO BRIDESTOWE

LINE RISES STEEPLY 1:77

TAVISTOCK

BRENTOR

LYDFORD

BRIDESTOWE

SOURTON

HIGHEST POINT ON SOUTHERN RLY SYSTEM

MELDON VIADUCT

ROYAL TOR

to Bude

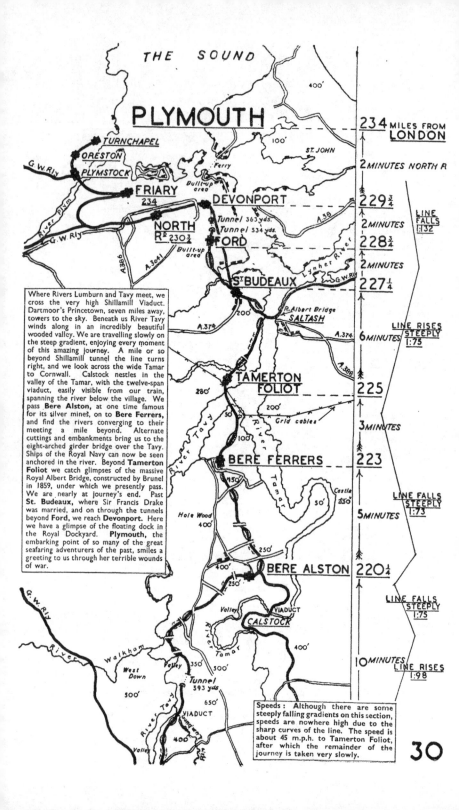

THE SOUND

# PLYMOUTH

TURNCHAPEL
ORESTON
PLYMSTOCK
G.W. Rly

FRIARY
234

DEVONPORT

NORTH
Rd 230¼
FORD

Tunnel 363 yds.
Tunnel 534 yds.

St BUDEAUX

SALTASH
R. Albert Bridge

TAMERTON
FOLIOT

Grid cables

BERE FERRERS

BERE ALSTON 220¼

CALSTOCK
VIADUCT

Tunnel 393 yds.

VIADUCT

West Down

234 MILES FROM LONDON
2 MINUTES NORTH R
229¾
2 MINUTES
228¼
2 MINUTES
227¼
6 MINUTES    LINE RISES STEEPLY 1:75
225
3 MINUTES
223
5 MINUTES    LINE FALLS STEEPLY 1:73
220¼    LINE FALLS STEEPLY 1:75
10 MINUTES   LINE RISES 1:98

LINE FALLS 1:32

Where Rivers Lumburn and Tavy meet, we cross the very high Shillamill Viaduct. Dartmoor's Princetown, seven miles away, towers to the sky. Beneath us River Tavy winds along in an incredibly beautiful wooded valley. We are travelling slowly on the steep gradient, enjoying every moment of this amazing journey. A mile or so beyond Shillamill tunnel the line turns right, and we look across the wide Tamar to Cornwall. Calstock nestles in the valley of the Tamar, with the twelve-span viaduct, easily visible from our train, spanning the river below the village. We pass Bere Alston, at one time famous for its silver mines, on to Bere Ferrers, and find the rivers converging to their meeting a mile beyond. Alternate cuttings and embankments bring us to the eight-arched girder bridge over the Tavy. Ships of the Royal Navy can now be seen anchored in the river. Beyond Tamerton Foliot we catch glimpses of the massive Royal Albert Bridge, constructed by Brunel in 1859, under which we presently pass. We are nearly at journey's end. Past St. Budeaux, where Sir Francis Drake was married, and on through the tunnels beyond Ford, we reach Devonport. Here we have a glimpse of the floating dock in the Royal Dockyard. Plymouth, the embarking point of so many of the great seafaring adventurers of the past, smiles a greeting to us through her terrible wounds of war.

Speeds: Although there are some steeply falling gradients on this section, speeds are nowhere high due to the sharp curves of the line. The speed is about 45 m.p.h. to Tamerton Foliot, after which the remainder of the journey is taken very slowly.

30

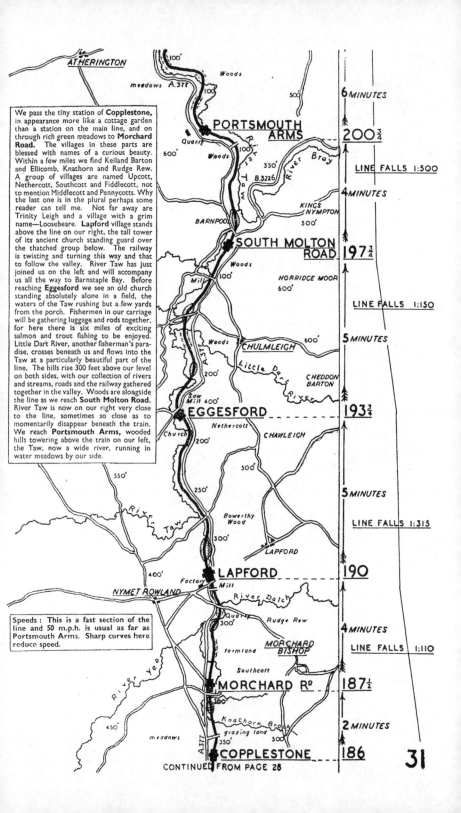

ATHERINGTON

meadows A.377

Woods

We pass the tiny station of **Copplestone**, in appearance more like a cottage garden than a station on the main line, and on through rich green meadows to **Morchard Road.** The villages in these parts are blessed with names of a curious beauty. Within a few miles we find Keiland Barton and Ellicomb, Knathorn and Rudge Rew. A group of villages are named Upcott, Nethercott, Southcott and Fiddlecott, not to mention Middlecott and Pennycotts. Why the last one is in the plural perhaps some reader can tell me. Not far away are Trinity Leigh and a village with a grim name—Loosebeare. **Lapford** village stands above the line on our right, the tall tower of its ancient church standing guard over the thatched group below. The railway is twisting and turning this way and that to follow the valley. River Taw has just joined us on the left and will accompany us all the way to Barnstaple Bay. Before reaching **Eggesford** we see an old church standing absolutely alone in a field, the waters of the Taw rushing but a few yards from the porch. Fishermen in our carriage will be gathering luggage and rods together, for here there is six miles of exciting salmon and trout fishing to be enjoyed. Little Dart River, another fisherman's paradise, crosses beneath us and flows into the Taw at a particularly beautiful part of the line. The hills rise 300 feet above our level on both sides, with our collection of rivers and streams, roads and the railway gathered together in the valley. Woods are alongside the line as we reach **South Molton Road.** River Taw is now on our right very close to the line, sometimes so close as to momentarily disappear beneath the train. We reach **Portsmouth Arms,** wooded hills towering above the train on our left, the Taw, now a wide river, running in water meadows by our side.

Quarry

600'

Woods

100'

B.3226

River Bray

River Taw

350'

KINGS NYMPTON

500'

BARNPOOL

**PORTSMOUTH ARMS**

**SOUTH MOLTON ROAD**

Woods

Mill

100'

HORRIDGE MOOR

600'

Woods

600'

**CHULMLEIGH**

Little Dart

CHEDDON BARTON

River

200'

Saw Mill 400'

**EGGESFORD**

Nethercott

CHAWLEIGH

Church

200'

500'

550'

250'

River Taw

Bowerthy Wood

300'

LAPFORD

400'

**LAPFORD**

Factory Mill

*NYMET ROWLAND*

River Dalch

Quarry 300'

Rudge Rew

**Speeds : This is a fast section of the line and 50 m.p.h. is usual as far as Portsmouth Arms. Sharp curves here reduce speed.**

River Yeo

farmland

**MORCHARD BISHOP**

Southcott

**MORCHARD Rᴅ**

300'

450'

Knathorn Brook

grazing land

350' 500'

meadows

A.377

**COPPLESTONE**

CONTINUED FROM PAGE 28

6 MINUTES

**200¾**

LINE FALLS 1:500

4 MINUTES

**197¾**

LINE FALLS 1:150

5 MINUTES

**193¾**

5 MINUTES

LINE FALLS 1:315

**190**

4 MINUTES

LINE FALLS 1:110

**187½**

2 MINUTES

**186**

**31**

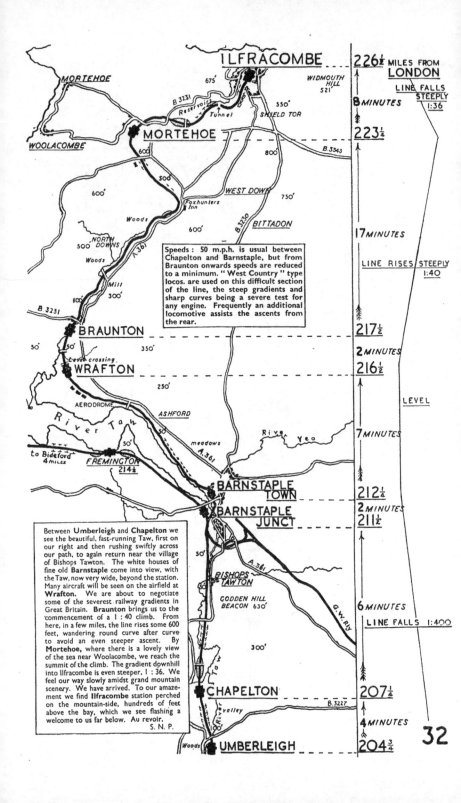

# Mile by Mile

## ON THE L.M.S.

by

S. N. PIKE, M.B.E.

MIDLAND REGION EDITION
BRITISH RAILWAYS

The journey between Euston and St. Pancras and the North and
North-West described in detail :—

- GRADIENTS OF THE LINE
- SPEED TESTS AND MILEAGES
- VIADUCTS, BRIDGES AND EMBANKMENTS
- TUNNELS, CUTTINGS AND CROSSOVERS
- STREAMS, RIVERS AND ROADS
- MINES, FACTORIES AND WORKS

with an account of features of interest and beauty to be seen
from the train.

*Published by*
STUART N. PIKE,
3, Canterbury House,
Worthing, Sussex

*Sole Distributors to the Trade* :—
Atlas Publishing and Distributing Co., Ltd.,
18, Bride Lane. London, E.C.4.

# PRINCIPAL STATIONS

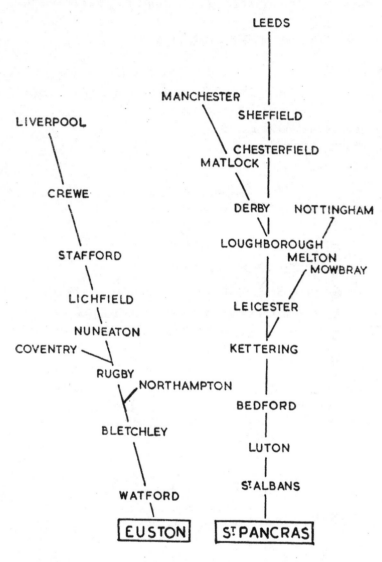

FOR INDEX TO ALL STATIONS
SEE PAGE 4

# Author's Note

In this, my third railway book, I have to again acknowledge, with grateful thanks, the valuable assistance I have received from all grades of railway officials. Those whose daily work it is to ensure speedy and comfortable travel on the Midland Region of British Railways have thrown themselves enthusiastically into the task of helping me with the construction of this little book.

Embodied in this edition are many helpful suggestions received from readers of my previous books " Mile by Mile on the Southern Railway" and " Mile by Mile on the L.N.E.R." To these correspondents I am extremely grateful, and if I have not adopted all the ideas put forward it is because I wished to keep all three booklets in line as to style, size and price, so that they all may be considered as companion editions and, with the forthcoming Western Region edition (G.W. Railway), form a set covering the most used main railway lines in the country.

I am indebted to the Railway Publishing Co. Ltd. for their kind permission to reproduce certain of the diagrams from their publication " Gradients of British Main Line Railways."

To save correspondence I would say here that I will advise all old and new post customers for my books when the G.W. Railway (Western Region) edition is ready for sale, and as other railway books by me become available.

3 Canterbury House,                                        S. N. P.
    Worthing, Sussex.

# Index to Stations

# Rivers we meet

# Canals

*For index of Tunnels and Water-Troughs en route see page 6*

# Tunnels en Route

# Water-Trough Installations en Route

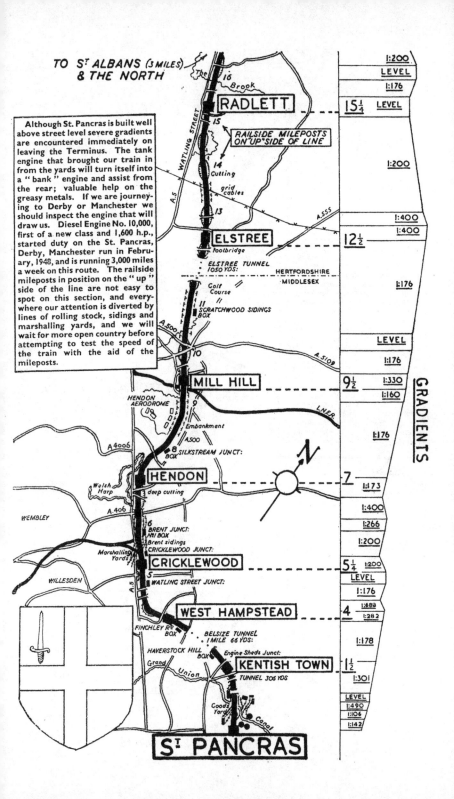

TO ST ALBANS (3 MILES)
& THE NORTH

The Brook

16

RADLETT

15

*RAILSIDE MILEPOSTS
ON "UP" SIDE OF LINE*

14
Cutting

grid cables

13

ELSTREE
Footbridge

ELSTREE TUNNEL
1050 YDS.

HERTFORDSHIRE
MIDDLESEX

Golf Course

11
SCRATCHWOOD SIDINGS
BOX

10

MILL HILL

HENDON
AERODROME

9

Embankment
A500

8
BOX
SILKSTREAM JUNCT:

HENDON

Welsh Harp

deep cutting

A.406

6
BRENT JUNCT:
N°1 BOX
Brent sidings
CRICKLEWOOD JUNCT:

Marshalling Yards

CRICKLEWOOD

WATLING STREET JUNCT:

WEST HAMPSTEAD

FINCHLEY RD
BOX

BELSIZE TUNNEL
1 MILE 66 YDS:

HAVERSTOCK HILL
BOX
Engine Sheds Junct:

Grand Union

KENTISH TOWN

TUNNEL 305 YDS

Goods Yard

Canal

ST PANCRAS

WEMBLEY

A4006

A 406

WILLESDEN

A.5

LNER

N

A.5109

A.500

A.5

WATLING STREET

A.5

A.555

**GRADIENTS**

| | |
|---|---|
| 1:200 | |
| LEVEL | |
| 1:176 | |
| LEVEL | 15¼ |
| 1:200 | |
| 1:400 | |
| 1:400 | 12½ |
| 1:176 | |
| LEVEL | |
| 1:176 | |
| 1:330 | 9½ |
| 1:160 | |
| 1:176 | |
| 1:173 | 7 |
| 1:400 | |
| 1:266 | |
| 1:200 | |
| 1:200 | 5¼ |
| LEVEL | |
| 1:176 | |
| 1:689 | 4 |
| 1:282 | |
| 1:178 | |
| 1:301 | 1½ |
| LEVEL | |
| 1:490 | |
| 1:106 | |
| 1:142 | |

Although St. Pancras is built well above street level severe gradients are encountered immediately on leaving the Terminus. The tank engine that brought our train in from the yards will turn itself into a "bank" engine and assist from the rear; valuable help on the greasy metals. If we are journeying to Derby or Manchester we should inspect the engine that will draw us. Diesel Engine No. 10,000, first of a new class and 1,600 h.p., started duty on the St. Pancras, Derby, Manchester run in February, 1948, and is running 3,000 miles a week on this route. The railside mileposts in position on the "up" side of the line are not easy to spot on this section, and everywhere our attention is diverted by lines of rolling stock, sidings and marshalling yards, and we will wait for more open country before attempting to test the speed of the train with the aid of the mileposts.

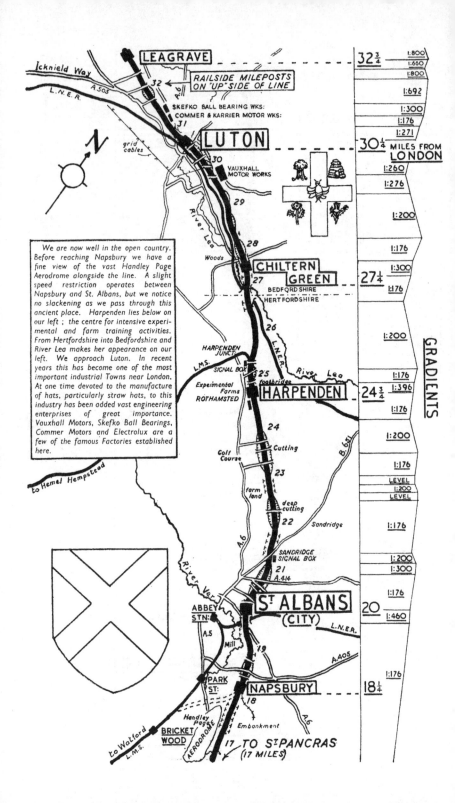

LEAGRAVE

Icknield Way

L.N.E.R.

**RAILSIDE MILEPOSTS ON 'UP' SIDE OF LINE**

32

SKEFKO BALL BEARING WKS:
COMMER & KARRIER MOTOR WKS:

31

**LUTON**

30

VAUXHALL MOTOR WORKS

29

grid cables

River Lea

28

Woods

**CHILTERN GREEN**

27

BEDFORDSHIRE
HERTFORDSHIRE

26

HARPENDEN JUNCT.

L.N.E.R.

River Lea

L.M.S.

SIGNAL BOX

25

Experimental Farms ROTHAMSTED

footbridge

**HARPENDEN**

to Hemel Hempstead

24

Golf Course

Cutting

B.651

23

farm land

deep cutting

22

Sandridge

A.6

SANDRIDGE SIGNAL BOX

21

A.414

River Ver

ABBEY STN:

A.5

**St. ALBANS**
(CITY)

L.N.E.R.

Mill

19

A.405

**PARK ST:**

**NAPSBURY**

to Watford

L.M.S.

**BRICKET WOOD**

Handley Page AERODROME

18

Embankment

A.6

17 **TO St PANCRAS**
(17 MILES)

We are now well in the open country. Before reaching Napsbury we have a fine view of the vast Handley Page Aerodrome alongside the line. A slight speed restriction operates between Napsbury and St. Albans, but we notice no slackening as we pass through this ancient place. Harpenden lies below on our left ; the centre for intensive experimental and farm training activities. From Hertfordshire into Bedfordshire and River Lea makes her appearance on our left. We approach Luton. In recent years this has become one of the most important industrial Towns near London. At one time devoted to the manufacture of hats, particularly straw hats, to this industry has been added vast engineering enterprises of great importance. Vauxhall Motors, Skefko Ball Bearings, Commer Motors and Electrolux are a few of the famous Factories established here.

**GRADIENTS**

32¾

1:800
1:660
1:800
1:692
1:300
1:176
1:271

30¼ **MILES FROM LONDON**

1:260
1:276
1:200
1:176
1:300
1:176

27¼

1:200
1:176
1:396
1:176

24¾

1:200
1:176
LEVEL
1:200
LEVEL
1:176
1:200
1:300
1:176

20

1:460
1:176

18¼

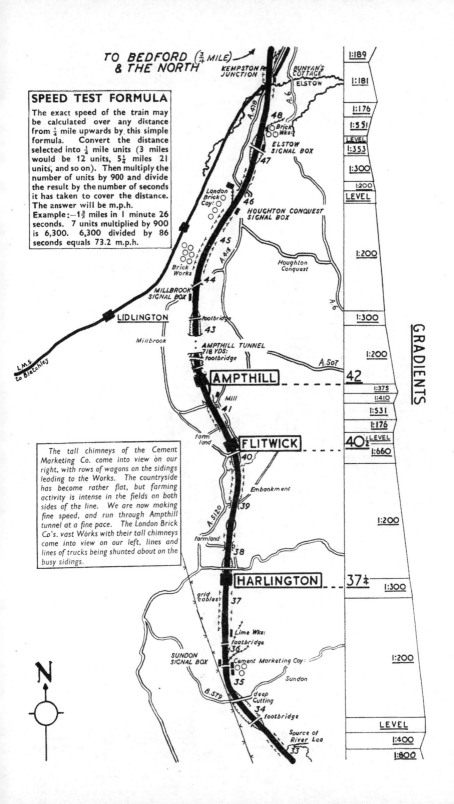

TO BEDFORD (¾ MILE) & THE NORTH

KEMPSTON JUNCTION

BUNYAN'S COTTAGE

ELSTOW

**SPEED TEST FORMULA**

The exact speed of the train may be calculated over any distance from ¼ mile upwards by this simple formula. Convert the distance selected into ¼ mile units (3 miles would be 12 units, 5¼ miles 21 units, and so on). Then multiply the number of units by 900 and divide the result by the number of seconds it has taken to cover the distance. The answer will be m.p.h.
Example:—1¾ miles in 1 minute 26 seconds. 7 units multiplied by 900 is 6,300. 6,300 divided by 86 seconds equals 73.2 m.p.h.

48

Brick Wks:

ELSTOW SIGNAL BOX

47

London Brick Coy:

46

HOUGHTON CONQUEST SIGNAL BOX

45

Houghton Conquest

Brick Works

44

MILLBROOK SIGNAL BOX

LIDLINGTON

footbridge

43

Millbrook

A.507

AMPTHILL TUNNEL 718 YDS:
footbridge

**AMPTHILL**

42

Mill

41

The tall chimneys of the Cement Marketing Co. come into view on our right, with rows of wagons on the sidings leading to the Works. The countryside has become rather flat, but farming activity is intense in the fields on both sides of the line. We are now making fine speed, and run through Ampthill tunnel at a fine pace. The London Brick Co's. vast Works with their tall chimneys come into view on our left, lines and lines of trucks being shunted about on the busy sidings.

farm land

**FLITWICK**

40½

40

Embankment

39

farmland

38

**HARLINGTON**

37½

grid cables

37

Lime Wks:
footbridge

36

SUNDON SIGNAL BOX

Cement Marketing Coy:

35

Sundon

B.579

deep Cutting

34

footbridge

Source of River Lea

33

LMS to Bletchley

N

**GRADIENTS**

1:189
1:181
1:176
1:551
LEVEL
1:353
1:300
1:200
LEVEL
1:200
1:300
1:200
1:375
1:410
1:531
1:176
LEVEL
1:660
1:200
1:300
1:200
LEVEL
1:400
1:800

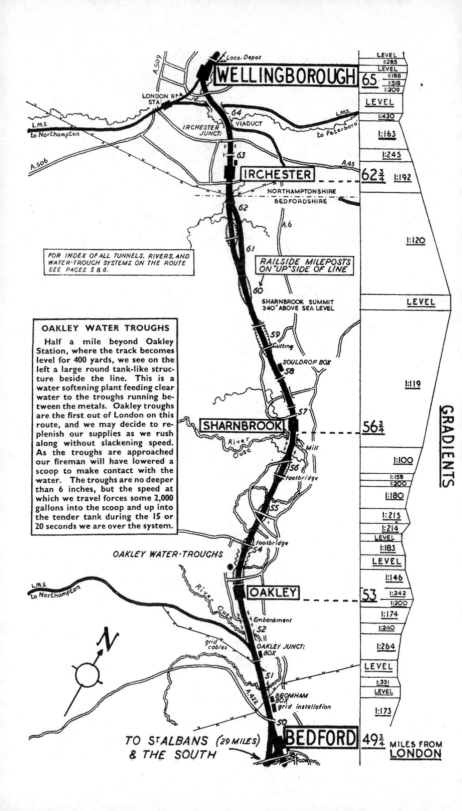

**OAKLEY WATER TROUGHS**

Half a mile beyond Oakley Station, where the track becomes level for 400 yards, we see on the left a large round tank-like structure beside the line. This is a water softening plant feeding clear water to the troughs running between the metals. Oakley troughs are the first out of London on this route, and we may decide to replenish our supplies as we rush along without slackening speed. As the troughs are approached our fireman will have lowered a scoop to make contact with the water. The troughs are no deeper than 6 inches, but the speed at which we travel forces some 2,000 gallons into the scoop and up into the tender tank during the 15 or 20 seconds we are over the system.

FOR INDEX OF ALL TUNNELS, RIVERS, AND WATER-TROUGH SYSTEMS ON THE ROUTE SEE PAGES 5 & 6.

*RAILSIDE MILEPOSTS ON "UP" SIDE OF LINE*

Loco. Depot

**WELLINGBOROUGH** 65

London Rd. STA.

L.M.S. to Northampton

A.509

A.506

*IRCHESTER JUNCT.*

64 VIADUCT

L.M.S. to Peterboro

63

**IRCHESTER** 62¾

A.45

NORTHAMPTONSHIRE
BEDFORDSHIRE

A.6

62

61

60

SHARNBROOK SUMMIT
340' ABOVE SEA LEVEL

59
*Cutting*

SOULDROP BOX
58

57

**SHARNBROOK** 56¾

*River Ouse*

*Mill*

56
*footbridge*

55

*footbridge*

54

*OAKLEY WATER-TROUGHS*

*River Ouse*

**OAKLEY** 53

*Embankment*

52

*grid cables*

OAKLEY JUNCT:
BOX

51

A.422

BROMHAM
BOX
*grid installation*

50

**BEDFORD** 49¾ MILES FROM **LONDON**

TO St ALBANS (29 MILES)
& THE SOUTH

N

**GRADIENTS**

| LEVEL |
| 1:285 |
| LEVEL |
| 1:188 |
| 1:518 |
| 1:209 |
| LEVEL |
| 1:420 |
| 1:163 |
| 1:245 |
| 1:192 |
| 1:120 |
| LEVEL |
| 1:119 |
| 1:100 |
| 1:158 |
| 1:200 |
| 1:180 |
| 1:215 |
| 1:214 |
| LEVEL |
| 1:183 |
| LEVEL |
| 1:146 |
| 1:242 |
| 1:200 |
| 1:174 |
| 1:240 |
| 1:264 |
| LEVEL |
| 1:331 |
| LEVEL |
| 1:173 |

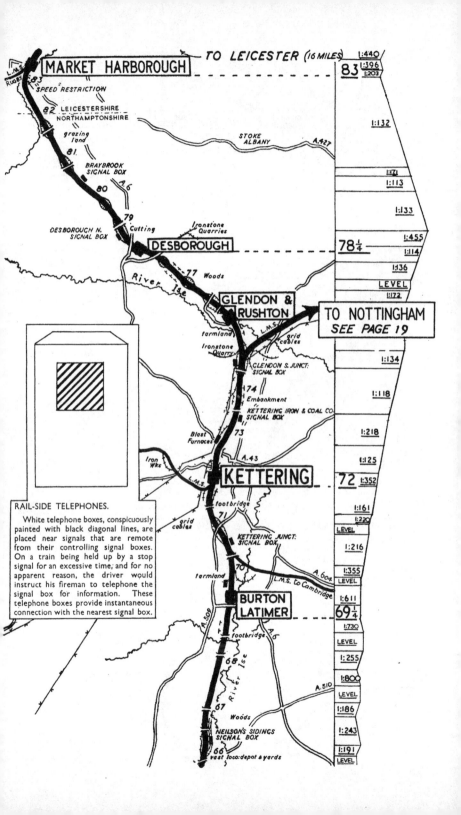

TO LEICESTER (16 MILES)  1:440

**MARKET HARBOROUGH**  83  1:396
1:203

L.M.S. RUGBY 83

SPEED RESTRICTION

82  LEICESTERSHIRE
NORTHAMPTONSHIRE  1:132

grazing land

STOKE ALBANY  A.427

81

BRAYBROOK SIGNAL BOX  1:71
1:113

80  A.6

79  1:133

DESBOROUGH N. SIGNAL BOX  Cutting

Ironstone Quarries  1:455

**DESBOROUGH**  78¼  1:114

1:136

77  Woods  LEVEL

River Ise

1:72

**GLENDON & RUSHTON**

**TO NOTTINGHAM**
**SEE PAGE 19**

farmland  L.M.S.  grid cables

Ironstone Quarry

CLENDON S. JUNCT: SIGNAL BOX  1:134

74  Embankment  1:118

KETTERING IRON & COAL CO. SIGNAL BOX

Blast Furnaces  73  1:218

Iron Wks.  1:125

A.43

L.M.S.  **KETTERING**  72  1:352

footbridge  1:161

71  1:220

grid cables  LEVEL

KETTERING JUNCT: SIGNAL BOX  1:216

farmland  70  1:355  A.604

L.M.S. to Cambridge  LEVEL

1:611

**BURTON**
**LATIMER**  69¼  1:730

footbridge  A.6  LEVEL

A.509  1:255

68  1:800

River Ise  LEVEL

A.510  1:186

67  Woods  1:243

NEILSON'S SIDINGS SIGNAL BOX  1:191

66  vast loco: depot & yards  LEVEL

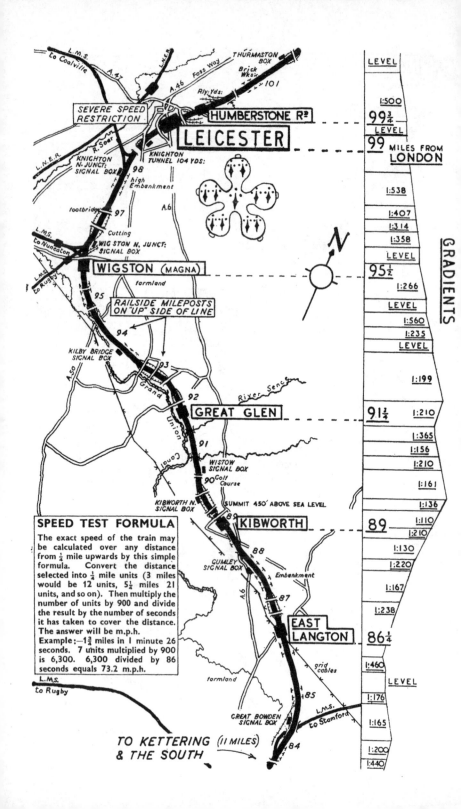

**TO KETTERING (11 MILES) & THE SOUTH**

### SPEED TEST FORMULA
The exact speed of the train may be calculated over any distance from ¼ mile upwards by this simple formula. Convert the distance selected into ¼ mile units (3 miles would be 12 units, 5¼ miles 21 units, and so on). Then multiply the number of units by 900 and divide the result by the number of seconds it has taken to cover the distance. The answer will be m.p.h.
Example:—1¾ miles in 1 minute 26 seconds. 7 units multiplied by 900 is 6,300. 6,300 divided by 86 seconds equals 73.2 m.p.h.

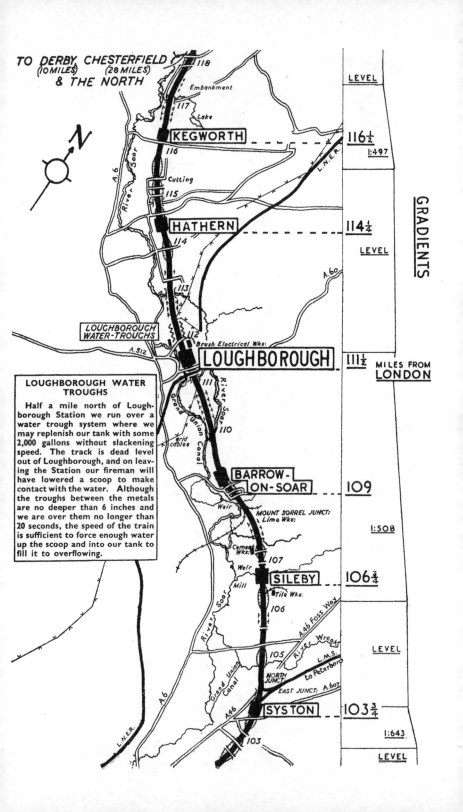

TO DERBY CHESTERFIELD
(10 MILES) (28 MILES)
& THE NORTH

*Embankment*

118

117

*Lake*

KEGWORTH

116

*River Soar*

*A.6*

*L.N.E.R.*

*Cutting*

115

HATHERN

114

113

LOUGHBOROUGH
WATER-TROUGHS

*A.512*

112

*Brush Electrical Wks.*

LOUGHBOROUGH

111

*River Soar*

*A.60*

*Grand Union Canal*

110

*grid cables*

## LOUGHBOROUGH WATER TROUGHS

Half a mile north of Lough-borough Station we run over a water trough system where we may replenish our tank with some 2,000 gallons without slackening speed. The track is dead level out of Loughborough, and on leaving the Station our fireman will have lowered a scoop to make contact with the water. Although the troughs between the metals are no deeper than 6 inches and we are over them no longer than 20 seconds, the speed of the train is sufficient to force enough water up the scoop and into our tank to fill it to overflowing.

BARROW-
ON-SOAR

*Weir*

*MOUNT SORREL JUNCT.
Lime Wks.*

*Cement Wks.*

107

*Weir*

SILEBY

106

*Tile Wks.*

*River Soar*

*Mill*

105

*River Wreak*

*A.46 Foss Way*

*L.M.S.*

*to Peterboro*

NORTH
JUNCT.

EAST JUNCT. *A.607*

*Grand Union Canal*

*A.46*

SYSTON

103

*A.6*

*L.N.E.R.*

### GRADIENTS

LEVEL

116½
1:497

114¼
LEVEL

111½  MILES FROM
LONDON

109

1:508

106¾

LEVEL

103¾
1:643

LEVEL

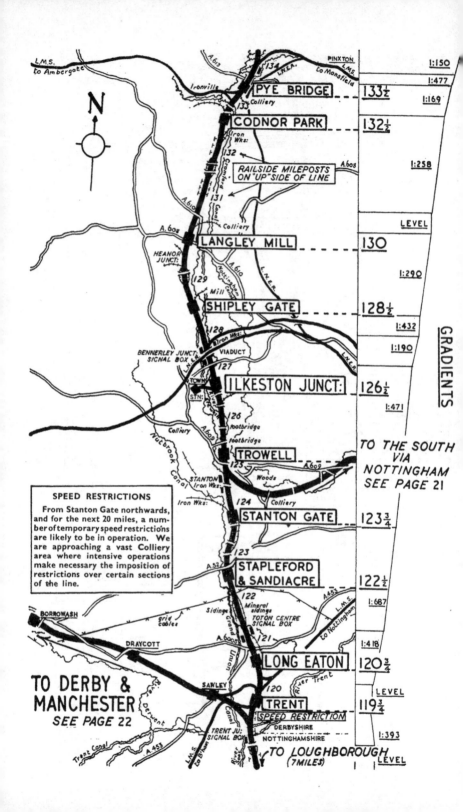

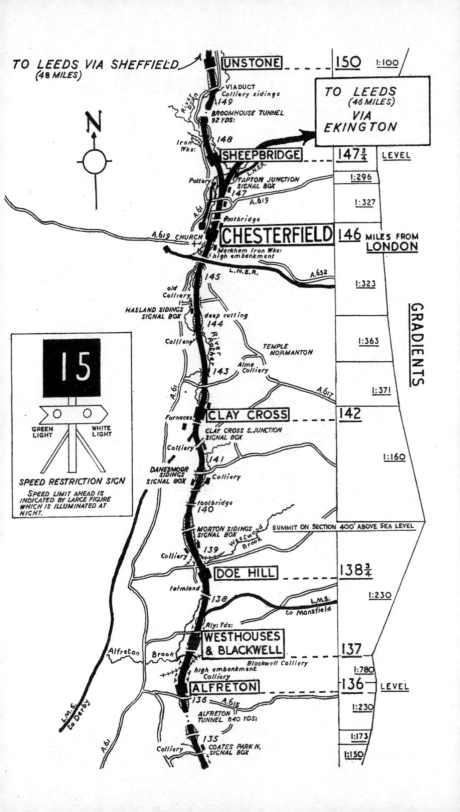

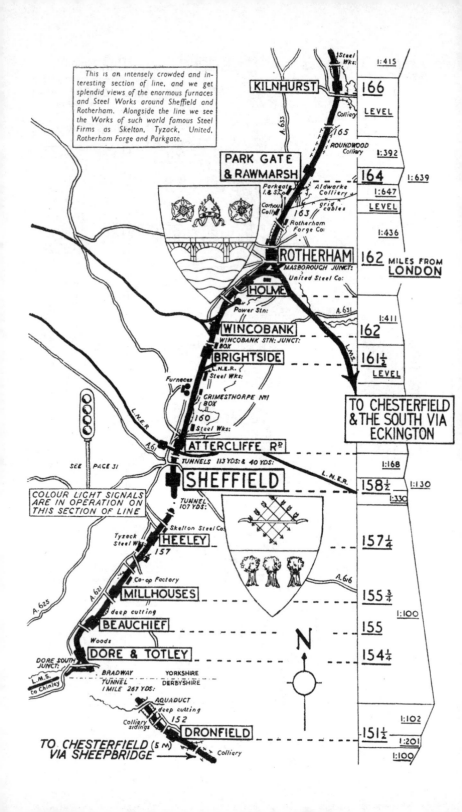

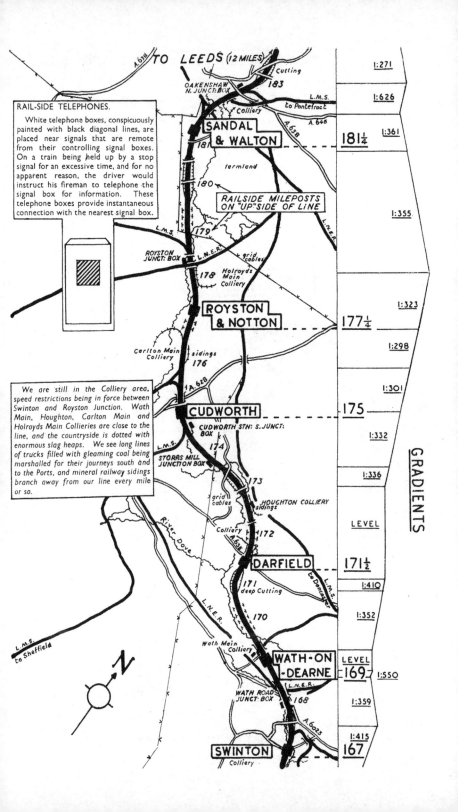

TO LEEDS (12 MILES)

Cutting
183

A.638

OAKENSHAW
N. JUNCT: BOX

L.M.S.
to Pontefract

A.645

Colliery

A.638

**SANDAL & WALTON**

181

farmland

180

**RAILSIDE MILEPOSTS ON "UP" SIDE OF LINE**

**RAIL-SIDE TELEPHONES.**

White telephone boxes, conspicuously painted with black diagonal lines, are placed near signals that are remote from their controlling signal boxes. On a train being held up by a stop signal for an excessive time, and for no apparent reason, the driver would instruct his fireman to telephone the signal box for information. These telephone boxes provide instantaneous connection with the nearest signal box.

L.M.S.

179

ROYSTON
JUNCT: BOX

L.N.E.R.

grid cables

178

Holroyds
Main
Colliery

**ROYSTON & NOTTON**

L.N.E.R.

Carlton Main
Colliery

sidings
176

A.628

We are still in the Colliery area, speed restrictions being in force between Swinton and Royston Junction. Wath Main, Houghton, Carlton Main and Holroyds Main Collieries are close to the line, and the countryside is dotted with enormous slag heaps. We see long lines of trucks filled with gleaming coal being marshalled for their journeys south and to the Ports, and mineral railway sidings branch away from our line every mile or so.

**CUDWORTH**

CUDWORTH STN: S. JUNCT:
BOX

L.M.S.

174

STORRS MILL
JUNCTION BOX

173

grid
cables

HOUGHTON COLLIERY
sidings

River Dove

Colliery

A.6?

172

**DARFIELD**

to Doncaster

L.M.S.

171

deep Cutting

L.N.E.R.

170

L.M.S.
to Sheffield

Wath Main
Colliery

**WATH-ON -DEARNE**

L.N.E.R.

WATH ROAD
JUNCT: BOX

168

A.6023

**SWINTON**

Colliery

**GRADIENTS**

| | |
|---|---|
| 1:271 | |
| 1:626 | |
| 1:361 | 181¼ |
| | 180 |
| 1:355 | |
| 1:323 | 177¼ |
| 1:298 | |
| 1:301 | |
| 175 | |
| 1:332 | |
| 1:336 | |
| LEVEL | |
| 171½ | |
| 1:410 | |
| 1:352 | |
| LEVEL | |
| 169 | 1:550 |
| 1:359 | |
| 1:415 | 167 |

# LEEDS

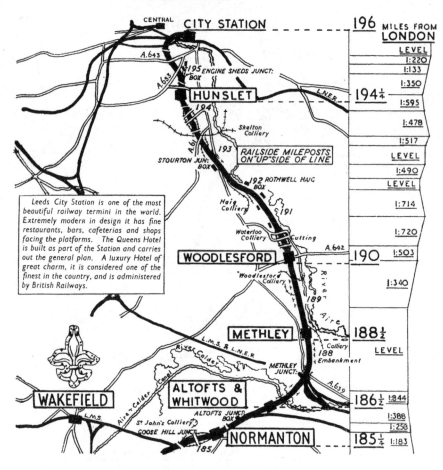

Leeds City Station is one of the most beautiful railway termini in the world. Extremely modern in design it has fine restaurants, bars, cafeterias and shops facing the platforms. The Queens Hotel is built as part of the Station and carries out the general plan. A luxury Hotel of great charm, it is considered one of the finest in the country, and is administered by British Railways.

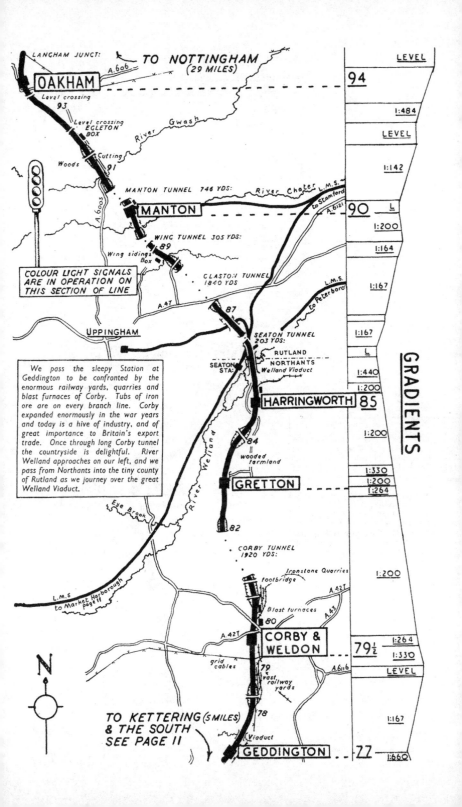

LANGHAM JUNCT:
TO NOTTINGHAM
(29 MILES)
A.606

**OAKHAM**

Level crossing
93

Level crossing
EGLETON BOX

River Gwash

Woods    Cutting
91

A.6003

MANTON TUNNEL 746 YDS:    River Chater    L.M.S.
to Stamford
A.6121

**MANTON**

WING TUNNEL 305 YDS:
89

Wing sidings
Box

CLASTON TUNNEL
1840 YDS

L.M.S.
to Peterboro

A.47

**COLOUR LIGHT SIGNALS
ARE IN OPERATION ON
THIS SECTION OF LINE**

87

**UPPINGHAM**

SEATON TUNNEL
203 YDS:

RUTLAND
NORTHANTS
Welland Viaduct

SEATON
STA:

We pass the sleepy Station at
Geddington to be confronted by the
enormous railway yards, quarries and
blast furnaces of Corby. Tubs of iron
ore are on every branch line. Corby
expanded enormously in the war years
and today is a hive of industry, and of
great importance to Britain's export
trade. Once through long Corby tunnel
the countryside is delightful. River
Welland approaches on our left, and we
pass from Northants into the tiny county
of Rutland as we journey over the great
Welland Viaduct.

**HARRINGWORTH**

84

wooded
farmland

River Welland

**GRETTON**

Eye Brook

82

CORBY TUNNEL
1920 YDS:

Ironstone Quarries

footbridge
A.42T

Blast furnaces    A.43

L.M.S
to Market Harborough
page 11

80

A.42T

**CORBY &
WELDON**

grid
cables

79
vast
railway
yards

A.6116

N

78

**TO KETTERING (5 MILES)
& THE SOUTH
SEE PAGE 11**

Viaduct

**GEDDINGTON**

**GRADIENTS**

LEVEL

94

1:484

LEVEL

1:142

90  L

1:200

1:164

1:167

1:167

L

1:440

1:200

85

1:200

1:200

1:330
1:200
1:264

1:200

1:264

79½  1:264

1:330

LEVEL

1:167

77  1:660

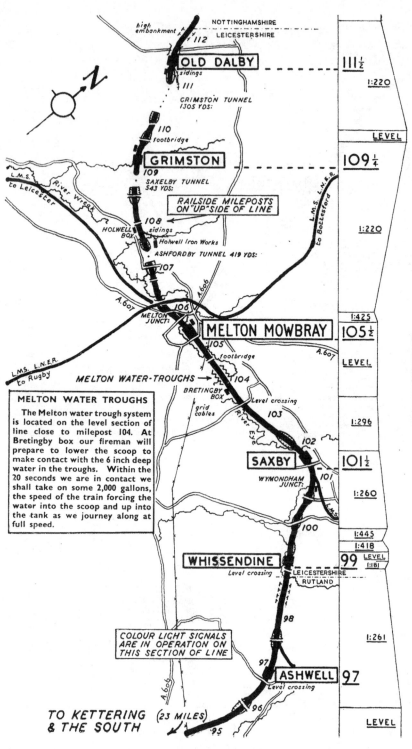

high embankment

112

NOTTINGHAMSHIRE
LEICESTERSHIRE

**OLD DALBY**

*sidings*

111

GRIMSTON TUNNEL 1305 YDS:

110

*footbridge*

**GRIMSTON**

109

SAXELBY TUNNEL 543 YDS:

**RAILSIDE MILEPOSTS ON "UP" SIDE OF LINE**

108

*sidings*

HOLWELL BOX

*Holwell Iron Works*

ASHFORDBY TUNNEL 419 YDS:

107

106

MELTON JUNCT:

**MELTON MOWBRAY**

105

*footbridge*

**MELTON WATER-TROUGHS**

104

BRETINGBY BOX

*Level crossing*

*grid cables*

103

102

**SAXBY**

WYMONDHAM JUNCT:

101

100

**WHISSENDINE**

*Level crossing*

LEICESTERSHIRE
RUTLAND

98

**COLOUR LIGHT SIGNALS ARE IN OPERATION ON THIS SECTION OF LINE**

97

**ASHWELL**

*Level crossing*

96

**TO KETTERING (23 MILES) & THE SOUTH**

95

L.M.S. to Leicester

River Wreak

A.607

A.606

LMS. L.N.E.R. to Rugby

L.M.S. L.N.E.R. to Bottesford

A.607

River Eye

A.606

**MELTON WATER TROUGHS**

The Melton water trough system is located on the level section of line close to milepost 104. At Bretingby box our fireman will prepare to lower the scoop to make contact with the 6 inch deep water in the troughs. Within the 20 seconds we are in contact we shall take on some 2,000 gallons, the speed of the train forcing the water into the scoop and up into the tank as we journey along at full speed.

**GRADIENTS**

111½    1:220

LEVEL

109¼    1:220

1:425

105½

LEVEL

1:296

101½

1:260

1:445
1:418

99   LEVEL
1:181

1:261

97

LEVEL

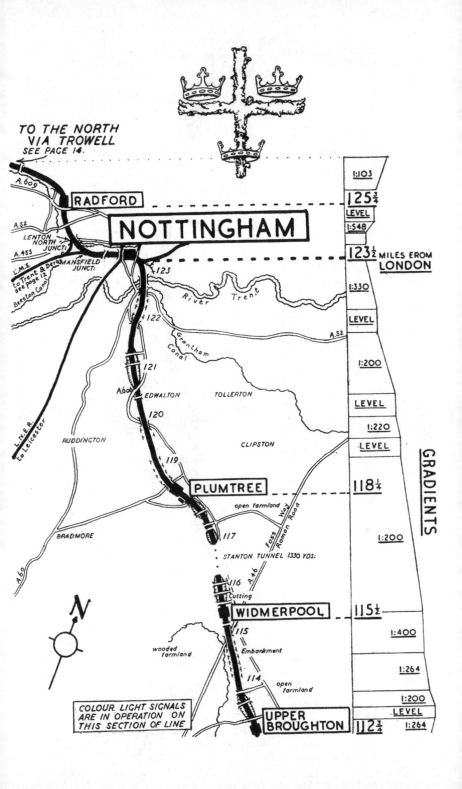

TO THE NORTH
VIA TROWELL
SEE PAGE 14.

A.609

RADFORD

NOTTINGHAM

A.52

LENTON
NORTH
JUNCT:

A.453

L.M.S.
to Trent & Derby
see page 12

MANSFIELD
JUNCT:

Beeston Canal

123

River Trent

122

Grantham Canal

121

A.606

EDWALTON

120

TOLLERTON

L.N.E.R.
to Leicester

RUDDINGTON

119

CLIPSTON

PLUMTREE

open farmland

117

BRADMORE

Foss Way Roman Road

STANTON TUNNEL 1330 YDS:

A.60

116

A.46

Cutting

N

WIDMERPOOL

115

wooded
farmland

Embankment

114

open
farmland

COLOUR LIGHT SIGNALS
ARE IN OPERATION ON
THIS SECTION OF LINE

UPPER
BROUGHTON

**GRADIENTS**

1:103

125¾

LEVEL

1:548

123½ MILES FROM
LONDON

1:330

LEVEL

1:200

LEVEL

1:220

LEVEL

118¼

1:200

115½

1:400

1:264

1:200

LEVEL

112¾

1:264

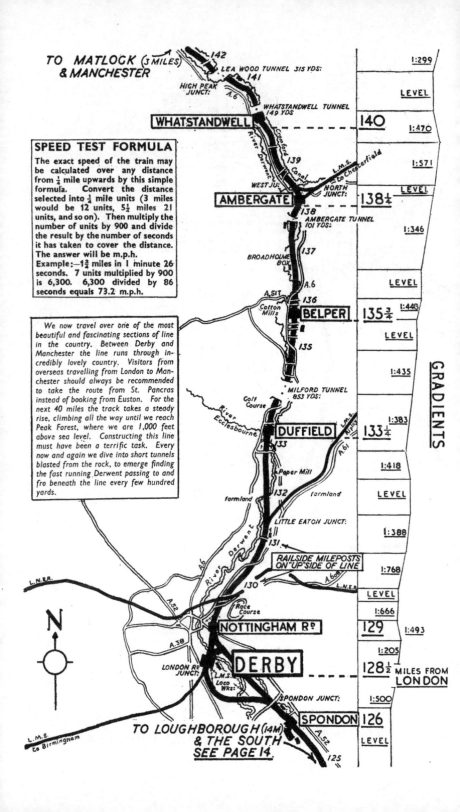

TO MATLOCK (3 MILES) & MANCHESTER

### SPEED TEST FORMULA

The exact speed of the train may be calculated over any distance from ¼ mile upwards by this simple formula. Convert the distance selected into ¼ mile units (3 miles would be 12 units, 5¼ miles 21 units, and so on). Then multiply the number of units by 900 and divide the result by the number of seconds it has taken to cover the distance. The answer will be m.p.h.
Example:—1¾ miles in 1 minute 26 seconds. 7 units multiplied by 900 is 6,300. 6,300 divided by 86 seconds equals 73.2 m.p.h.

We now travel over one of the most beautiful and fascinating sections of line in the country. Between Derby and Manchester the line runs through incredibly lovely country. Visitors from overseas travelling from London to Manchester should always be recommended to take the route from St. Pancras instead of booking from Euston. For the next 40 miles the track takes a steady rise, climbing all the way until we reach Peak Forest, where we are 1,000 feet above sea level. Constructing this line must have been a terrific task. Every now and again we dive into short tunnels blasted from the rock, to emerge finding the fast running Derwent passing to and fro beneath the line every few hundred yards.

LEA WOOD TUNNEL 315 YDS.
142
141
HIGH PEAK JUNCT.
A.6
WHATSTANDWELL TUNNEL 149 YDS.
WHATSTANDWELL 140
139
Cromford Canal
L.M.S. to Chesterfield
WEST JU:
NORTH JUNCT.
AMBERGATE 138½
138
AMBERGATE TUNNEL 101 YDS.
137
BROADHOLME BOX
A.6
A.517
136
Cotton Mills
BELPER 135¾
135
MILFORD TUNNEL 853 YDS.
Golf Course
River Ecclesbourne
DUFFIELD 133¼
133
A.61
Paper Mill
132
farmland   farmland
LITTLE EATON JUNCT.
131
RAILSIDE MILEPOSTS ON 'UP' SIDE OF LINE
A.608   L.N.E.R.
130
River Derwent
Race Course
NOTTINGHAM RD 129
DERBY 128½   MILES FROM LONDON
LONDON RD JUNCT.
L.M.S. Loco Wks.
SPONDON JUNCT.
SPONDON 126
TO LOUGHBOROUGH (14M) & THE SOUTH SEE PAGE 14.
125
L.N.E.R.
A.52
A.38
L.M.S. to Birmingham
N

GRADIENTS

| 1:299 |
| LEVEL |
| 1:470 |
| 1:571 |
| LEVEL |
| 1:346 |
| LEVEL |
| 1:446 |
| LEVEL |
| 1:435 |
| 1:383 |
| 1:418 |
| LEVEL |
| 1:388 |
| 1:768 |
| LEVEL |
| 1:666 |
| 1:493 |
| 1:205 |
| 1:500 |
| LEVEL |

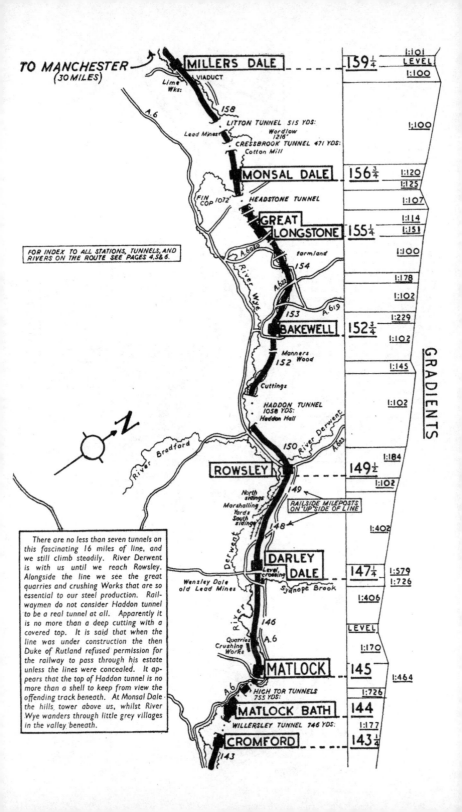

TO MANCHESTER
(30 MILES)

MILLERS DALE  159¼

Lime Wks:

VIADUCT

158

LITTON TUNNEL 515 YDS:
Wardlow 1216'
Lead Mines
CRESSBROOK TUNNEL 471 YDS:
Cotton Mill

MONSAL DALE  156¾

FIN COP 1072'   HEADSTONE TUNNEL

GREAT
LONGSTONE  155¼

FOR INDEX TO ALL STATIONS, TUNNELS, AND
RIVERS ON THE ROUTE SEE PAGES 4, 5 & 6.

farmland
154

River Wye

153

BAKEWELL  152¾

Manners Wood
152

Cuttings

HADDON TUNNEL
1058 YDS:
Haddon Hall

150        River Derwent

River Bradford

ROWSLEY  149½

149

North sidings
Marshalling Yards
South sidings

148    RAILSIDE MILEPOSTS
ON 'UP' SIDE OF LINE

Derwent

DARLEY
DALE  147¼

Level crossing

Wensley Dale
old Lead Mines          Sydnope Brook

River

146

Quarries
Crushing
Works

A.6

MATLOCK  145

HIGH TOR TUNNELS
755 YDS:

MATLOCK BATH  144

WILLERSLEY TUNNEL 746 YDS:

CROMFORD  143¼

143

GRADIENTS

1:101
LEVEL
1:100

1:100

1:120
1:125
1:107
1:114
1:151
1:100
1:178
1:102
1:229
1:102
1:145
1:102
1:184
1:102
1:402
1:579
1:726
1:406
LEVEL
1:170
1:464
1:726
1:177

There are no less than seven tunnels on this fascinating 16 miles of line, and we still climb steadily. River Derwent is with us until we reach Rowsley. Alongside the line we see the great quarries and crushing Works that are so essential to our steel production. Railwaymen do not consider Haddon tunnel to be a real tunnel at all. Apparently it is no more than a deep cutting with a covered top. It is said that when the line was under construction the then Duke of Rutland refused permission for the railway to pass through his estate unless the lines were concealed. It appears that the top of Haddon tunnel is no more than a shell to keep from view the offending track beneath. At Monsal Dale the hills tower above us, whilst River Wye wanders through little grey villages in the valley beneath.

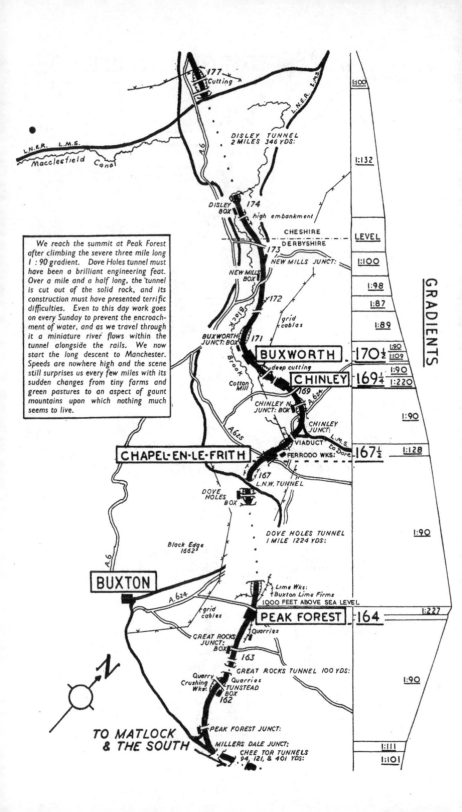

We reach the summit at Peak Forest after climbing the severe three mile long 1 : 90 gradient. Dove Holes tunnel must have been a brilliant engineering feat. Over a mile and a half long, the tunnel is cut out of the solid rock, and its construction must have presented terrific difficulties. Even to this day work goes on every Sunday to prevent the encroachment of water, and as we travel through it a miniature river flows within the tunnel alongside the rails. We now start the long descent to Manchester. Speeds are nowhere high and the scene still surprises us every few miles with its sudden changes from tiny farms and green pastures to an aspect of gaunt mountains upon which nothing much seems to live.

# MANCHESTER

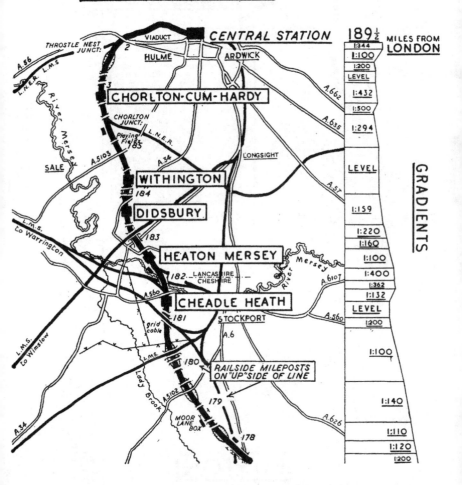

THROSTLE NEST JUNCT:

VIADUCT

CENTRAL STATION

A.56

L.N.E.R. L.M.S.

HULME

ARDWICK

A.662

River Mersey

2

A.635

CHORLTON-CUM-HARDY

CHORLTON JUNCT:

L.N.E.R.

Playing Fields

3

185

SALE

A.5103

A.34

LONGSIGHT

A.57

WITHINGTON

184

L.M.S. To Warrington

DIDSBURY

183

HEATON MERSEY

182. LANCASHIRE
CHESHIRE

River Mersey

A.6107

A.560

CHEADLE HEATH

181

STOCKPORT

A.560

L.M.S. To Wimslow

grid cable

A.6

LEVEL

1:200

1:100

A.34

Lady Brook

L.M.S.

180

A.5102

RAILSIDE MILEPOSTS
ON "UP" SIDE OF LINE

179

A.626

MOOR LANE BOX

178

189½ MILES FROM LONDON

1:344
1:100
1:200
LEVEL
1:432
1:500
1:294

LEVEL

1:159

1:220
1:160
1:100
1:400
1:362
1:132
LEVEL

GRADIENTS

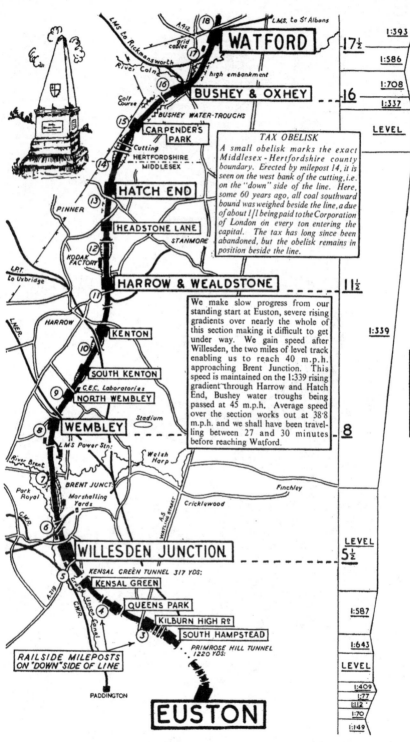

TAX OBELISK
A small obelisk marks the exact Middlesex-Hertfordshire county boundary. Erected by milepost 14, it is seen on the west bank of the cutting, i.e. on the "down" side of the line. Here, some 60 years ago, all coal southward bound was weighed beside the line, a due of about 1/1 being paid to the Corporation of London on every ton entering the capital. The tax has long since been abandoned, but the obelisk remains in position beside the line.

We make slow progress from our standing start at Euston, severe rising gradients over nearly the whole of this section making it difficult to get under way. We gain speed after Willesden, the two miles of level track enabling us to reach 40 m.p.h. approaching Brent Junction. This speed is maintained on the 1:339 rising gradient through Harrow and Hatch End, Bushey water troughs being passed at 45 m.p.h. Average speed over the section works out at 38·8 m.p.h. and we shall have been travelling between 27 and 30 minutes before reaching Watford.

RAILSIDE MILEPOSTS ON "DOWN" SIDE OF LINE

WATFORD
BUSHEY & OXHEY
CARPENDER'S PARK
HATCH END
HEADSTONE LANE
HARROW & WEALDSTONE
KENTON
SOUTH KENTON
NORTH WEMBLEY
WEMBLEY
BRENT JUNCT.
WILLESDEN JUNCTION
KENSAL GREEN
QUEENS PARK
KILBURN HIGH RD.
SOUTH HAMPSTEAD
EUSTON
PADDINGTON

GRADIENTS

1:393
17½
1:586
1:708
16
1:337
LEVEL

11½
1:339

8

LEVEL
5½

1:587

1:643
LEVEL
1:409
1:77
1:112
1:70
1:149

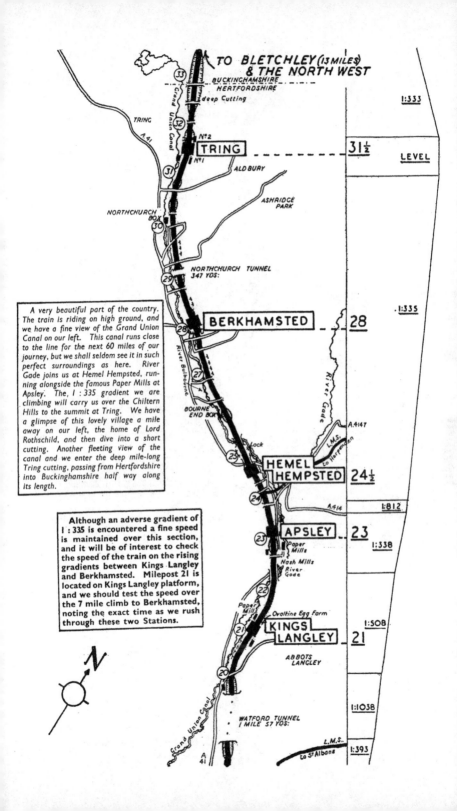

TO BLETCHLEY (13 MILES)
& THE NORTH WEST

BUCKINGHAMSHIRE
HERTFORDSHIRE

deep cutting

1:333

TRING
A.41

Grand Union Canal

No 2

TRING

31½

LEVEL

No 1

ALDBURY

ASHRIDGE PARK

NORTHCHURCH BOX

NORTHCHURCH TUNNEL
347 YDS.

1:335

BERKHAMSTED

28

River Gade

A very beautiful part of the country. The train is riding on high ground, and we have a fine view of the Grand Union Canal on our left. This canal runs close to the line for the next 60 miles of our journey, but we shall seldom see it in such perfect surroundings as here. River Gade joins us at Hemel Hempsted, running alongside the famous Paper Mills at Apsley. The, 1 : 335 gradient we are climbing will carry us over the Chiltern Hills to the summit at Tring. We have a glimpse of this lovely village a mile away on our left, the home of Lord Rothschild, and then dive into a short cutting. Another fleeting view of the canal and we enter the deep mile-long Tring cutting, passing from Hertfordshire into Buckinghamshire half way along its length.

River Bulbourne

BOURNE END BOX

A.4147

L.M.S. to Harpenden

Lock

HEMEL HEMPSTED

24½

Although an adverse gradient of 1 : 335 is encountered a fine speed is maintained over this section, and it will be of interest to check the speed of the train on the rising gradients between Kings Langley and Berkhamsted. Milepost 21 is located on Kings Langley platform, and we should test the speed over the 7 mile climb to Berkhamsted, noting the exact time as we rush through these two Stations.

A.414

1:812

APSLEY

23

Paper Mills

1:338

Nash Mills
River Gade

Paper Mills

Ovaltine Egg Farm

KINGS LANGLEY

1:508

21

ABBOTS LANGLEY

N

ABBOTS LANGLEY

Grand Union Canal

1:1038

WATFORD TUNNEL
1 MILE 57 YDS.

A.41

L.M.S. to St Albans

1:393

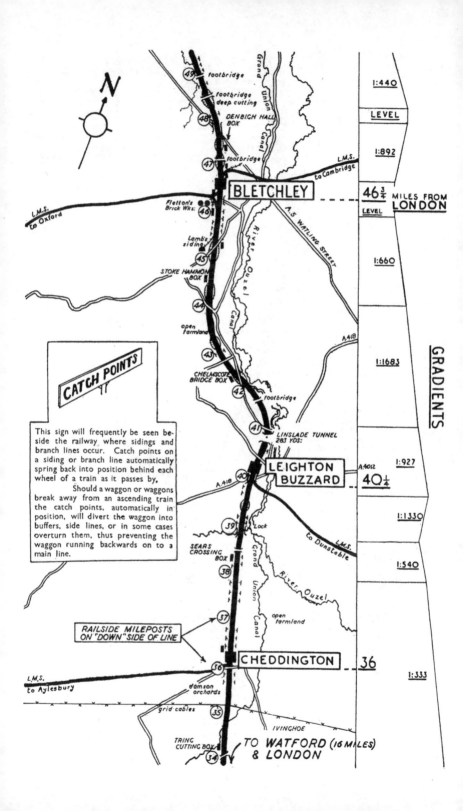

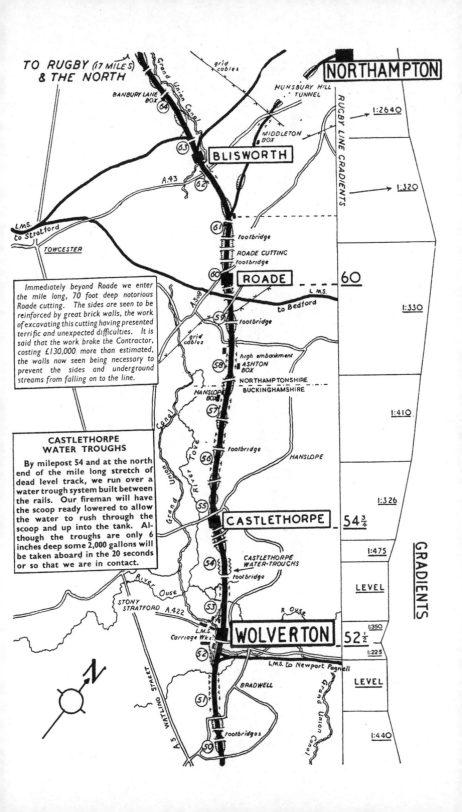

TO RUGBY (17 MILES) & THE NORTH

grid cables

NORTHAMPTON

BANBURY LANE BOX (64)

Grand Union Canal

HUNSBURY HILL TUNNEL

MIDDLETON BOX

RUGBY LINE GRADIENTS

→ 1:2640

(63)

BLISWORTH

(62)

A.43

→ 1:320

LMS. to Stratford

(61)

footbridge

TOWCESTER

ROADE CUTTING

footbridge

1:330

(60)

ROADE

60

L.MS. to Bedford

*Immediately beyond Roade we enter the mile long, 70 foot deep notorious Roade cutting. The sides are seen to be reinforced by great brick walls, the work of excavating this cutting having presented terrific and unexpected difficulties. It is said that the work broke the Contractor, costing £130,000 more than estimated, the walls now seen being necessary to prevent the sides and underground streams from falling on to the line.*

(59)

footbridge

grid cables

(58)

high embankment

ASHTON BOX

NORTHAMPTONSHIRE

BUCKINGHAMSHIRE

HANSLOPE BOX

(57)

1:410

CASTLETHORPE WATER TROUGHS

By milepost 54 and at the north end of the mile long stretch of dead level track, we run over a water trough system built between the rails. Our fireman will have the scoop ready lowered to allow the water to rush through the scoop and up into the tank. Although the troughs are only 6 inches deep some 2,000 gallons will be taken aboard in the 20 seconds or so that we are in contact.

Grand Union Canal

River Tove

(56)

footbridge

HANSLOPE

(55)

1:326

CASTLETHORPE

54¾

(54)

CASTLETHORPE WATER-TROUGHS

1:475

footbridge

LEVEL

River Ouse

STONY STRATFORD A.422

(53)

R. Ouse

WOLVERTON

52½

1:350

L.MS. Carriage Wks.

(52)

1:225

L.MS. to Newport Pagnell

LEVEL

A.5 WATLING STREET

BRADWELL

Grand Union Canal

(51)

GRADIENTS

(50)

footbridges

1:440

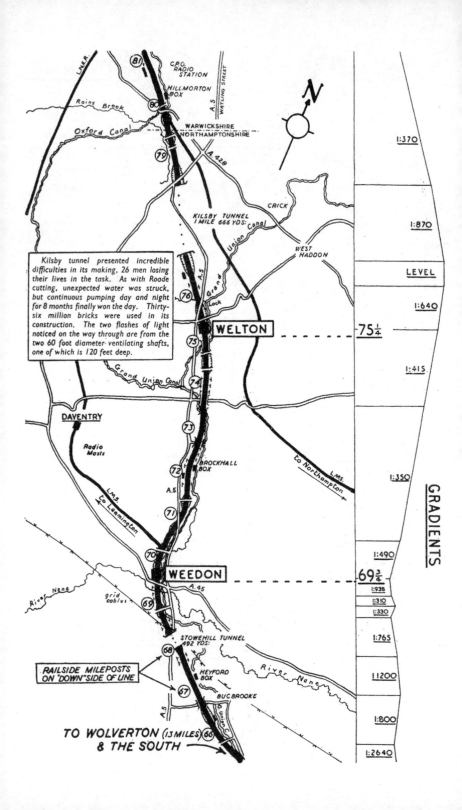

Kilsby tunnel presented incredible difficulties in its making, 26 men losing their lives in the task. As with Roade cutting, unexpected water was struck, but continuous pumping day and night for 8 months finally won the day. Thirty-six million bricks were used in its construction. The two flashes of light noticed on the way through are from the two 60 foot diameter ventilating shafts, one of which is 120 feet deep.

RAILSIDE MILEPOSTS ON "DOWN" SIDE OF LINE

TO WOLVERTON (13 MILES) & THE SOUTH

GRADIENTS

1:370
1:870
LEVEL
1:640
1:415
1:350
1:490
1:938
1:310
1:330
1:765
1:1200
1:800
1:2640

75¼
69¾

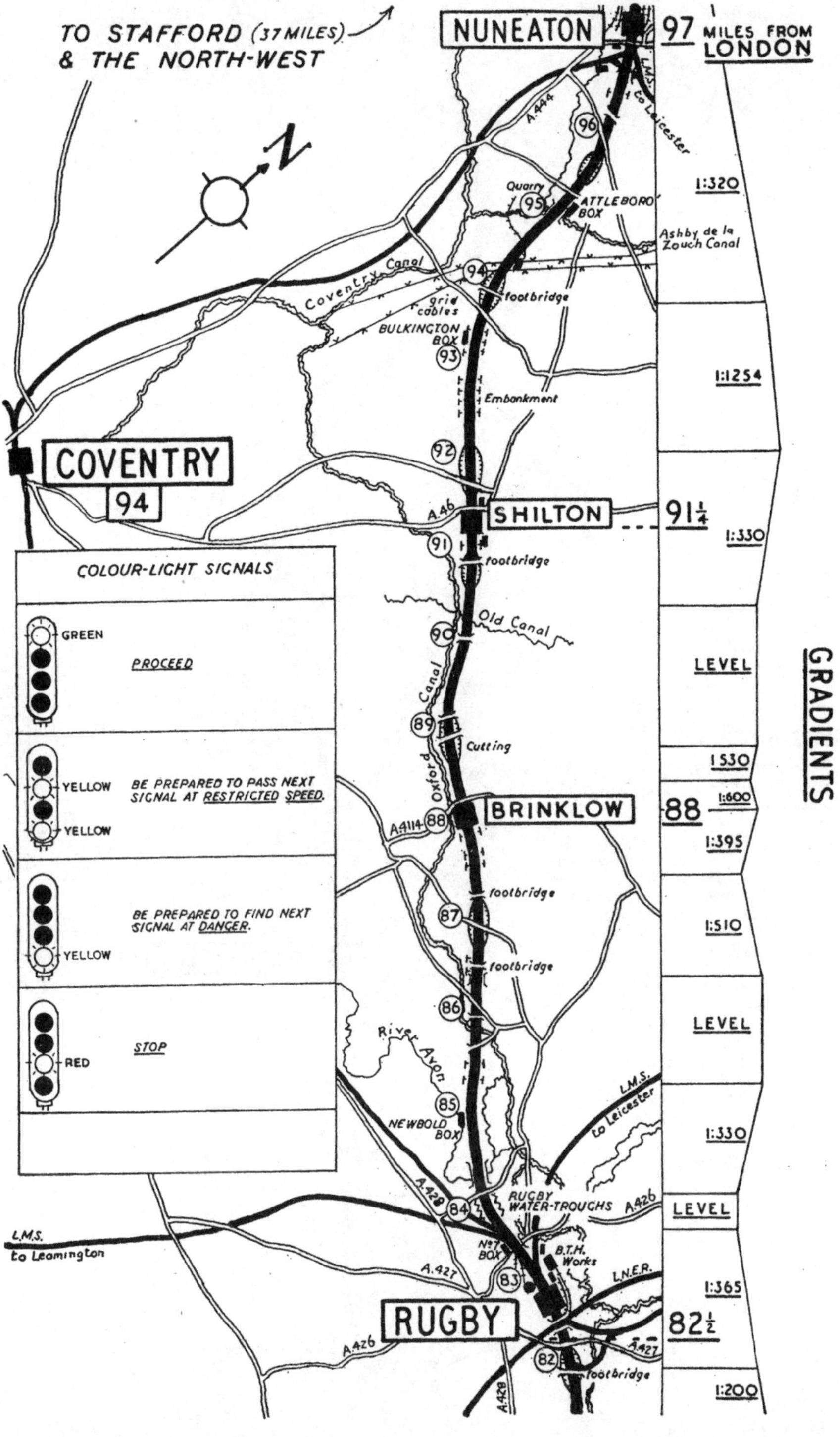

TO STAFFORD (37 MILES)
& THE NORTH-WEST

NUNEATON

97 MILES FROM
LONDON

96

to Leicester

A.444

1:320

Quarry

95

ATTLEBORO
BOX

Ashby de la
Zouch Canal

Coventry Canal

94

footbridge

grid
cables

1:1254

BULKINGTON
BOX

93

Embankment

COVENTRY

94

92

A.46

SHILTON

91¼

1:330

91

footbridge

90

Old Canal

LEVEL

**COLOUR-LIGHT SIGNALS**

| | GREEN | | PROCEED |
|---|---|---|---|

89

Cutting

1:530

1:600

| | YELLOW | BE PREPARED TO PASS NEXT |
| | | SIGNAL AT RESTRICTED SPEED. |
| | YELLOW | |

A.4114 88

BRINKLOW

88

1:395

| | | BE PREPARED TO FIND NEXT |
| | | SIGNAL AT DANGER. |
| | YELLOW | |

footbridge

87

1:510

footbridge

86

LEVEL

| | RED | STOP |

River Avon

85

NEWBOLD
BOX

L.M.S.
to Leicester

1:330

A.428

84

RUGBY
WATER-TROUGHS

A.426

LEVEL

L.M.S.
to Leamington

A.427

No.7
BOX

B.T.H.
Works

L.N.E.R.

1:365

83

82½

RUGBY

A.426

A.427

A.428

82

footbridge

1:200

GRADIENTS

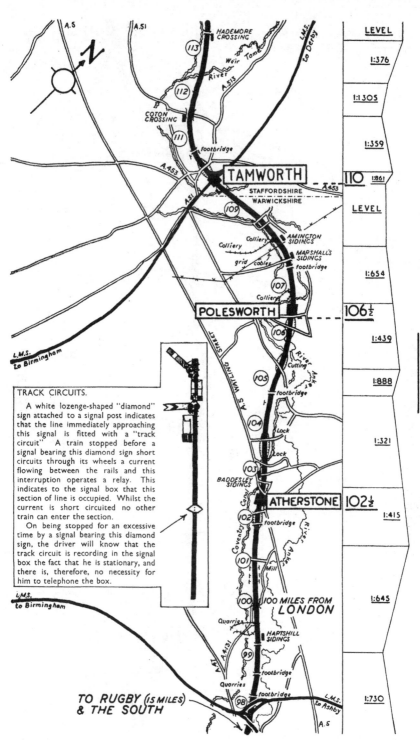

LEVEL

1:376

1:1305

1:359

110   1:861

LEVEL

1:654

106½

1:439

1:888

1:321

102½

1:415

1:645

1:730

GRADIENTS

A.S

A.51

HADEMORE
CROSSING

113

Weir Tame

River A.513

112

COTON
CROSSING

111

footbridge

A.453

TAMWORTH

STAFFORDSHIRE

WARWICKSHIRE

A.453

L.M.S.
to Derby

109

Colliery

Colliery

AMINGTON
SIDINGS

MARSHALL'S
SIDINGS

grid   cables

footbridge

107

Colliery

POLESWORTH

106

L.M.S.
to Birmingham

105

River
Anker

Cutting

footbridge

**TRACK CIRCUITS.**

A white lozenge-shaped "diamond"
sign attached to a signal post indicates
that the line immediately approaching
this signal is fitted with a "track
circuit." A train stopped before a
signal bearing this diamond sign short
circuits through its wheels a current
flowing between the rails and this
interruption operates a relay. This
indicates to the signal box that this
section of line is occupied. Whilst the
current is short circuited no other
train can enter the section.

On being stopped for an excessive
time by a signal bearing this diamond
sign, the driver will know that the
track circuit is recording in the signal
box the fact that he is stationary, and
there is, therefore, no necessity for
him to telephone the box.

104

Lock

Lock

103

BADDESLEY
SIDINGS

ATHERSTONE

102

footbridge

101

Mill

L.M.S.
to Birmingham

100

100 MILES FROM
LONDON

Quarries

HARTSHILL
SIDINGS

A.47

99

footbridge

Quarries

footbridge

98

TO RUGBY (15 MILES)
& THE SOUTH

L.M.S.
to Ashby

A.S

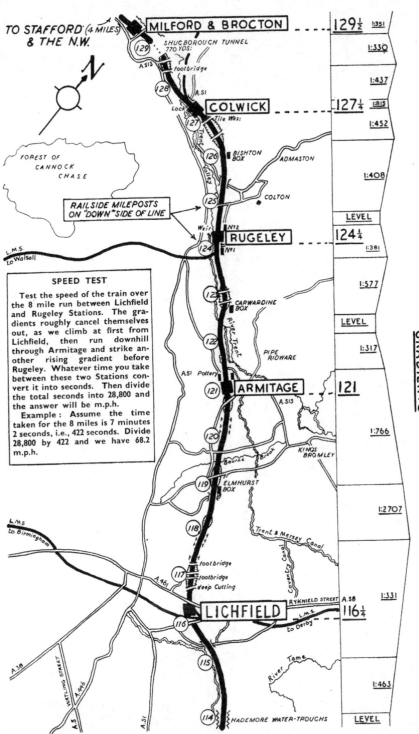

TO STAFFORD (4 MILES) & THE N.W.

N

FOREST OF CANNOCK CHASE

RAILSIDE MILEPOSTS ON "DOWN" SIDE OF LINE

MILFORD & BROCTON    129½    1:351

SHUGBOROUGH TUNNEL 770 YDS.

129

A.513

footbridge

128    A.51    1:330

Lock    1:437

COLWICK    127¼    1:815

127    Tile Wks:    1:452

126    BISHTON BOX    ADMASTON

Trent Valley    1:408

125    COLTON

Weir    LEVEL

Nº2    124¼    124¼

RUGELEY    1:381

124    Nº1

L.M.S. To Walsall

123    1:577

CARWARDINE BOX    LEVEL

122    River Trent    1:317

PIPE RIDWARE

A.51 Pottery    121    121

121    ARMITAGE    A.513

120    1:766

KINGS BROMLEY

Bourne Brook

119    ELMHURST BOX

118    1:2707

Trent & Mersey Canal

L.M.S. To Birmingham

footbridge    117    Coventry Canal

A.461    footbridge

deep Cutting

RYKNIELD STREET A.38    1:331

116    LICHFIELD    116¼

L.M.S. To Derby

115

River Tame    1:463

114    HADEMORE WATER-TROUGHS    LEVEL

A.38    WATLING STREET    A.446    A.5    A.51

## SPEED TEST

Test the speed of the train over the 8 mile run between Lichfield and Rugeley Stations. The gradients roughly cancel themselves out, as we climb at first from Lichfield, then run downhill through Armitage and strike another rising gradient before Rugeley. Whatever time you take between these two Stations convert it into seconds. Then divide the total seconds into 28,800 and the answer will be m.p.h.

Example : Assume the time taken for the 8 miles is 7 minutes 2 seconds, i.e., 422 seconds. Divide 28,800 by 422 and we have 68.2 m.p.h.

GRADIENTS

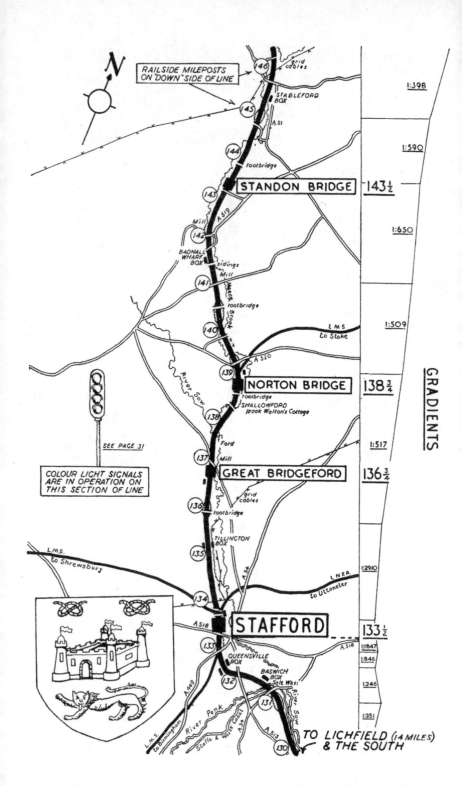

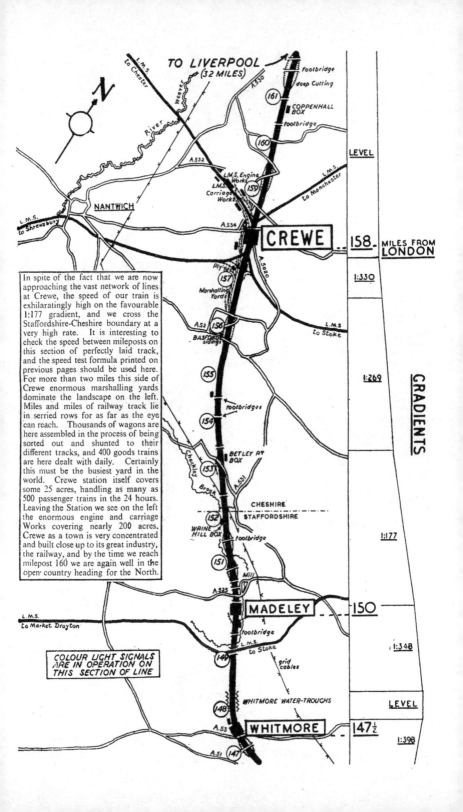

**TO LIVERPOOL**
**(32 MILES)**

N

L.M.S. to Chester

River Weaver

A.550

footbridge
deep Cutting
161
COPPENHALL BOX
footbridge
160

A.532

L.M.S. Engine Works
L.M.S. Carriage Works
159

L.M.S. to Monchester

NANTWICH

A.534

L.M.S. to Shrewsbury

**CREWE**

A.5020

Ply Yd
157
Marshalling Yards

A.52
156
BASFORD sidings

L.M.S. to Stoke

155

footbridges

154

Checkley Brook
153
BETLEY R? BOX
A.531

CHESHIRE
152
STAFFORDSHIRE

WRINE HILL BOX
footbridge

151

Mill

A.525

L.M.S. to Market Drayton

**MADELEY**

footbridge

149
L.M.S. to Stoke

grid cables

148
WHITMORE WATER-TROUGHS

A.53
**WHITMORE**

A.51
147

LEVEL

**158** MILES FROM LONDON

1:330

1:269

1:177

**GRADIENTS**

**150**

1:348

LEVEL

**147½**

1:398

In spite of the fact that we are now approaching the vast network of lines at Crewe, the speed of our train is exhilaratingly high on the favourable 1:177 gradient, and we cross the Staffordshire-Cheshire boundary at a very high rate. It is interesting to check the speed between mileposts on this section of perfectly laid track, and the speed test formula printed on previous pages should be used here. For more than two miles this side of Crewe enormous marshalling yards dominate the landscape on the left. Miles and miles of railway track lie in serried rows for as far as the eye can reach. Thousands of wagons are here assembled in the process of being sorted out and shunted to their different tracks, and 400 goods trains are here dealt with daily. Certainly this must be the busiest yard in the world. Crewe station itself covers some 25 acres, handling as many as 500 passenger trains in the 24 hours. Leaving the Station we see on the left the enormous engine and carriage Works covering nearly 200 acres. Crewe as a town is very concentrated and built close up to its great industry, the railway, and by the time we reach milepost 160 we are again well in the open country heading for the North.

COLOUR LIGHT SIGNALS ARE IN OPERATION ON THIS SECTION OF LINE

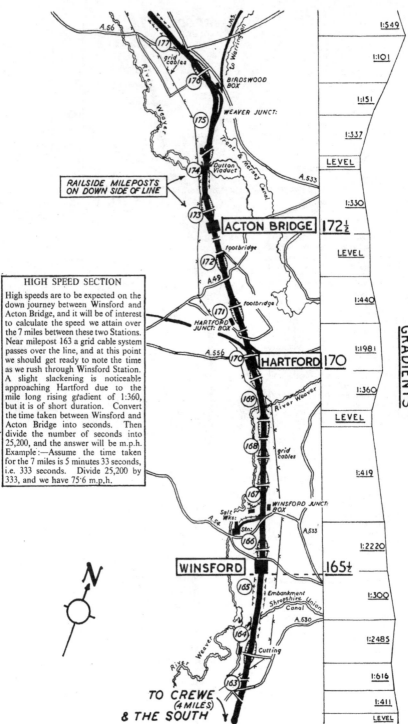

HIGH SPEED SECTION

High speeds are to be expected on the down journey between Winsford and Acton Bridge, and it will be of interest to calculate the speed we attain over the 7 miles between these two Stations. Near milepost 163 a grid cable system passes over the line, and at this point we should get ready to note the time as we rush through Winsford Station. A slight slackening is noticeable approaching Hartford due to the mile long rising gradient of 1:360, but it is of short duration. Convert the time taken between Winsford and Acton Bridge into seconds. Then divide the number of seconds into 25,200, and the answer will be m.p.h. Example :—Assume the time taken for the 7 miles is 5 minutes 33 seconds, i.e. 333 seconds. Divide 25,200 by 333, and we have 75·6 m.p.h.

RAILSIDE MILEPOSTS ON DOWN SIDE OF LINE

BIRDSWOOD BOX

WEAVER JUNCT:

Dutton Viaduct

ACTON BRIDGE 172½

footbridge

footbridge

HARTFORD JUNCT: BOX

HARTFORD 170

River Weaver

grid cables

WINSFORD JUNCT: BOX

Salt Wks:

Stn.

WINSFORD 165½

Embankment
Shropshire Union Canal

Cutting

TO CREWE
(4 MILES)
& THE SOUTH

N

GRADIENTS

1:549
1:101
1:151
1:337
LEVEL
1:330
LEVEL
1:440
1:1981
1:360
LEVEL
1:419
1:2220
1:300
1:2485
1:616
1:411
LEVEL

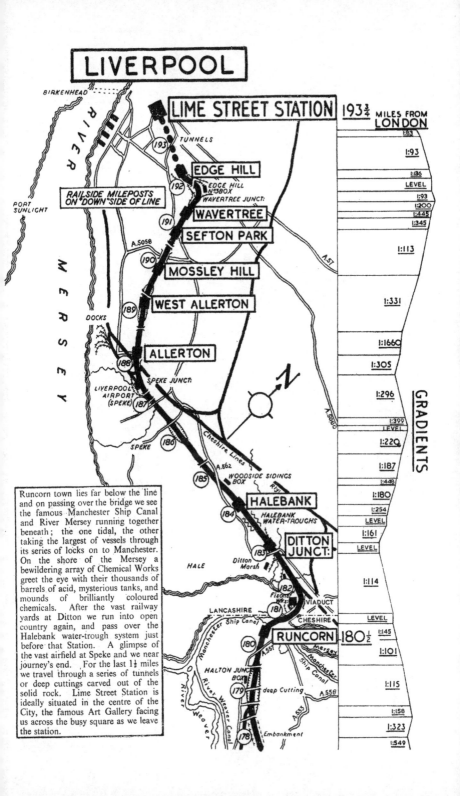

# LIVERPOOL

BIRKENHEAD

RIVER

PORT SUNLIGHT

## LIME STREET STATION 193¾ MILES FROM LONDON

193 TUNNELS

EDGE HILL

192 EDGE HILL N°380X
WAVERTREE JUNCT:

**RAILSIDE MILEPOSTS ON "DOWN" SIDE OF LINE**

191

## WAVERTREE

## SEFTON PARK

A.5058

190

## MOSSLEY HILL

189

## WEST ALLERTON

DOCKS

M E R S E Y

188

## ALLERTON

SPEKE JUNCT:

LIVERPOOL AIRPORT (SPEKE)

187

SPEKE

186

Cheshire Lines

185 A.562

WOODSIDE SIDINGS BOX

Runcorn town lies far below the line and on passing over the bridge we see the famous Manchester Ship Canal and River Mersey running together beneath; the one tidal, the other taking the largest of vessels through its series of locks on to Manchester. On the shore of the Mersey a bewildering array of Chemical Works greet the eye with their thousands of barrels of acid, mysterious tanks, and mounds of brilliantly coloured chemicals. After the vast railway yards at Ditton we run into open country again, and pass over the Halebank water-trough system just before that Station. A glimpse of the vast airfield at Speke and we near journey's end. For the last 1½ miles we travel through a series of tunnels or deep cuttings carved out of the solid rock. Lime Street Station is ideally situated in the centre of the City, the famous Art Gallery facing us across the busy square as we leave the station.

184

## HALEBANK
HALEBANK WATER-TROUGHS

183

## DITTON JUNCT:

HALE

Ditton Marsh

182

Fisons Wks

181

LANCASHIRE
CHESHIRE

VIADUCT

## RUNCORN 180½

180 A.557

Manchester Ship Canal

Mersey

Manchester Ship Canal

HALTON JUNCT BOX

179

deep Cutting A.558

River Weaver Canal

River Weaver

178 Embankment

### GRADIENTS

| 1:83 |
| 1:93 |
| 1:86 |
| LEVEL |
| 1:93 |
| 1:200 |
| 1:445 |
| 1:345 |
| 1:113 |
| 1:331 |
| 1:1660 |
| 1:305 |
| 1:296 |
| 1:399 |
| LEVEL |
| 1:220 |
| 1:187 |
| 1:448 |
| 1:180 |
| 1:254 |
| LEVEL |
| 1:161 |
| LEVEL |
| 1:114 |
| LEVEL |
| 1:145 |
| 1:101 |
| 1:115 |
| 1:158 |
| 1:323 |
| 1:549 |

A.57

A.5080

A.533

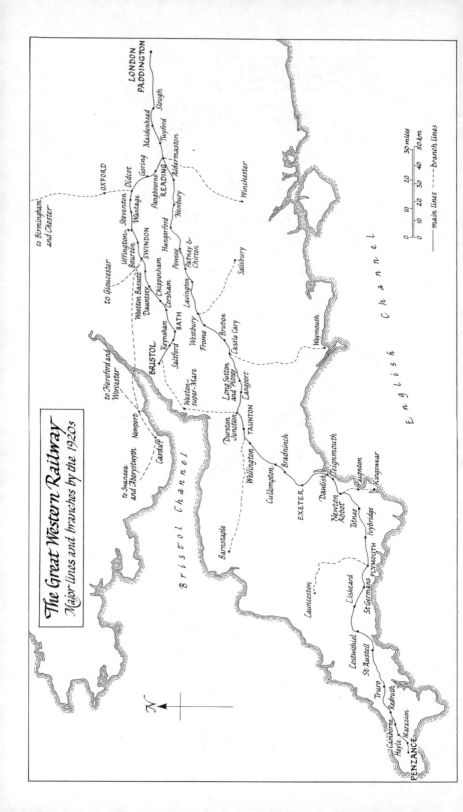

# Mile by Mile

## ON THE G.W.R.

Maps by Reginald Piggott; research by Matt Thompson

**PADDINGTON EDITION**

The journey between London and the South-West described in detail:–

- **GRADIENTS OF THE LINE**
- **MILEAGES**
- **VIADUCTS, BRIDGES AND EMBANKMENTS**
- **TUNNELS, CUTTINGS AND CROSSOVERS**
- **STREAMS, RIVERS AND ROADS**
- **TOWNS, VILLAGES AND CHURCHES**
- **MINES, FACTORIES AND WORKS**

With an account of features of interest and beauty to be seen from the train.

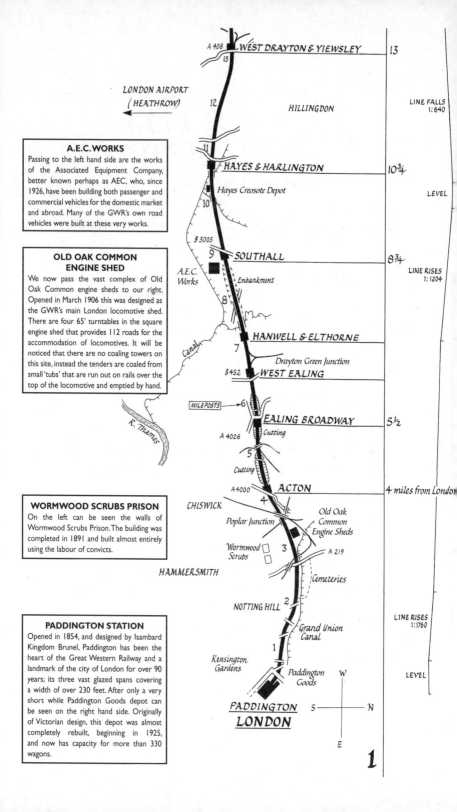

### A.E.C. WORKS
Passing to the left hand side are the works of the Associated Equipment Company, better known perhaps as AEC, who, since 1926, have been building both passenger and commercial vehicles for the domestic market and abroad. Many of the GWR's own road vehicles were built at these very works.

### OLD OAK COMMON ENGINE SHED
We now pass the vast complex of Old Oak Common engine sheds to our right. Opened in March 1906 this was designed as the GWR's main London locomotive shed. There are four 65' turntables in the square engine shed that provides 112 roads for the accommodation of locomotives. It will be noticed that there are no coaling towers on this site, instead the tenders are coaled from small 'tubs' that are run out on rails over the top of the locomotive and emptied by hand.

### WORMWOOD SCRUBS PRISON
On the left can be seen the walls of Wormwood Scrubs Prison. The building was completed in 1891 and built almost entirely using the labour of convicts.

### PADDINGTON STATION
Opened in 1854, and designed by Isambard Kingdom Brunel, Paddington has been the heart of the Great Western Railway and a landmark of the city of London for over 90 years; its three vast glazed spans covering a width of over 230 feet. After only a very short while Paddington Goods depot can be seen on the right hand side. Originally of Victorian design, this depot was almost completely rebuilt, beginning in 1925, and now has capacity for more than 330 wagons.

A 408   WEST DRAYTON & YIEWSLEY   13

LONDON AIRPORT (HEATHROW)   12

HILLINGDON   LINE FALLS 1:640

11   HAYES & HARLINGTON   10¾   LEVEL

Hayes Creosote Depot   10

B 3005   9   SOUTHALL   8¾   LINE RISES 1:1204

A.E.C. Works   Embankment

8

Canal   7   HANWELL & ELTHORNE

Drayton Green Junction

B 452   WEST EALING

R. Thames   MILE POSTS   6   EALING BROADWAY   5½

A 4026   Cutting

5

Cutting

A 4000   4   ACTON   4 miles from London

CHISWICK   Old Oak Common Engine Sheds

Poplar Junction

Wormwood Scrubs   3   A 219

HAMMERSMITH   Cemeteries

NOTTING HILL   2   Grand Union Canal   LINE RISES 1:1760

Kensington Gardens   1

Paddington Goods   W   LEVEL

PADDINGTON   S — N
LONDON

E

1

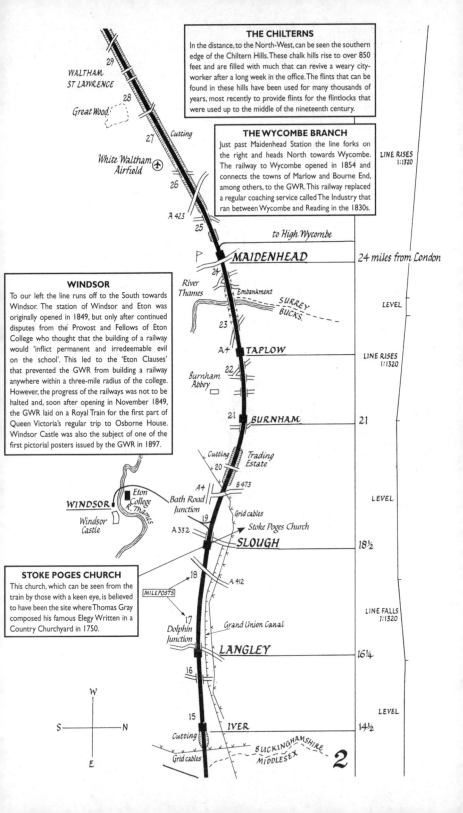

### THE CHILTERNS

In the distance, to the North-West, can be seen the southern edge of the Chiltern Hills. These chalk hills rise to over 850 feet and are filled with much that can revive a weary city-worker after a long week in the office. The flints that can be found in these hills have been used for many thousands of years, most recently to provide flints for the flintlocks that were used up to the middle of the nineteenth century.

### THE WYCOMBE BRANCH

Just past Maidenhead Station the line forks on the right and heads North towards Wycombe. The railway to Wycombe opened in 1854 and connects the towns of Marlow and Bourne End, among others, to the GWR. This railway replaced a regular coaching service called The Industry that ran between Wycombe and Reading in the 1830s.

### WINDSOR

To our left the line runs off to the South towards Windsor. The station of Windsor and Eton was originally opened in 1849, but only after continued disputes from the Provost and Fellows of Eton College who thought that the building of a railway would 'inflict permanent and irredeemable evil on the school'. This led to the 'Eton Clauses' that prevented the GWR from building a railway anywhere within a three-mile radius of the college. However, the progress of the railways was not to be halted and, soon after opening in November 1849, the GWR laid on a Royal Train for the first part of Queen Victoria's regular trip to Osborne House. Windsor Castle was also the subject of one of the first pictorial posters issued by the GWR in 1897.

### STOKE POGES CHURCH

This church, which can be seen from the train by those with a keen eye, is believed to have been the site where Thomas Gray composed his famous Elegy Written in a Country Churchyard in 1750.

WALTHAM ST LAWRENCE

29

28 Great Wood

27 Cutting

White Waltham Airfield

26

A 423

25

to High Wycombe

LINE RISES 1:1320

MAIDENHEAD — 24 miles from London

24

River Thames — Embankment

SURREY BUCKS

LEVEL

23

A4 — TAPLOW

22

Burnham Abbey

LINE RISES 1:1320

21 — BURNHAM — 21

Cutting

20 — Trading Estate

A4 — Bath Road Junction — B 473

19 — Grid cables — Stoke Poges Church

A 332

WINDSOR — Eton College — R. Thames

Windsor Castle

SLOUGH — 18½

LEVEL

18 — A 412

MILEPOSTS

17 — Grand Union Canal — LINE FALLS 1:1320

Dolphin Junction

LANGLEY — 16¼

16

15 — IVER — 14½

LEVEL

Cutting

Grid cables — BUCKINGHAMSHIRE MIDDLESEX

W
S — N
E

2

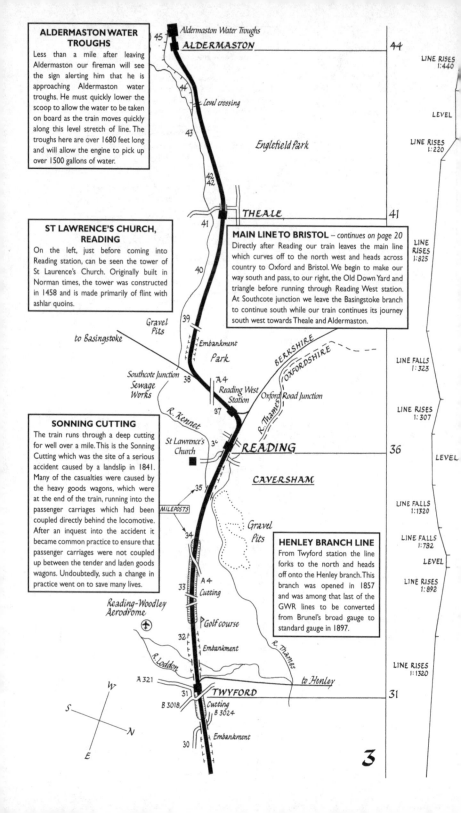

## ALDERMASTON WATER TROUGHS

Less than a mile after leaving Aldermaston our fireman will see the sign alerting him that he is approaching Aldermaston water troughs. He must quickly lower the scoop to allow the water to be taken on board as the train moves quickly along this level stretch of line. The troughs here are over 1680 feet long and will allow the engine to pick up over 1500 gallons of water.

## ST LAWRENCE'S CHURCH, READING

On the left, just before coming into Reading station, can be seen the tower of St Laurence's Church. Originally built in Norman times, the tower was constructed in 1458 and is made primarily of flint with ashlar quoins.

**MAIN LINE TO BRISTOL** – *continues on page 20* Directly after Reading our train leaves the main line which curves off to the north west and heads across country to Oxford and Bristol. We begin to make our way south and pass, to our right, the Old Down Yard and triangle before running through Reading West station. At Southcote junction we leave the Basingstoke branch to continue south while our train continues its journey south west towards Theale and Aldermaston.

## SONNING CUTTING

The train runs through a deep cutting for well over a mile. This is the Sonning Cutting which was the site of a serious accident caused by a landslip in 1841. Many of the casualties were caused by the heavy goods wagons, which were at the end of the train, running into the passenger carriages which had been coupled directly behind the locomotive. After an inquest into the accident it became common practice to ensure that passenger carriages were not coupled up between the tender and laden goods wagons. Undoubtedly, such a change in practice went on to save many lives.

## HENLEY BRANCH LINE

From Twyford station the line forks to the north and heads off onto the Henley branch. This branch was opened in 1857 and was among that last of the GWR lines to be converted from Brunel's broad gauge to standard gauge in 1897.

### Map labels

Aldermaston Water Troughs
ALDERMASTON
45
44
LINE RISES 1:440
Level crossing
44
43
Englefield Park
LEVEL
LINE RISES 1:220
42
42
THEALE
41
41
40
LINE RISES 1:825
Gravel Pits
39
to Basingstoke
Embankment
Park
BERKSHIRE
OXFORDSHIRE
LINE FALLS 1:323
Southcote Junction
Sewage Works
38
A4
Reading West Station
Oxford Road Junction
R. Thames
LINE RISES 1:307
37
R. Kennet
St Lawrence's Church
3½
READING
36
LEVEL
35
CAVERSHAM
MILEPOSTS
34
Gravel Pits
LINE FALLS 1:1320
LINE FALLS 1:792
LEVEL
A4 Cutting
33
LINE RISES 1:892
Reading-Woodley Aerodrome
32
Golf course
Embankment
R. Loddon
R. Thames
LINE RISES 1:1320
A 321
31
TWYFORD
31
B 3018
Cutting
B 3024
to Henley
30
Embankment

W
S
N
E

3

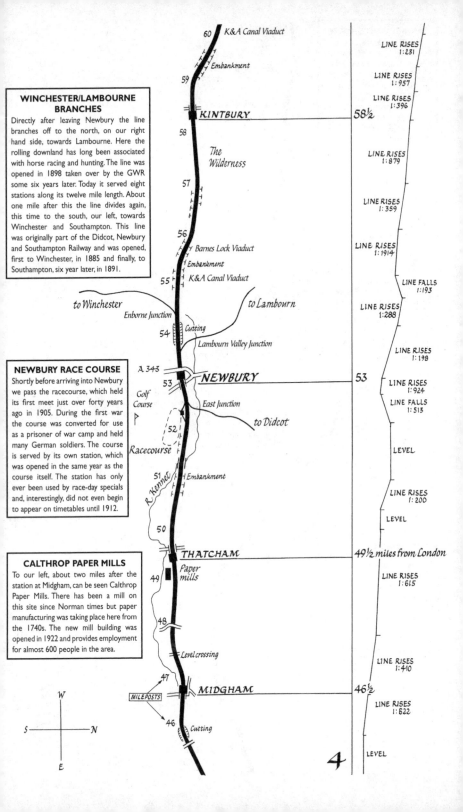

**60** K&A Canal Viaduct

Embankment

**59**

## WINCHESTER/LAMBOURNE BRANCHES

Directly after leaving Newbury the line branches off to the north, on our right hand side, towards Lambourne. Here the rolling downland has long been associated with horse racing and hunting. The line was opened in 1898 taken over by the GWR some six years later. Today it served eight stations along its twelve mile length. About one mile after this the line divides again, this time to the south, our left, towards Winchester and Southampton. This line was originally part of the Didcot, Newbury and Southampton Railway and was opened, first to Winchester, in 1885 and finally, to Southampton, six year later, in 1891.

**KINTBURY**

**58**

*The Wilderness*

**57**

**56**

Barnes Lock Viaduct

Embankment

**55** K&A Canal Viaduct

*to Winchester*

*to Lambourn*

Enborne Junction

**54** Cutting

Lambourn Valley Junction

## NEWBURY RACE COURSE

Shortly before arriving into Newbury we pass the racecourse, which held its first meet just over forty years ago in 1905. During the first war the course was converted for use as a prisoner of war camp and held many German soldiers. The course is served by its own station, which was opened in the same year as the course itself. The station has only ever been used by race-day specials and, interestingly, did not even begin to appear on timetables until 1912.

A 343

**53** **NEWBURY**

*Golf Course*

East Junction

**52**

*to Didcot*

*Racecourse*

**51** *R. Kennet* Embankment

**50**

**THATCHAM**

## CALTHROP PAPER MILLS

To our left, about two miles after the station at Midgham, can be seen Calthrop Paper Mills. There has been a mill on this site since Norman times but paper manufacturing was taking place here from the 1740s. The new mill building was opened in 1922 and provides employment for almost 600 people in the area.

**49** Paper mills

**48**

Level crossing

**47**

MILEPOSTS

**MIDGHAM**

**46** Cutting

W
S — N
E

LINE RISES 1:231

LINE RISES 1:957

LINE RISES 1:396

**58½**

LINE RISES 1:879

LINE RISES 1:359

LINE RISES 1:914

LINE FALLS 1:193

LINE RISES 1:288

LINE RISES 1:198

**53**

LINE RISES 1:924

LINE FALLS 1:513

LEVEL

LINE RISES 1:200

LEVEL

**49½ miles from London**

LINE RISES 1:615

LINE RISES 1:410

**46½**

LINE RISES 1:622

**4**

LEVEL

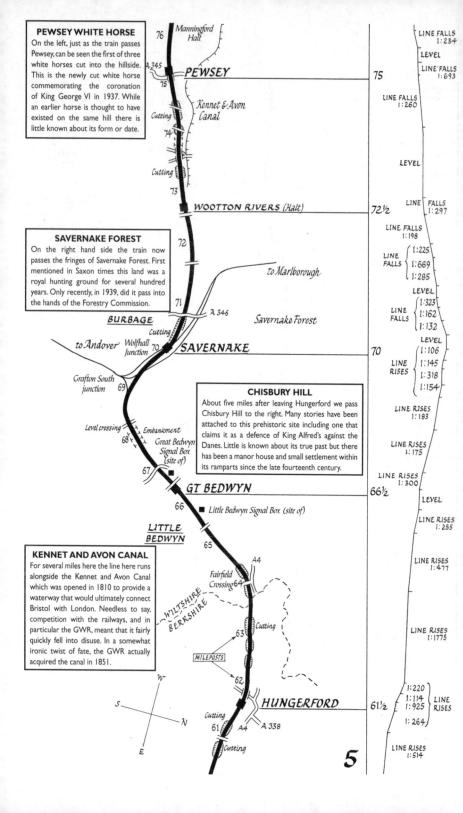

**PEWSEY WHITE HORSE**
On the left, just as the train passes Pewsey, can be seen the first of three white horses cut into the hillside. This is the newly cut white horse commemorating the coronation of King George VI in 1937. While an earlier horse is thought to have existed on the same hill there is little known about its form or date.

**SAVERNAKE FOREST**
On the right hand side the train now passes the fringes of Savernake Forest. First mentioned in Saxon times this land was a royal hunting ground for several hundred years. Only recently, in 1939, did it pass into the hands of the Forestry Commission.

**CHISBURY HILL**
About five miles after leaving Hungerford we pass Chisbury Hill to the right. Many stories have been attached to this prehistoric site including one that claims it as a defence of King Alfred's against the Danes. Little is known about its true past but there has been a manor house and small settlement within its ramparts since the late fourteenth century.

**KENNET AND AVON CANAL**
For several miles here the line here runs alongside the Kennet and Avon Canal which was opened in 1810 to provide a waterway that would ultimately connect Bristol with London. Needless to say, competition with the railways, and in particular the GWR, meant that it fairly quickly fell into disuse. In a somewhat ironic twist of fate, the GWR actually acquired the canal in 1851.

Manningford Halt

76

A.345

PEWSEY

75

Kennet & Avon Canal

Cutting

74

Cutting

73

WOOTTON RIVERS (Halt)

72

to Marlborough

71

BURBAGE

A.346

Savernake Forest

Cutting

to Andover

Wolfhall Junction

70

SAVERNAKE

Grafton South junction

69

Level crossing

Embankment

68

Great Bedwyn Signal Box (site of)

67

GT BEDWYN

66

Little Bedwyn Signal Box (site of)

LITTLE BEDWYN

65

A4

Fairfield Crossing

64

WILTSHIRE

BERKSHIRE

Cutting

63

MILEPOSTS

62

HUNGERFORD

Cutting

61

A4

A.338

Cutting

W

S

N

E

**5**

LINE FALLS 1:234

LEVEL

LINE FALLS 1:693

75

LINE FALLS 1:260

LEVEL

72½

LINE FALLS 1:297

LINE FALLS 1:198

LINE FALLS {1:225 / 1:669 / 1:285}

LEVEL

LINE FALLS {1:323 / 1:162 / 1:132}

LEVEL

LINE RISES {1:106 / 1:145 / 1:318 / 1:154}

70

LINE RISES 1:183

LINE RISES 1:175

LINE RISES 1:300

66½

LEVEL

LINE RISES 1:255

LINE RISES 1:477

LINE RISES 1:1775

LINE RISES {1:220 / 1:114 / 1:925 / 1:264}

61½

LINE RISES 1:514

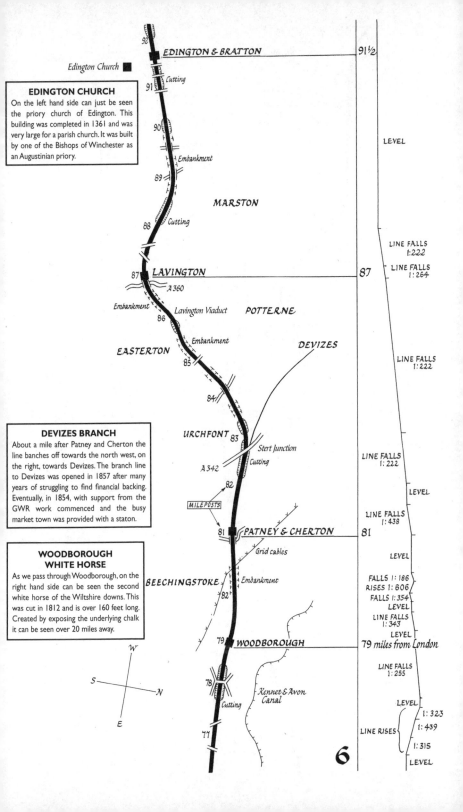

**EDINGTON & BRATTON**

91½

*Cutting*

Edington Church ■

### EDINGTON CHURCH
On the left hand side can just be seen the priory church of Edington. This building was completed in 1361 and was very large for a parish church. It was built by one of the Bishops of Winchester as an Augustinian priory.

92

91

90

*Embankment*

89

**MARSTON**

88

*Cutting*

LEVEL

LINE FALLS 1:222

**LAVINGTON**

87

87

LINE FALLS 1:264

*A 360*

*Embankment*

**POTTERNE**

86 *Lavington Viaduct*

*Embankment*

**EASTERTON**

85

**DEVIZES**

LINE FALLS 1:222

84

**URCHFONT**

83

*Stert Junction*

LINE FALLS 1:222

### DEVIZES BRANCH
About a mile after Patney and Cherton the line branches off towards the north west, on the right, towards Devizes. The branch line to Devizes was opened in 1857 after many years of struggling to find financial backing. Eventually, in 1854, with support from the GWR work commenced and the busy market town was provided with a staton.

*A 342*

*Cutting*

82

LEVEL

**MILEPOSTS**

LINE FALLS 1:438

81

**PATNEY & CHERTON**

81

*Grid cables*

LEVEL

### WOODBOROUGH WHITE HORSE
As we pass through Woodborough, on the right hand side can be seen the second white horse of the Wiltshire downs. This was cut in 1812 and is over 160 feet long. Created by exposing the underlying chalk it can be seen over 20 miles away.

**BEECHINGSTOKE**

*Embankment*

82

FALLS 1:186
RISES 1:606
FALLS 1:354
LEVEL
LINE FALLS 1:343
LEVEL

79 **WOODBOROUGH**

79 miles from London

W

S — N

E

*Kennet & Avon Canal*

78

*Cutting*

LINE FALLS 1:255

LEVEL
1:323
LINE RISES { 1:439
1:315
LEVEL

77

**6**

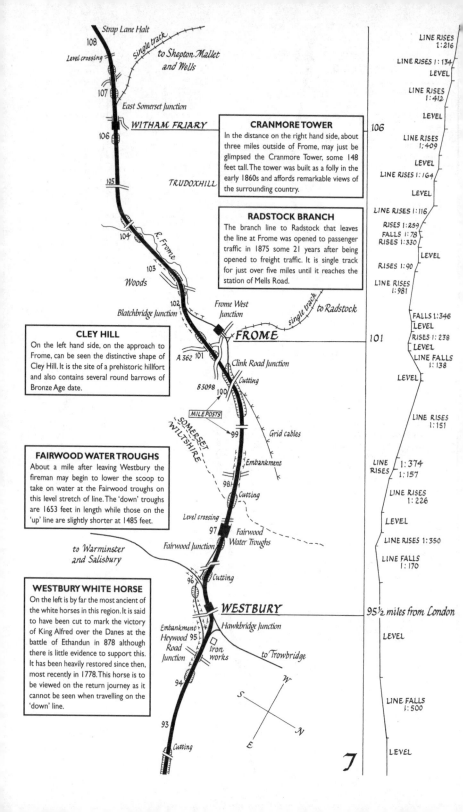

Strap Lane Halt

108

Level crossing

single track

to Shepton Mallet and Wells

107

East Somerset Junction

WITHAM FRIARY

106

105

TRUDOXHILL

R. Frome

104

103

Woods

102

Blatchbridge Junction

Frome West Junction

single track   to Radstock

FROME

A 362   101

Clink Road Junction

Cutting

B 5098   100

MILE POSTS

99

Grid cables

SOMERSET
WILTSHIRE

Embankment

98

Cutting

Level crossing

97

Fairwood Junction

Fairwood
Water Troughs

to Warminster
and Salisbury

96   Cutting

WESTBURY

Hawkbridge Junction

Embankment

Heywood 95
Road
Junction

Iron
works

to Trowbridge

94

W
S          N
E

93

Cutting

106

101

95½ miles from London

**CRANMORE TOWER**

In the distance on the right hand side, about three miles outside of Frome, may just be glimpsed the Cranmore Tower, some 148 feet tall. The tower was built as a folly in the early 1860s and affords remarkable views of the surrounding country.

**RADSTOCK BRANCH**

The branch line to Radstock that leaves the line at Frome was opened to passenger traffic in 1875 some 21 years after being opened to freight traffic. It is single track for just over five miles until it reaches the station of Mells Road.

**CLEY HILL**

On the left hand side, on the approach to Frome, can be seen the distinctive shape of Cley Hill. It is the site of a prehistoric hillfort and also contains several round barrows of Bronze Age date.

**FAIRWOOD WATER TROUGHS**

About a mile after leaving Westbury the fireman may begin to lower the scoop to take on water at the Fairwood troughs on this level stretch of line. The 'down' troughs are 1653 feet in length while those on the 'up' line are slightly shorter at 1485 feet.

**WESTBURY WHITE HORSE**

On the left is by far the most ancient of the white horses in this region. It is said to have been cut to mark the victory of King Alfred over the Danes at the battle of Ethandun in 878 although there is little evidence to support this. It has been heavily restored since then, most recently in 1778. This horse is to be viewed on the return journey as it cannot be seen when travelling on the 'down' line.

LINE RISES 1:216

LINE RISES 1:134

LEVEL

LINE RISES 1:412

LEVEL

LINE RISES 1:409

LEVEL

LINE RISES 1:164

LEVEL

LINE RISES 1:116

RISES 1:259
FALLS 1:78
RISES 1:330

LEVEL

RISES 1:90

LINE RISES 1:981

FALLS 1:346
LEVEL
RISES 1:238
LEVEL
LINE FALLS 1:138

LEVEL

LINE RISES 1:151

LINE RISES   1:374
1:157

LINE RISES 1:226

LEVEL

LINE RISES 1:350

LINE FALLS 1:170

LEVEL

LINE FALLS 1:500

LEVEL

7

**GLASTONBURY TOR**
On the right hand side, just after Keinton Mandeville station can be seen the distinctive landmark of Glastonbury Tor. The Tor itself rises out of the flat levels and is surmounted by the tower of St. Michael's church. The site has strong associations with King Arthur and the Holy Grail and archaeology suggests that there has been occupation on the site reaching far back into prehistory.

**THE FOSSE WAY**
At this point the line crosses a road that runs along the route of the Fosse way. The Fosse Way was one of the main Roman roads in the country and ran from Exeter (known as Isca Dumnoniorum) in the west all the way to Lincoln (Lindum Colonia) in the north east. Over its 182 miles of length it is reputed to be never more than six miles off a straight line.

**CASTLE CARY**
At Castle Cary junction the line divides; our train continues westward while the other line, fully opened in 1856, heads south towards Yeovil and, eventually, Weymouth.

**BRUTON GRAMMAR SCHOOL**
On the right hand side can be seen the buildings of Bruton grammar school. This school was founded in the early 1500s by Richard FitzJames and owns a copy of the Magna Carta dating from 1297.

124 ¼
Cutting
R. Cary
123
CHARLTON ADAM
CHARLTON MACKRELL
122
Embankment
A.37
121
Cutting
120
KEINTON MANDEVILLE
Fosse Way
R. Brue
119
Cutting
118
Embankment
117
ALFORD (Halt
Embankment
to Yeovil & Dorchester
116
Castle Cary Junction
CASTLE CARY
115
MILE POSTS
114 ¼
to Shepton Mallet
A.359
Cutting
to Wincanton
113
EVERCREECH
112
BRUTON
111
Embankment
Cutting
R. Brue
110
UPTON NOBLE
109

W
S
N
E

LINE FALLS 1:264
LEVEL
122
LINE RISES 1:330
120 miles from London
LEVEL
LINE FALLS 1:660
LEVEL
LINE FALLS 1:264
117
LINE FALLS 1:330
LINE RISES 1:366
LEVEL
115
RISES 1:100
LEVEL
LINE FALLS 1:143
LEVEL
LINE FALLS 1:358
LEVEL
LINE FALLS 1:79
LEVEL
LINE FALLS 1:98
112
LEVEL
LINE FALLS 1:93
LINE FALLS 1:140
LEVEL
LINE FALLS 1:98
LEVEL
LINE FALLS 1:81
LEVEL

**8**

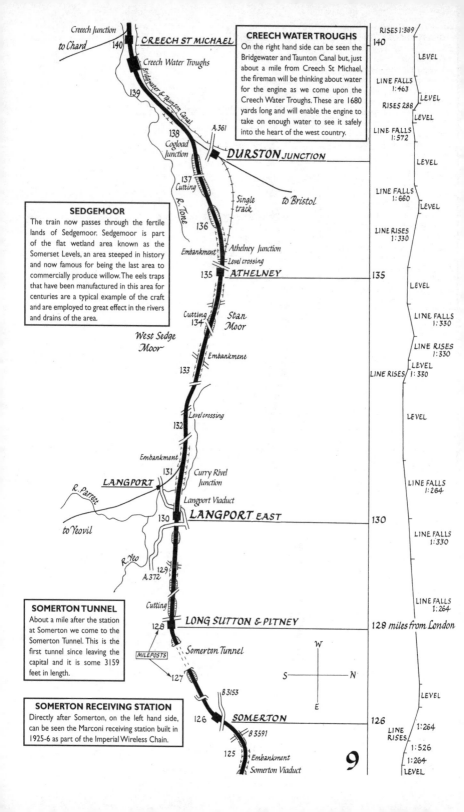

**CREECH WATER TROUGHS**
On the right hand side can be seen the Bridgewater and Taunton Canal but, just about a mile from Creech St Michael, the fireman will be thinking about water for the engine as we come upon the Creech Water Troughs. These are 1680 yards long and will enable the engine to take on enough water to see it safely into the heart of the west country.

**SEDGEMOOR**
The train now passes through the fertile lands of Sedgemoor. Sedgemoor is part of the flat wetland area known as the Somerset Levels, an area steeped in history and now famous for being the last area to commercially produce willow. The eels traps that have been manufactured in this area for centuries are a typical example of the craft and are employed to great effect in the rivers and drains of the area.

**SOMERTON TUNNEL**
About a mile after the station at Somerton we come to the Somerton Tunnel. This is the first tunnel since leaving the capital and it is some 3159 feet in length.

**SOMERTON RECEIVING STATION**
Directly after Somerton, on the left hand side, can be seen the Marconi receiving station built in 1925-6 as part of the Imperial Wireless Chain.

Creech Junction
to Chard
140
CREECH ST MICHAEL
Creech Water Troughs
Bridgewater & Taunton Canal
139
138
Cogload Junction
A 361
DURSTON Junction
137 Cutting
R. Tone
Single track
to Bristol
136
Embankment
Athelney Junction
Level crossing
135
ATHELNEY
Cutting 134
Stan Moor
West Sedge Moor
Embankment
133
Level crossing
132
Embankment
131
Curry Rivel Junction
LANGPORT
R. Parrett
Langport Viaduct
130
LANGPORT EAST
to Yeovil
R. Yeo
129
A 372
Cutting
128
LONG SUTTON & PITNEY
MILEPOSTS
Somerton Tunnel
127
B 3153
126
SOMERTON
B 3591
125
Embankment
Somerton Viaduct

W
S — N
E

**9**

RISES 1:389
140
LEVEL
LINE FALLS 1:463
LEVEL
RISES 288
LEVEL
LINE FALLS 1:572
LEVEL
LINE FALLS 1:660
LEVEL
LINE RISES 1:330
135
LEVEL
LINE FALLS 1:330
LINE RISES 1:330
LEVEL
LINE RISES 1:330
LEVEL
LINE FALLS 1:264
130
LINE FALLS 1:330
LINE FALLS 1:264
128 miles from London
LEVEL
126
LINE RISES 1:264
1:526
1:264
LEVEL

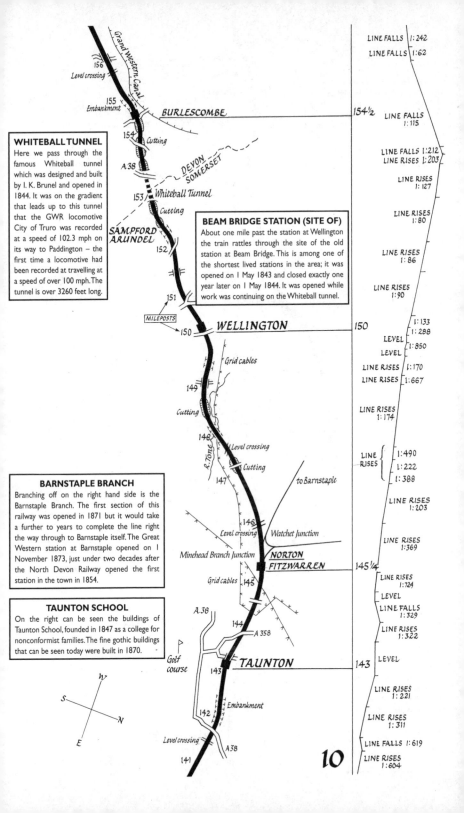

LINE FALLS 1:242
LINE FALLS 1:62

156
Level crossing

155
Embankment

BURLESCOMBE

154½ LINE FALLS 1:115

154 Cutting

DEVON
SOMERSET

A 38

Grand Western Canal

LINE FALLS 1:212
LINE RISES 1:203

LINE RISES 1:127

153 Whiteball Tunnel

Cutting

LINE RISES 1:80

SAMPFORD
ARUNDEL

152

LINE RISES 1:86

**WHITEBALL TUNNEL**
Here we pass through the famous Whiteball tunnel which was designed and built by I. K. Brunel and opened in 1844. It was on the gradient that leads up to this tunnel that the GWR locomotive City of Truro was recorded at a speed of 102.3 mph on its way to Paddington – the first time a locomotive had been recorded at travelling at a speed of over 100 mph. The tunnel is over 3260 feet long.

**BEAM BRIDGE STATION (SITE OF)**
About one mile past the station at Wellington the train rattles through the site of the old station at Beam Bridge. This is among one of the shortest lived stations in the area; it was opened on 1 May 1843 and closed exactly one year later on 1 May 1844. It was opened while work was continuing on the Whiteball tunnel.

LINE RISES 1:90

151

MILEPOSTS

150 WELLINGTON 150
1:133
1:288
LEVEL 1:850
LEVEL

Grid cables

LINE RISES 1:170
LINE RISES 1:667

149

Cutting

LINE RISES 1:174

148 Level crossing

R. Tone

Cutting

LINE RISES { 1:490
1:222
1:388

147

to Barnstaple

LINE RISES 1:203

**BARNSTAPLE BRANCH**
Branching off on the right hand side is the Barnstaple Branch. The first section of this railway was opened in 1871 but it would take a further to years to complete the line right the way through to Barnstaple itself. The Great Western station at Barnstaple opened on 1 November 1873, just under two decades after the North Devon Railway opened the first station in the town in 1854.

146 Level crossing Watchet Junction

LINE RISES 1:369

Minehead Branch Junction

NORTON
FITZWARREN 145¼

LINE RISES 1:724
LEVEL
LINE FALLS 1:329

Grid cables 145

144 A 358

LINE RISES 1:322

143 LEVEL

**TAUNTON SCHOOL**
On the right can be seen the buildings of Taunton School, founded in 1847 as a college for nonconformist families. The fine gothic buildings that can be seen today were built in 1870.

A 38

Golf
course 143 TAUNTON 143

LINE RISES 1:221

142 Embankment

LINE RISES 1:311

N
W — S
E

Level crossing
A 38
141

LINE FALLS 1:619

LINE RISES 1:604

**10**

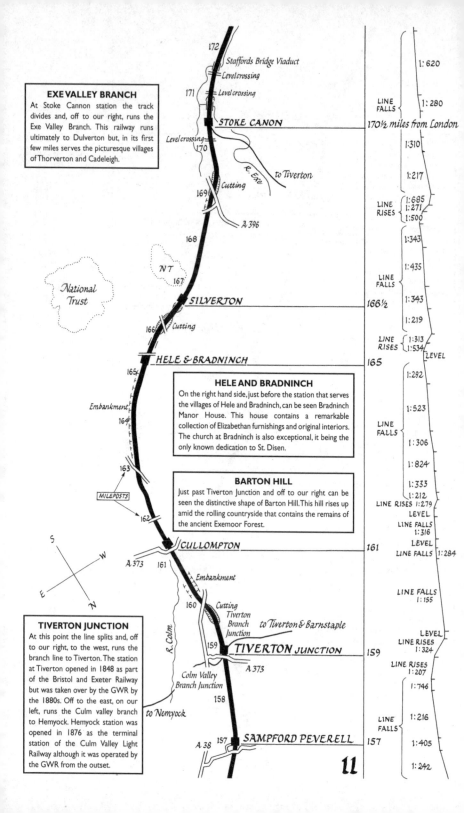

**EXE VALLEY BRANCH**
At Stoke Cannon station the track divides and, off to our right, runs the Exe Valley Branch. This railway runs ultimately to Dulverton but, in its first few miles serves the picturesque villages of Thorverton and Cadeleigh.

**HELE AND BRADNINCH**
On the right hand side, just before the station that serves the villages of Hele and Bradninch, can be seen Bradninch Manor House. This house contains a remarkable collection of Elizabethan furnishings and original interiors. The church at Bradninch is also exceptional, it being the only known dedication to St. Disen.

**BARTON HILL**
Just past Tiverton Junction and off to our right can be seen the distinctive shape of Barton Hill. This hill rises up amid the rolling countryside that contains the remains of the ancient Exemoor Forest.

**TIVERTON JUNCTION**
At this point the line splits and, off to our right, to the west, runs the branch line to Tiverton. The station at Tiverton opened in 1848 as part of the Bristol and Exeter Railway but was taken over by the GWR by the 1880s. Off to the east, on our left, runs the Culm valley branch to Hemyock. Hemyock station was opened in 1876 as the terminal station of the Culm Valley Light Railway although it was operated by the GWR from the outset.

172
Staffords Bridge Viaduct
Level crossing
171
Level crossing
**STOKE CANON**
Level crossing
170
R. Exe
to Tiverton
169
Cutting
A 396
168
NT
167
**SILVERTON**
National Trust
166
Cutting
**HELE & BRADNINCH**
165
Embankment
164
163
MILEPOSTS
162
**CULLOMPTON**
161
A 373
Embankment
160
Cutting
Tiverton Branch Junction
to Tiverton & Barnstaple
159
**TIVERTON** JUNCTION
A 373
R. Colm
Colm Valley Branch Junction
158
to Hemyock
A 38
157
**SAMPFORD PEVERELL**

S
W
E
N

1: 620
LINE FALLS
1: 280
170½ miles from London
1:310
1:217
LINE RISES
1:685
1:271
1:500
1:343
1:435
LINE FALLS
166½
1:343
1:219
LINE RISES
1:313
1:534
LEVEL
165
1:292
1:523
LINE FALLS
1:306
1:824
1:333
1:212
LINE RISES 1:279
LEVEL
LINE FALLS
1:316
161
LEVEL
LINE FALLS 1:284
LINE FALLS
1:155
LEVEL
LINE RISES
1:324
159
LINE RISES
1:207
1:746
1:216
LINE FALLS
157
1:405
1:242

**11**

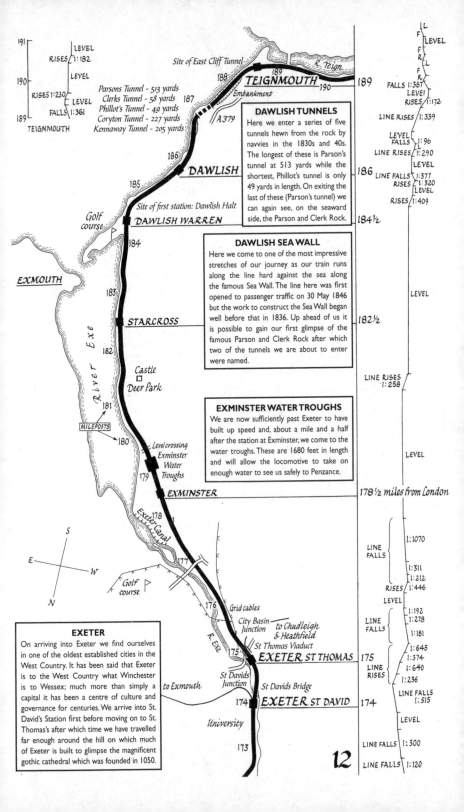

191

190
RISES 1:230

LEVEL
RISES 1:182
LEVEL

LEVEL

189
FALLS 1:361
TEIGNMOUTH

Site of East Cliff Tunnel

R. Teign

188
190
**TEIGNMOUTH** — 189

Embankment

187
A379

Parsons Tunnel - 513 yards
Clerks Tunnel - 58 yards
Phillot's Tunnel - 49 yards
Coryton Tunnel - 227 yards
Kennaway Tunnel - 205 yards

186

185
**DAWLISH**

Golf course

**DAWLISH WARREN**

Site of first station: Dawlish Halt

184

183

*River Exe*

EXMOUTH

182
**STARCROSS**

Castle □
Deer Park

181

180
*MILEPOSTS*

Level crossing
Exminster
Water
Troughs

179
**EXMINSTER**

Exeter Canal

178

177

Golf course

176
Grid cables
City Basin
Junction
*to Chudleigh
& Heathfield*
St Thomas Viaduct

175
**EXETER ST THOMAS** — 175

St Davids
Junction
R. Exe

*to Exmouth*

St Davids Bridge

174
**EXETER ST DAVID** — 174

University

173

### DAWLISH TUNNELS
Here we enter a series of five tunnels hewn from the rock by navvies in the 1830s and 40s. The longest of these is Parson's tunnel at 513 yards while the shortest, Phillot's tunnel is only 49 yards in length. On exiting the last of these (Parson's tunnel) we can again see, on the seaward side, the Parson and Clerk Rock.

### DAWLISH SEA WALL
Here we come to one of the most impressive stretches of our journey as our train runs along the line hard against the sea along the famous Sea Wall. The line here was first opened to passenger traffic on 30 May 1846 but the work to construct the Sea Wall began well before that in 1836. Up ahead of us it is possible to gain our first glimpse of the famous Parson and Clerk Rock after which two of the tunnels we are about to enter were named.

### EXMINSTER WATER TROUGHS
We are now sufficiently past Exeter to have built up speed and, about a mile and a half after the station at Exminster, we come to the water troughs. These are 1680 feet in length and will allow the locomotive to take on enough water to see us safely to Penzance.

### EXETER
On arriving into Exeter we find ourselves in one of the oldest established cities in the West Country. It has been said that Exeter is to the West Country what Winchester is to Wessex; much more than simply a capital it has been a centre of culture and governance for centuries. We arrive into St. David's Station first before moving on to St. Thomas's after which time we have travelled far enough around the hill on which much of Exeter is built to glimpse the magnificent gothic cathedral which was founded in 1050.

189
190
L
F
R
F
R
L
L
LEVEL

FALLS 1:367
LEVEL
RISES 1:172

LINE RISES 1:339

LEVEL
FALLS 1:96
LINE RISES 1:290

186
LEVEL
LINE FALLS 1:377
RISES 1:320
LEVEL
RISES 1:409

184½

LEVEL

182½

LINE RISES 1:258

LEVEL

178½ miles from London

LINE FALLS { 1:1070
1:311
1:212
RISES 1:446
LEVEL

LINE FALLS { 1:192
1:278
1:181

175
1:645
1:374
LINE RISES { 1:640
1:236
LINE FALLS 1:515

174
LEVEL

LINE FALLS 1:300

LINE FALLS 1:120

**12**

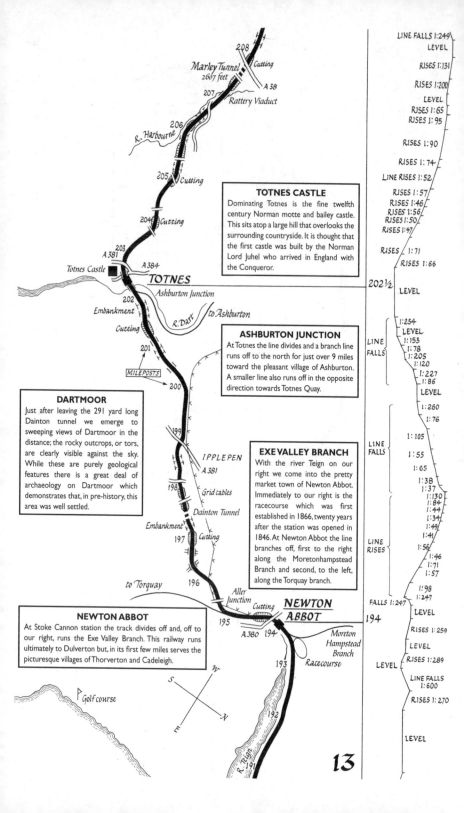

**TOTNES CASTLE**
Dominating Totnes is the fine twelfth century Norman motte and bailey castle. This sits atop a large hill that overlooks the surrounding countryside. It is thought that the first castle was built by the Norman Lord Juhel who arrived in England with the Conqueror.

**ASHBURTON JUNCTION**
At Totnes the line divides and a branch line runs off to the north for just over 9 miles toward the pleasant village of Ashburton. A smaller line also runs off in the opposite direction towards Totnes Quay.

**DARTMOOR**
Just after leaving the 291 yard long Dainton tunnel we emerge to sweeping views of Dartmoor in the distance; the rocky outcrops, or tors, are clearly visible against the sky. While these are purely geological features there is a great deal of archaeology on Dartmoor which demonstrates that, in pre-history, this area was well settled.

**EXE VALLEY BRANCH**
With the river Teign on our right we come into the pretty market town of Newton Abbot. Immediately to our right is the racecourse which was first established in 1866, twenty years after the station was opened in 1846. At Newton Abbot the line branches off, first to the right along the Moretonhampstead Branch and second, to the left, along the Torquay branch.

**NEWTON ABBOT**
At Stoke Cannon station the track divides off and, off to our right, runs the Exe Valley Branch. This railway runs ultimately to Dulverton but, in its first few miles serves the picturesque villages of Thorverton and Cadeleigh.

Map labels:

208
Marley Tunnel 2607 feet
Cutting
A 38
207
Rattery Viaduct
206
R. Harbourne
205 Cutting
204 Cutting
203
A 381
A 384
Totnes Castle
**TOTNES**
Ashburton Junction
202
to Ashburton
R. Dart
Embankment
Cutting
201
MILEPOSTS
200
199
IPPLEPEN
A 381
198
Grid cables
Dainton Tunnel
Embankment
197 Cutting
196
to Torquay
Aller Junction
Cutting
195
A 380 194
193
192
R. Teign 191
Golf course
N S E W (compass)

Gradient profile (right side):
LINE FALLS 1:249
LEVEL
RISES 1:131
RISES 1:200
LEVEL
RISES 1:65
RISES 1:95
RISES 1:90
RISES 1:74
LINE RISES 1:52
RISES 1:57
RISES 1:46
RISES 1:56
RISES 1:50
RISES 1:47
RISES 1:71
RISES 1:66
202½ LEVEL
1:254 LEVEL
LINE FALLS
1:153
1:78
1:205
1:120
1:227
1:86
LEVEL
1:260
1:76
1:105
LINE FALLS 1:55
1:65
1:38
1:37
1:130
1:84
1:44
1:34
1:49
1:41
LINE RISES 1:56
1:46
1:57
1:98
FALLS 1:247
194 LEVEL
RISES 1:259
LEVEL
RISES 1:289
LEVEL
LINE FALLS 1:600
RISES 1:270
LEVEL

**NEWTON ABBOT**
194
Moreton Hampstead Branch
Racecourse

**13**

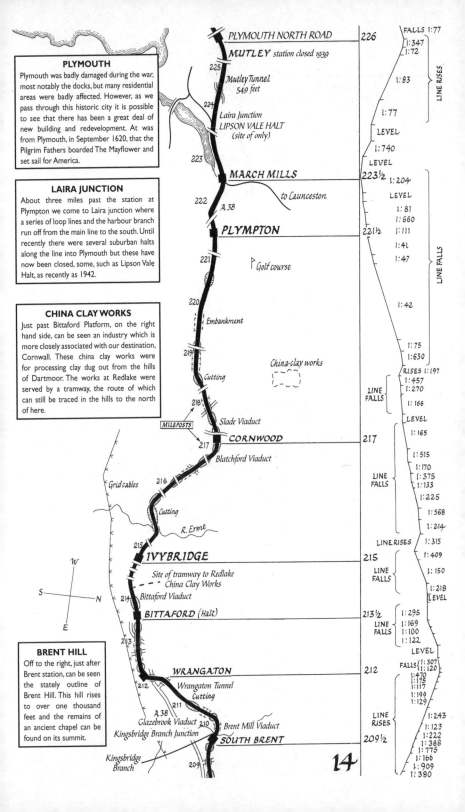

**PLYMOUTH NORTH ROAD** 226

*MUTLEY station closed 1939*

225

*Mutley Tunnel 549 feet*

224

*Laira Junction*
**LIPSON VALE HALT**
*(site of only)*

223

**MARCH MILLS** 223½

*to Launceston*

222

A 38

**PLYMPTON** 221½

221

⌐ *Golf course*

220

‖ *Embankment*

219

*Cutting*

*China-clay works*

218

*Slade Viaduct*

[MILEPOSTS]

217 **CORNWOOD** 217

*Blatchford Viaduct*

216

*Grid cables*

*Cutting*

*R. Erme*

215

**IVYBRIDGE** 215

*Site of tramway to Redlake*
*China Clay Works*

214 *Bittaford Viaduct*

**BITTAFORD (Halt)** 213½

213

**WRANGATON** 212

*Wrangaton Tunnel*
*Cutting*

212

211

A 38
*Glazebrook Viaduct* 210  *Brent Mill Viaduct*
*Kingsbridge Branch Junction*
**SOUTH BRENT** 209½

*Kingsbridge Branch*

209

**14**

## PLYMOUTH

Plymouth was badly damaged during the war, most notably the docks, but many residential areas were badly affected. However, as we pass through this historic city it is possible to see that there has been a great deal of new building and redevelopment. At was from Plymouth, in September 1620, that the Pilgrim Fathers boarded The Mayflower and set sail for America.

## LAIRA JUNCTION

About three miles past the station at Plympton we come to Laira junction where a series of loop lines and the harbour branch run off from the main line to the south. Until recently there were several suburban halts along the line into Plymouth but these have now been closed, some, such as Lipson Vale Halt, as recently as 1942.

## CHINA CLAY WORKS

Just past Bittaford Platform, on the right hand side, can be seen an industry which is more closely associated with our destination, Cornwall. These china clay works were for processing clay dug out from the hills of Dartmoor. The works at Redlake were served by a tramway, the route of which can still be traced in the hills to the north of here.

## BRENT HILL

Off to the right, just after Brent station, can be seen the stately outline of Brent Hill. This hill rises to over one thousand feet and the remains of an ancient chapel can be found on its summit.

W
S — N
E

FALLS 1:77
1:347
1:72

1:83

1:77

LEVEL

1:740

LEVEL

1:204

LEVEL

1:81
1:660
1:111
1:41
1:47

1:42

1:75
1:630

RISES 1:197
1:457
1:270
1:166

LEVEL

1:165
1:515
1:170
1:375
1:133
1:225
1:568
1:214

LINE RISES 1:315
1:409
1:150
1:218
LEVEL

1:295
1:169
1:100
1:122

LEVEL

FALLS 1:307
1:120
1:470
1:175
1:117
1:199
1:129

1:243
1:123
1:222
1:388
1:775
1:166
1:909
1:380

LINE RISES

LINE FALLS

LINE FALLS

LINE FALLS

LINE FALLS

LINE FALLS

LINE RISES

LINE FALLS

LINE FALLS

LINE RISES

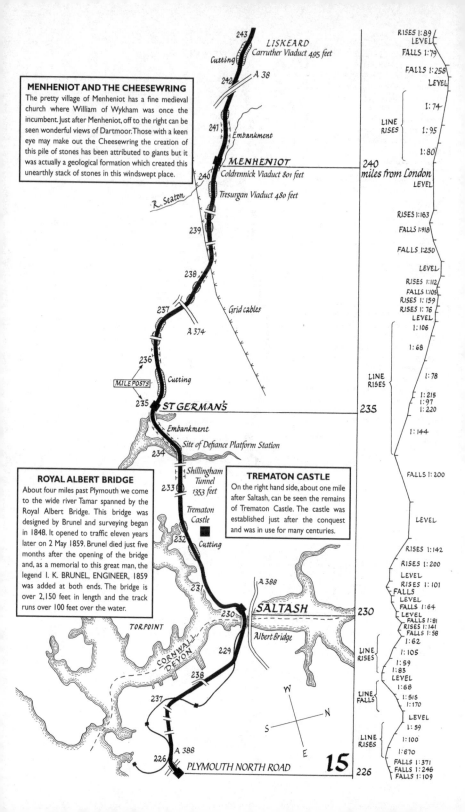

243

LISKEARD
Carruther Viaduct 495 feet

Cutting

242      A 38

241

Embankment

MENHENIOT

240
Coldrennick Viaduct 801 feet

Tresurgan Viaduct 480 feet

R. Seaton

239

238

237          Grid cables

A 374

236

Cutting

MILE POSTS

235   ST GERMAN'S

Embankment

234          Site of Defiance Platform Station

Shillingham
Tunnel
233   1353 feet

Trematon
Castle

232          Cutting

231

A 388

230   SALTASH

TORPOINT   Albert Bridge

229
CORNWALL
DEVON
238

237

W
N
S
E

226   A 388

PLYMOUTH NORTH ROAD          15

**MENHENIOT AND THE CHEESEWRING**
The pretty village of Menheniot has a fine medieval church where William of Wykham was once the incumbent. Just after Menheniot, off to the right can be seen wonderful views of Dartmoor. Those with a keen eye may make out the Cheesewring the creation of this pile of stones has been attributed to giants but it was actually a geological formation which created this unearthly stack of stones in this windswept place.

**ROYAL ALBERT BRIDGE**
About four miles past Plymouth we come to the wide river Tamar spanned by the Royal Albert Bridge. This bridge was designed by Brunel and surveying began in 1848. It opened to traffic eleven years later on 2 May 1859. Brunel died just five months after the opening of the bridge and, as a memorial to this great man, the legend I. K. BRUNEL, ENGINEER, 1859 was added at both ends. The bridge is over 2,150 feet in length and the track runs over 100 feet over the water.

**TREMATON CASTLE**
On the right hand side, about one mile after Saltash, can be seen the remains of Trematon Castle. The castle was established just after the conquest and was in use for many centuries.

RISES 1:89
LEVEL
FALLS 1:79

FALLS 1:258
LEVEL

1:74

LINE
RISES          1:95

1:80

240
miles from London
LEVEL

RISES 1:163

FALLS 1:918

FALLS 1:250

LEVEL
RISES 1:112
FALLS 1:105
RISES 1:159
RISES 1:76
LEVEL
1:106

1:68

1:78

LINE
RISES          1:215
1:97
1:220

1:144

235

FALLS 1:200

LEVEL

RISES 1:142

RISES 1:200
LEVEL
RISES 1:101
FALLS
LEVEL
FALLS 1:64
LEVEL
FALLS 1:81
RISES 1:141
FALLS 1:58

230          1:62

LINE          1:105
RISES          1:59
1:83
LEVEL
1:68
LINE          1:515
FALLS          1:170

LEVEL
1:59
LINE          1:100
RISES          1:670

FALLS 1:371
FALLS 1:246
226   FALLS 1:109

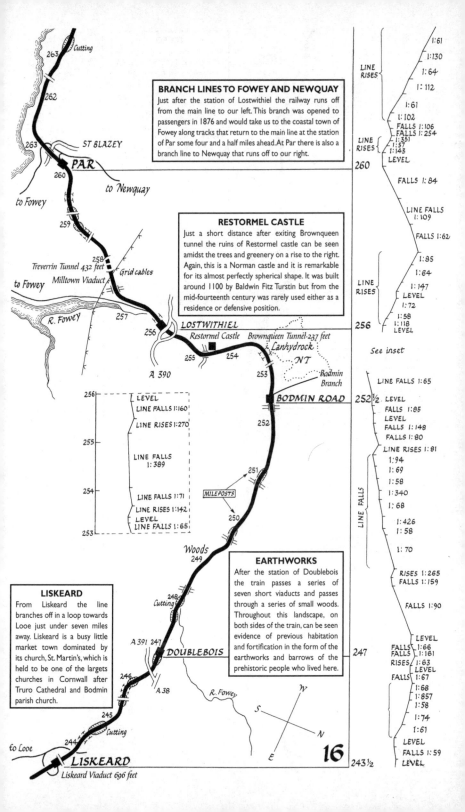

**BRANCH LINES TO FOWEY AND NEWQUAY**

Just after the station of Lostwithiel the railway runs off from the main line to our left. This branch was opened to passengers in 1876 and would take us to the coastal town of Fowey along tracks that return to the main line at the station of Par some four and a half miles ahead. At Par there is also a branch line to Newquay that runs off to our right.

**RESTORMEL CASTLE**

Just a short distance after exiting Brownqueen tunnel the ruins of Restormel castle can be seen amidst the trees and greenery on a rise to the right. Again, this is a Norman castle and it is remarkable for its almost perfectly spherical shape. It was built around 1100 by Baldwin Fitz Turstin but from the mid-fourteenth century was rarely used either as a residence or defensive position.

**LISKEARD**

From Liskeard the line branches off in a loop towards Looe just under seven miles away. Liskeard is a busy little market town dominated by its church, St. Martin's, which is held to be one of the largest churches in Cornwall after Truro Cathedral and Bodmin parish church.

**EARTHWORKS**

After the station of Doublebois the train passes a series of seven short viaducts and passes through a series of small woods. Throughout this landscape, on both sides of the train, can be seen evidence of previous habitation and fortification in the form of the earthworks and barrows of the prehistoric people who lived here.

263 *Cutting*
262
263
ST BLAZEY
PAR
260
*to Newquay*
*to Fowey*
259
258
*Treverrin Tunnel 432 feet*
*Grid cables*
*Milltown Viaduct*
*to Fowey*
*R. Fowey*
257
256
LOSTWITHIEL
*Restormel Castle*
*Brownqueen Tunnel 237 feet*
*Lanhydrock*
255 254
253 *NT*
A 390
*Badmin Branch*
BODMIN ROAD
252
251
*MILE POSTS*
250
*Woods*
249
248 *Cutting*
A 391 247
DOUBLEBOIS
246
A 38
A 38
*R. Fowey*
245
244 *Cutting*
*to Looe*
LISKEARD
*Liskeard Viaduct 696 feet*

256 LEVEL
LINE FALLS 1:160
LINE RISES 1:270
255
LINE FALLS 1:389
254
LINE FALLS 1:71
LINE RISES 1:142
LEVEL
253 LINE FALLS 1:65

W
S
N
E

**16**

1:61
1:130
1:64
1:112
LINE RISES
1:61
1:102
FALLS 1:106
FALLS 1:254
1:351
1:57
1:143
LINE RISES
LEVEL
260
FALLS 1:84
LINE FALLS 1:109
FALLS 1:62
1:85
1:64
1:147
LINE RISES
LEVEL
1:72
1:58
1:118
256
LEVEL
See inset
LINE FALLS 1:65
252½ LEVEL
FALLS 1:85
LEVEL
FALLS 1:148
FALLS 1:80
LINE RISES 1:81
1:94
1:69
1:58
1:340
1:68
LINE FALLS
1:426
1:58
1:70
RISES 1:265
FALLS 1:159
FALLS 1:90
LEVEL
FALLS 1:66
FALLS 1:161
RISES 1:63
LEVEL
FALLS 1:67
247
1:68
1:857
1:58
1:74
1:61
LEVEL
FALLS 1:59
LEVEL
243½

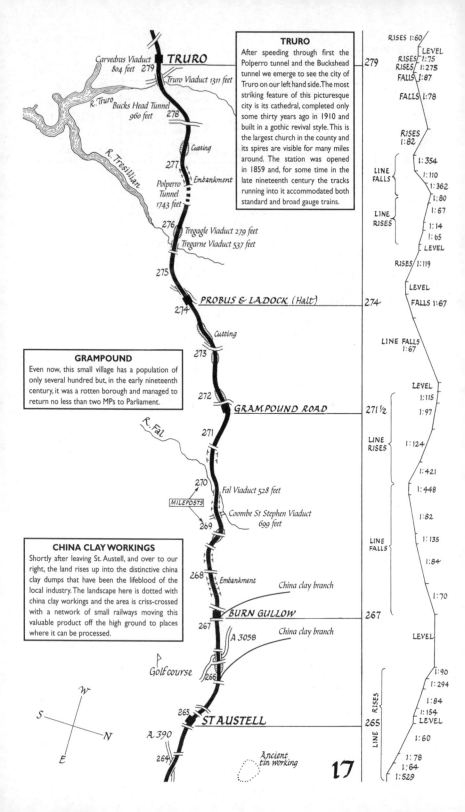

Carvedras Viaduct
804 feet  279

**TRURO**

Truro Viaduct 1311 feet

R. Truro  Bucks Head Tunnel
960 feet  278

R. Tresillian

*Cutting*

277

*Embankment*

Polperro
Tunnel
1743 feet

276

Tregagle Viaduct 279 feet
Tregarne Viaduct 537 feet

275

**PROBUS & LADOCK** (Halt)  274

274

*Cutting*

273

272

**GRAMPOUND ROAD**  271½

R. Fal

271

270

MILEPOSTS  Fal Viaduct 528 feet

Coombe St Stephen Viaduct
699 feet

269

268  *Embankment*

China clay branch

**BURN GULLOW**  267

267

A 3058  China clay branch

Golf course

266

265

**ST AUSTELL**  265

A 390

264

Ancient
tin working

**17**

## TRURO

After speeding through first the Polperro tunnel and the Buckshead tunnel we emerge to see the city of Truro on our left hand side. The most striking feature of this picturesque city is its cathedral, completed only some thirty years ago in 1910 and built in a gothic revival style. This is the largest church in the county and its spires are visible for many miles around. The station was opened in 1859 and, for some time in the late nineteenth century the tracks running into it accommodated both standard and broad gauge trains.

## GRAMPOUND

Even now, this small village has a population of only several hundred but, in the early nineteenth century, it was a rotten borough and managed to return no less than two MPs to Parliament.

## CHINA CLAY WORKINGS

Shortly after leaving St. Austell, and over to our right, the land rises up into the distinctive china clay dumps that have been the lifeblood of the local industry. The landscape here is dotted with china clay workings and the area is criss-crossed with a network of small railways moving this valuable product off the high ground to places where it can be processed.

W  N
S  E

RISES 1:60
LEVEL
RISES 1:75
RISES 1:275
FALLS 1:87
FALLS 1:78

RISES
1:82

1:354
LINE  1:110
FALLS  1:362
1:80
1:67
LINE  1:14
RISES  1:65
LEVEL

RISES 1:119

LEVEL
FALLS 1:67

LINE FALLS
1:67

LEVEL
1:115
1:97

LINE
RISES  1:124

1:421
1:448

1:82

LINE
FALLS  1:135

1:84

1:70

LEVEL

1:90
1:294
1:84
1:154
LEVEL

LINE
RISES  1:60

1:78
1:64
1:529

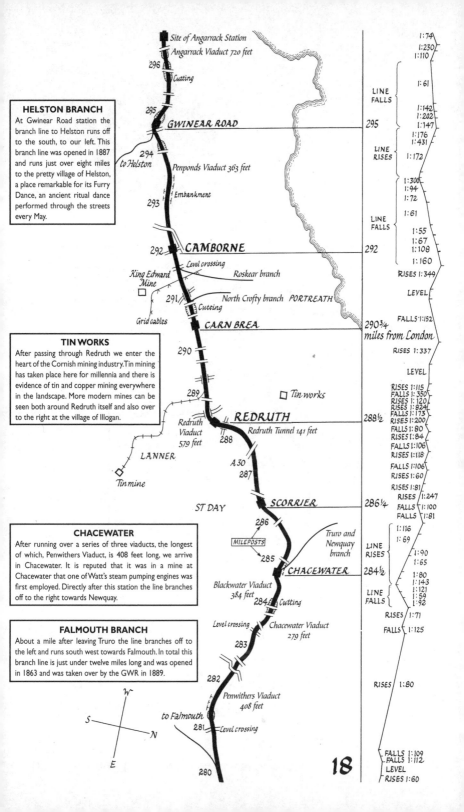

Site of Angarrack Station
Angarrack Viaduct 720 feet

296

Cutting

295

**GWINEAR ROAD**

294
to Helston

Penponds Viaduct 363 feet

293
Embankment

292 **CAMBORNE**

Level crossing
Roskear branch

King Edward Mine

291
North Crofty branch   **PORTREATH**

Cutting

Grid cables

**CARN BREA**

290

289

Tin works

**REDRUTH**

Redruth Viaduct 579 feet
288   Redruth Tunnel 141 feet

LANNER

A 30
287

Tin mine

ST DAY   **SCORRIER**

286

MILEPOSTS

285
Truro and Newquay branch

**CHACEWATER**

Blackwater Viaduct 384 feet

284.5   Cutting

Level crossing   Chacewater Viaduct 279 feet

283

282

Penwithers Viaduct 408 feet

to Falmouth
281   Level crossing

280

**18**

---

### Gradient column (right)

1:74
1:230
1:110

LINE FALLS
1:61
1:142
1:202
1:147

295

1:176
1:431
LINE RISES   1:172

1:300
1:94
1:72
1:61

LINE FALLS
1:55
1:67
1:108
1:160

292

RISES 1:349

LEVEL

290¾
miles from London   FALLS 1:152

RISES 1:337

LEVEL

RISES 1:115
FALLS 1:350
RISES 1:120
RISES 1:824
FALLS 1:173
288½   RISES 1:200
FALLS 1:80
RISES 1:84
FALLS 1:106
RISES 1:118

FALLS 1:106
RISES 1:60

RISES 1:81

286¼   RISES 1:247
FALLS 1:100
FALLS 1:81

1:116
1:69
LINE RISES
1:90
1:65

284½   1:80
1:143
LINE   1:121
FALLS   1:59
1:92

RISES 1:71

FALLS 1:125

RISES 1:80

FALLS 1:109
FALLS 1:112
LEVEL
RISES 1:60

---

### HELSTON BRANCH
At Gwinear Road station the branch line to Helston runs off to the south, to our left. This branch line was opened in 1887 and runs just over eight miles to the pretty village of Helston, a place remarkable for its Furry Dance, an ancient ritual dance performed through the streets every May.

### TIN WORKS
After passing through Redruth we enter the heart of the Cornish mining industry. Tin mining has taken place here for millennia and there is evidence of tin and copper mining everywhere in the landscape. More modern mines can be seen both around Redruth itself and also over to the right at the village of Illogan.

### CHACEWATER
After running over a series of three viaducts, the longest of which, Penwithers Viaduct, is 408 feet long, we arrive in Chacewater. It is reputed that it was in a mine at Chacewater that one of Watt's steam pumping engines was first employed. Directly after this station the line branches off to the right towards Newquay.

### FALMOUTH BRANCH
About a mile after leaving Truro the line branches off to the left and runs south west towards Falmouth. In total this branch line is just under twelve miles long and was opened in 1863 and was taken over by the GWR in 1889.

W
S
N
E

## PENZANCE

We arrive at our destination after over 300 miles of travel through the varied landscapes of many of the most beautiful counties in the country. The station was first opened in 1852 but a more modern building was erected in 1879 and since that time it has served many tens of thousands of holiday makers and countless tons of freight. From here the tourist may explore the villages in the surrounding countryside, visit the Lands End or even travel across the water to the Scilly Isles. Our journey at an end, we disembark and set out to enjoy what has been known for generations as The Cornish Riviera.

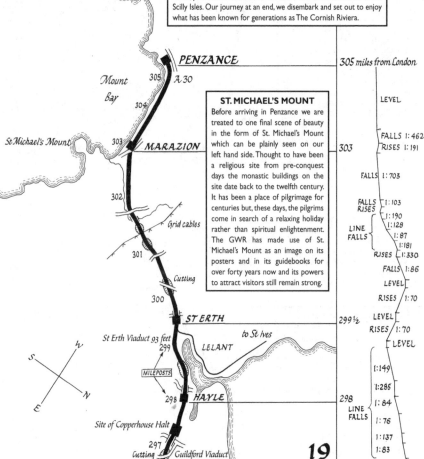

*NEWLYN*

**PENZANCE**

*Mount Bay*

305

A 30

304

*St Michael's Mount*

303

**MARAZION**

302

*Grid cables*

301

*Cutting*

300

**ST ERTH**

*St Erth Viaduct 93 feet*
299

*MILEPOSTS*

298

**HAYLE**

*Site of Copperhouse Halt*

297

*Cutting*  *Guildford Viaduct 369 feet*

*to St Ives*

*LELANT*

## ST. MICHAEL'S MOUNT

Before arriving in Penzance we are treated to one final scene of beauty in the form of St. Michael's Mount which can be plainly seen on our left hand side. Thought to have been a religious site from pre-conquest days the monastic buildings on the site date back to the twelfth century. It has been a place of pilgrimage for centuries but, these days, the pilgrims come in search of a relaxing holiday rather than spiritual enlightenment. The GWR has made use of St. Michael's Mount as an image on its posters and in its guidebooks for over forty years now and its powers to attract visitors still remain strong.

305 miles from London

LEVEL

FALLS 1: 462
RISES 1: 191

303

FALLS 1: 703

FALLS 1: 103
RISES

1: 190
1: 128

LINE FALLS

1: 87
1: 181

RISES 1: 330

FALLS 1: 86

LEVEL

RISES 1: 70

299½    LEVEL
RISES 1: 70
LEVEL

1: 149

1: 285

298    1: 84
LINE FALLS

1: 76

1: 137

1: 83

**19**

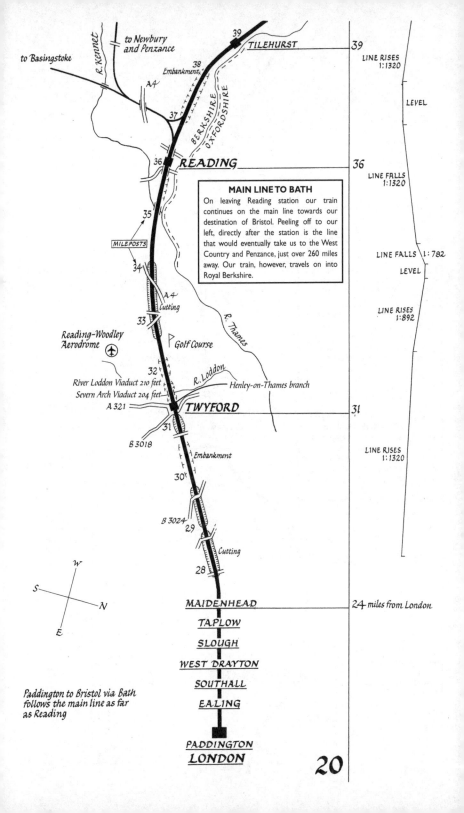

to Basingstoke

R. Kennet

to Newbury and Penzance

39
TILEHURST

39
LINE RISES 1:1320

38
Embankment
A4

LEVEL

37

BERKSHIRE
OXFORDSHIRE

36
READING

36
LINE FALLS 1:1320

35

**MAIN LINE TO BATH**

On leaving Reading station our train continues on the main line towards our destination of Bristol. Peeling off to our left, directly after the station is the line that would eventually take us to the West Country and Penzance, just over 260 miles away. Our train, however, travels on into Royal Berkshire.

LINE FALLS 1:782

LEVEL

MILEPOSTS

34

A4 Cutting

R. Thames

LINE RISES 1:892

33

Reading–Woodley Aerodrome ✈

▷ Golf Course

32

R. Loddon

River Loddon Viaduct 210 feet
Severn Arch Viaduct 204 feet

Henley-on-Thames branch

A 321

**TWYFORD**

31

31
B 3018

Embankment

LINE RISES 1:1320

30

B 3024

29

Cutting

28

**MAIDENHEAD**

24 miles from London

**TAPLOW**

**SLOUGH**

**WEST DRAYTON**

**SOUTHALL**

**EALING**

W
S — N
E

Paddington to Bristol via Bath follows the main line as far as Reading

**PADDINGTON
LONDON**

**20**

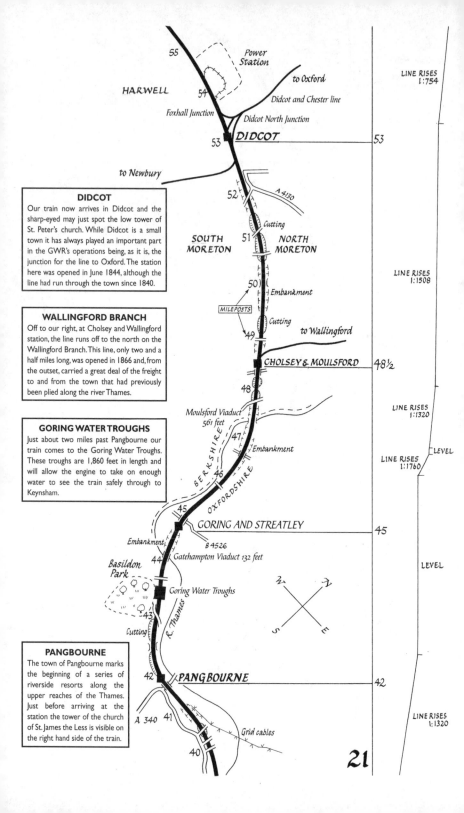

LINE RISES
1:754

55

Power
Station

to Oxford

HARWELL

54

Didcot and Chester line

Foxhall Junction

Didcot North Junction

53

DIDCOT

53

to Newbury

**DIDCOT**

Our train now arrives in Didcot and the
sharp-eyed may just spot the low tower of
St. Peter's church. While Didcot is a small
town it has always played an important part
in the GWR's operations being, as it is, the
junction for the line to Oxford. The station
here was opened in June 1844, although the
line had run through the town since 1840.

52

A 4130

Cutting

SOUTH
MORETON

51

NORTH
MORETON

LINE RISES
1:1508

50

Embankment

MILEPOSTS

Cutting

**WALLINGFORD BRANCH**

Off to our right, at Cholsey and Wallingford
station, the line runs off to the north on the
Wallingford Branch. This line, only two and a
half miles long, was opened in 1866 and, from
the outset, carried a great deal of the freight
to and from the town that had previously
been plied along the river Thames.

49

to Wallingford

CHOLSEY & MOULSFORD

48½

48

Moulsford Viaduct
561 feet

LINE RISES
1:1320

**GORING WATER TROUGHS**

Just about two miles past Pangbourne our
train comes to the Goring Water Troughs.
These troughs are 1,860 feet in length and
will allow the engine to take on enough
water to see the train safely through to
Keynsham.

47

Embankment

LEVEL

46

LINE RISES
1:1760

BERKSHIRE

OXFORDSHIRE

45

GORING AND STREATLEY

45

Embankment

B 4526

44

Gatehampton Viaduct 132 feet

LEVEL

Basildon
Park

Goring Water Troughs

N

43

W        E

Cutting

R. Thames

S

**PANGBOURNE**

The town of Pangbourne marks
the beginning of a series of
riverside resorts along the
upper reaches of the Thames.
Just before arriving at the
station the tower of the church
of St. James the Less is visible on
the right hand side of the train.

42

PANGBOURNE

42

A 340

41

Grid cables

LINE RISES
1:1320

40

**21**

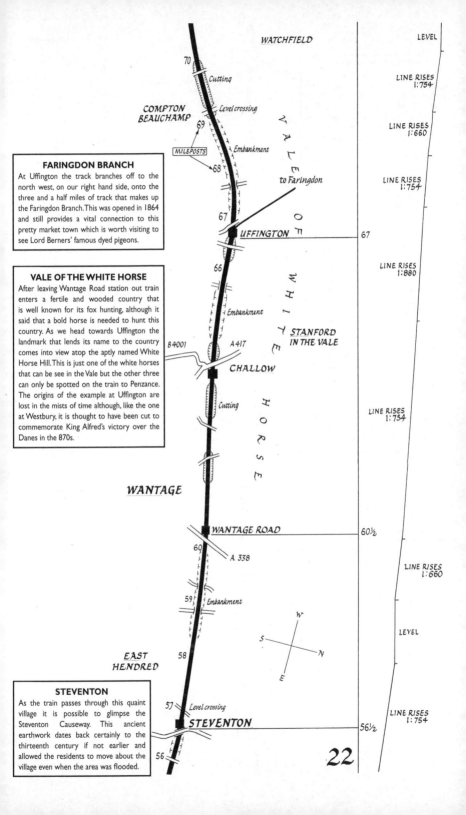

WATCHFIELD

LEVEL

LINE RISES 1:754

70

Cutting

COMPTON BEAUCHAMP

Level crossing

LINE RISES 1:660

69

MILEPOSTS

Embankment

68

to Faringdon

LINE RISES 1:754

V A L E   O F   W H I T E   H O R S E

### FARINGDON BRANCH

At Uffington the track branches off to the north west, on our right hand side, onto the three and a half miles of track that makes up the Faringdon Branch. This was opened in 1864 and still provides a vital connection to this pretty market town which is worth visiting to see Lord Berners' famous dyed pigeons.

67

UFFINGTON

67

66

### VALE OF THE WHITE HORSE

After leaving Wantage Road station out train enters a fertile and wooded country that is well known for its fox hunting, although it said that a bold horse is needed to hunt this country. As we head towards Uffington the landmark that lends its name to the country comes into view atop the aptly named White Horse Hill. This is just one of the white horses that can be see in the Vale but the other three can only be spotted on the train to Penzance. The origins of the example at Uffington are lost in the mists of time although, like the one at Westbury, it is thought to have been cut to commemorate King Alfred's victory over the Danes in the 870s.

LINE RISES 1:880

Embankment

STANFORD IN THE VALE

B 4001

A 417

CHALLOW

Cutting

LINE RISES 1:754

WANTAGE

WANTAGE ROAD

60½

60

A 338

LINE RISES 1:660

59

Embankment

LEVEL

EAST HENDRED

58

W

S

N

E

### STEVENTON

As the train passes through this quaint village it is possible to glimpse the Steventon Causeway. This ancient earthwork dates back certainly to the thirteenth century if not earlier and allowed the residents to move about the village even when the area was flooded.

57

Level crossing

STEVENTON

56½

LINE RISES 1:754

56

**22**

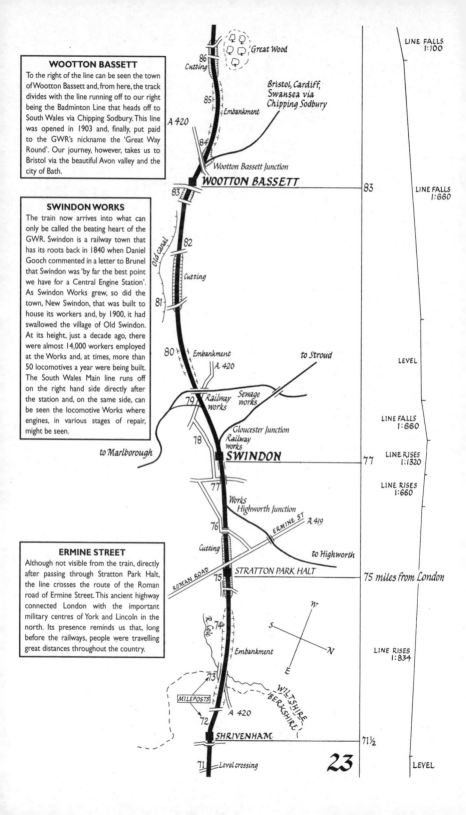

**LINE FALLS 1:100**

*Great Wood*

86
*Cutting*

## WOOTTON BASSETT
To the right of the line can be seen the town of Wootton Bassett and, from here, the track divides with the line running off to our right being the Badminton Line that heads off to South Wales via Chipping Sodbury. This line was opened in 1903 and, finally, put paid to the GWR's nickname the 'Great Way Round'. Our journey, however, takes us to Bristol via the beautiful Avon valley and the city of Bath.

85

*Embankment*

*Bristol, Cardiff, Swansea via Chipping Sodbury*

A 420

84

*Wootton Bassett Junction*

### WOOTTON BASSETT

83

**LINE FALLS 1:660**

83

## SWINDON WORKS
The train now arrives into what can only be called the beating heart of the GWR. Swindon is a railway town that has its roots back in 1840 when Daniel Gooch commented in a letter to Brunel that Swindon was 'by far the best point we have for a Central Engine Station'. As Swindon Works grew, so did the town, New Swindon, that was built to house its workers and, by 1900, it had swallowed the village of Old Swindon. At its height, just a decade ago, there were almost 14,000 workers employed at the Works and, at times, more than 50 locomotives a year were being built. The South Wales Main line runs off on the right hand side directly after the station and, on the same side, can be seen the locomotive Works where engines, in various stages of repair, might be seen.

*Old canal*

82

*Cutting*

81

80 *Embankment*

A 420

*to Stroud*

**LEVEL**

79 *Railway works*

*Sewage works*

78

*Gloucester Junction Railway works*

*to Marlborough*

### SWINDON

77

**LINE FALLS 1:660**

77

**LINE RISES 1:1320**

77

*Works*
*Highworth Junction*

**LINE RISES 1:660**

76

ERMINE ST   A 419

*to Highworth*

## ERMINE STREET
Although not visible from the train, directly after passing through Stratton Park Halt, the line crosses the route of the Roman road of Ermine Street. This ancient highway connected London with the important military centres of York and Lincoln in the north. Its presence reminds us that, long before the railways, people were travelling great distances throughout the country.

*Cutting*

*ROMAN ROAD*

75 **STRATTON PARK HALT**

**75 miles from London**

74 *R. Cole*

*N*
*S*
*W*
*E*

*Embankment*

**LINE RISES 1:834**

73

*MILEPOSTS*

A 420

72

*WILTSHIRE*
*BERKSHIRE*

### SHRIVENHAM

71½

71 *Level crossing*

**23**

**LEVEL**

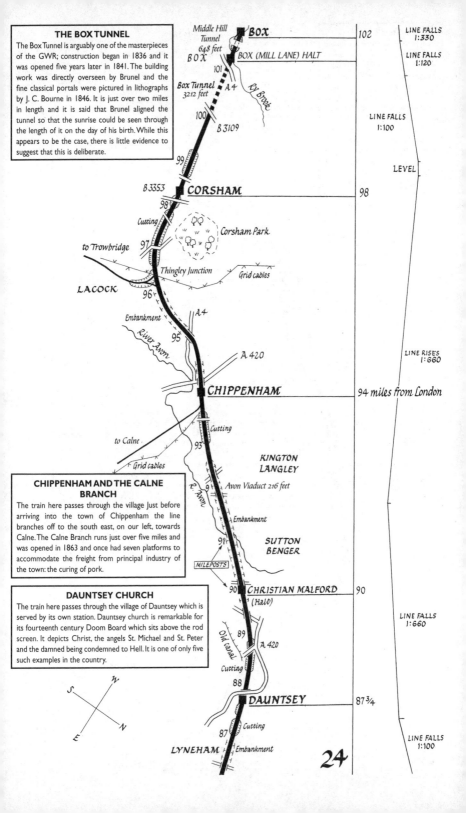

## THE BOX TUNNEL

The Box Tunnel is arguably one of the masterpieces of the GWR; construction began in 1836 and it was opened five years later in 1841. The building work was directly overseen by Brunel and the fine classical portals were pictured in lithographs by J. C. Bourne in 1846. It is just over two miles in length and it is said that Brunel aligned the tunnel so that the sunrise could be seen through the length of it on the day of his birth. While this appears to be the case, there is little evidence to suggest that this is deliberate.

## CHIPPENHAM AND THE CALNE BRANCH

The train here passes through the village Just before arriving into the town of Chippenham the line branches off to the south east, on our left, towards Calne. The Calne Branch runs just over five miles and was opened in 1863 and once had seven platforms to accommodate the freight from principal industry of the town: the curing of pork.

## DAUNTSEY CHURCH

The train here passes through the village of Dauntsey which is served by its own station. Dauntsey church is remarkable for its fourteenth century Doom Board which sits above the rod screen. It depicts Christ, the angels St. Michael and St. Peter and the damned being condemned to Hell. It is one of only five such examples in the country.

Middle Hill Tunnel 648 feet

**BOX**

BOX

BOX (MILL LANE) HALT

101

Box Tunnel 3212 feet

A4

By Brook

100

B 3109

99

B 3353

**CORSHAM**

98

Cutting

Corsham Park

97

to Trowbridge

Thingley Junction

Grid cables

**LACOCK**

96

Embankment

River Avon

95

A4

A 420

**CHIPPENHAM**

Cutting

to Calne

93

Grid cables

KINGTON LANGLEY

R. Avon

Avon Viaduct 216 feet

Embankment

91

SUTTON BENGER

MILEPOSTS

90

**CHRISTIAN MALFORD**

(Halt)

89

Old Canal

A 420

Cutting

88

**DAUNTSEY**

87

Cutting

**LYNEHAM**

Embankment

102    LINE FALLS 1:330

LINE FALLS 1:120

LINE FALLS 1:100

LEVEL

98

LINE RISES 1:660

94 miles from London

90    LINE FALLS 1:660

87¾

LINE FALLS 1:100

**24**

N    W    S    E

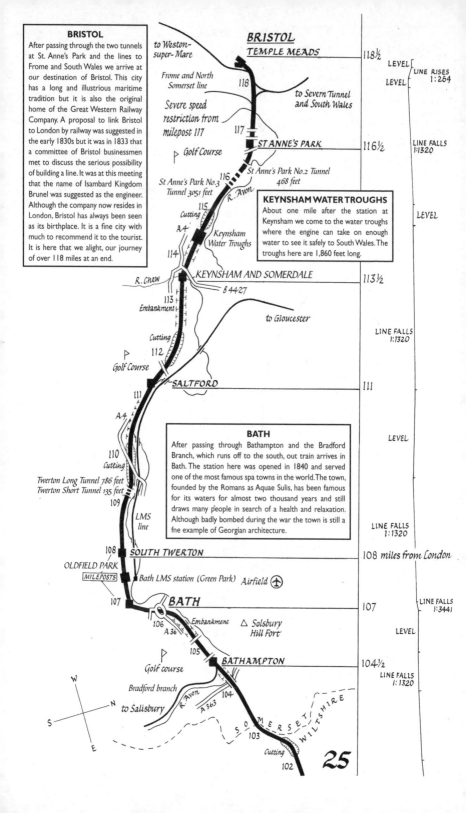

**BRISTOL**

After passing through the two tunnels at St. Anne's Park and the lines to Frome and South Wales we arrive at our destination of Bristol. This city has a long and illustrious maritime tradition but it is also the original home of the Great Western Railway Company. A proposal to link Bristol to London by railway was suggested in the early 1830s but it was in 1833 that a committee of Bristol businessmen met to discuss the serious possibility of building a line. It was at this meeting that the name of Isambard Kingdom Brunel was suggested as the engineer. Although the company now resides in London, Bristol has always been seen as its birthplace. It is a fine city with much to recommend it to the tourist. It is here that we alight, our journey of over 118 miles at an end.

**KEYNSHAM WATER TROUGHS**

About one mile after the station at Keynsham we come to the water troughs where the engine can take on enough water to see it safely to South Wales. The troughs here are 1,860 feet long.

**BATH**

After passing through Bathampton and the Bradford Branch, which runs off to the south, out train arrives in Bath. The station here was opened in 1840 and served one of the most famous spa towns in the world. The town, founded by the Romans as Aquae Sulis, has been famous for its waters for almost two thousand years and still draws many people in search of a health and relaxation. Although badly bombed during the war the town is still a fne example of Georgian architecture.

*BRISTOL TEMPLE MEADS*

to Weston-super-Mare

*Frome and North Somerset line*

to Severn Tunnel and South Wales

118½ — LEVEL / LINE RISES 1:264
LEVEL

118

*Severe speed restriction from milepost 117*

117

ST ANNE'S PARK — 116½ — LINE FALLS 1:1320

▷ Golf Course

116

St Anne's Park No.2 Tunnel 468 feet

St Anne's Park No.3 Tunnel 3051 feet — R. Avon

LEVEL

115 — *Cutting*

A4

*Keynsham Water Troughs*

114

R. Chew

KEYNSHAM AND SOMERDALE — 113½

B 4427

113 — *Embankment*

to Gloucester

LINE FALLS 1:1320

*Cutting*

112

▷ Golf Course

111 — SALTFORD — 111

A4

110 — *Cutting*

LEVEL

*Twerton Long Tunnel 786 feet*
*Twerton Short Tunnel 135 feet*

109 — LMS line

108 — SOUTH TWERTON — 108 miles from London

OLDFIELD PARK — MILEPOSTS — Bath LMS station (Green Park)  Airfield ✈

LINE FALLS 1:1320

107 — *BATH* — 107 — LINE FALLS 1:3441

106 — A 36 — *Embankment* — △ Solsbury Hill Fort

105 — LEVEL

BATHAMPTON — 104½ — LINE FALLS 1:1320

*Golf course*

*Bradford branch*

to Salisbury — R. Avon — A 363 — 104

103 — SOMERSET  WILTSHIRE

*Cutting*

102

**25**

W N S E (compass)

# Principal Stations of the GWR

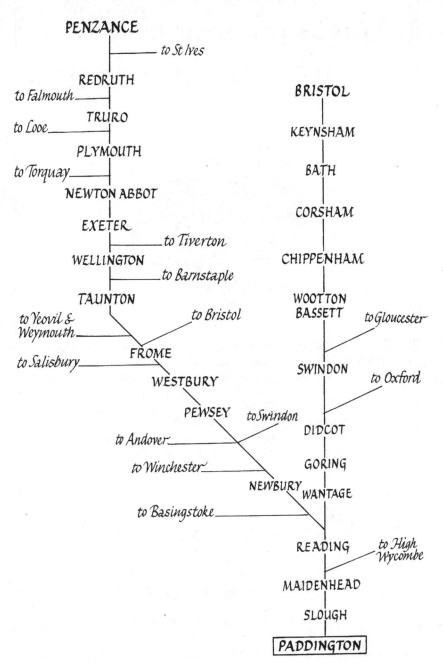

# This is the way to
## RHEUMATIC RELIEF

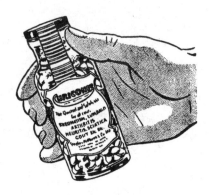

'Curicones' have proved a turning point in the life of many a Rheumatic sufferer. This great treatment has brought freedom from the cruel pains of Rheumatism, Gout, Lumbago, Sciatica, Neuritis, Synovitis, Fibrositis, Swollen Joints, and kindred ills. The large volume of testimony, accumulated over years, is ample tribute to the power of 'CURICONES.' Such testimony cannot be denied. **It is your assurance of the substantial relief that 'Curicones' have brought to others.** All ingredients in 'Curicones' are fully approved by the British Pharmaceutical Authorities. Begin a course of 'Curicones' today.

## FROM ALL CHEMISTS

# 'Good Mornings'
# begin with Gillette

Life and soul of the carriage, behold Mr. Gay who
boasts that his blades make him bright for the day!

*For*

**EXPRESS RELIEF**

*from*

**TRAIN HEADACHE**

**'GENASPRIN'**

*is safe, convenient
and sure*

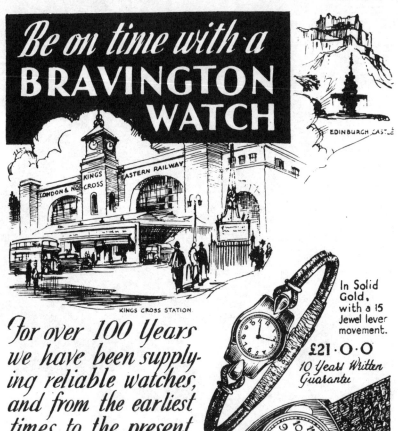

# Be on time with a BRAVINGTON WATCH

EDINBURGH CASTLE

KINGS CROSS STATION

*For over 100 Years we have been supplying reliable watches, and from the earliest times to the present day, they have been famous for their ability to stand up to the day in, day out service required of a watch.*

In Solid Gold, with a 15 Jewel lever movement.

**£21·0·0**

*10 Years Written Guarantee*

*The Popular Model*

Nickel Chrome & Steel.
Superior 15 Jewel lever movement
An accurate & reliable timekeeper.
*Ten Years Written Guarantee* **£5·15·0**